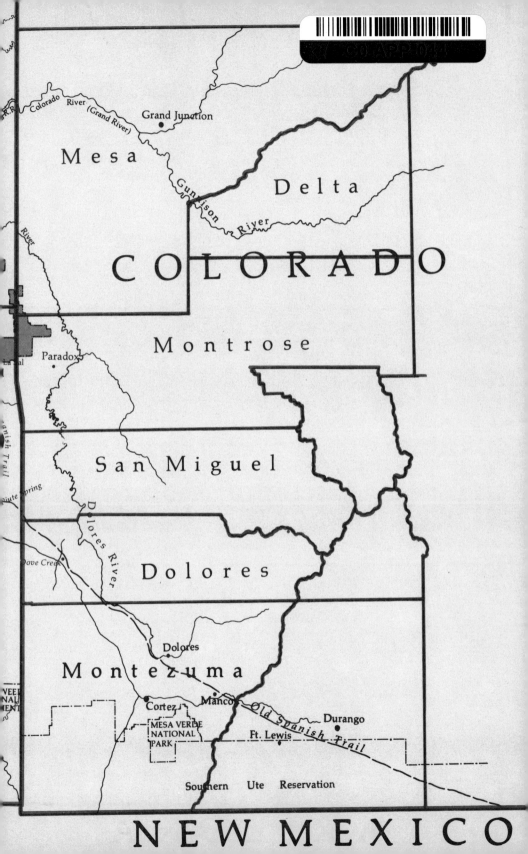

Look
to the
Mountains

Look to the Mountains

Southeastern Utah and the
La Sal National Forest

by Charles S. Peterson

With Cooperation of the
Manti-La Sal National Forest

Brigham Young University Press

Library of Congress Cataloging in Publication Data
Peterson, Charles S
 Look to the Mountains
 Bibliography: P.
 1. Manti-La Sal National Forest, Utah and Colo.—
History 2. Utah—History. I. Title
F832.M3P47 917.92'59 74-18031
ISBN 0-8425-0152-5

Library of Congress Catalog Card Number: 74-18031
International Standard Book Number: 0-8425-0152-5
© 1975 Brigham Young University Press. All rights reserved
Brigham Young University Press, Provo, Utah 84602
Printed in the United States of America
75 3M 1041

Contents

Acknowledgments

I am grateful for the kind assistance given me in the preparation of this book. Work on it has taken me to numerous libraries and archives and has required considerable work in the field. The entire process has been brightened and enlivened by pleasant and instructive contact with a wide variety of individuals. For much of the fact and more of the understanding and insight I am indebted to friends who have encouraged and helped me. Such errors as have been incorporated are quite naturally my own.

Financial assistance from two sources has made it possible for me to proceed. The original research and writing on which this book rests were done under a contract with the Manti-La Sal National Forest. Final writing and preparation have been carried on by means of a Mineral Leasing research grant from Utah State University.

Where personal assistance is concerned my obligations extend first to Forest Service personnel. Especially helpful were David M. Moon, administrative officer of the Manti-La Sal National Forest, and George F. McLaughlin and Robert B. Terrill, respectively forest supervisor and former supervisor of the Manti-La Sal Forest. Also generous in their time and information have been former Forest officers including James Jacobs, Howard W. Balsley, and J. W. Humphrey, whose long list of Forest Service achievements include stints as supervisor on both the La Sal and the Manti forests.

Many people in southeastern Utah have shared their knowledge of the country with me. I am especially indebted to Albert R. Lyman, now deceased, and Lynn Lyman of Blanding and Charlie Redd of La Sal.

Elsewhere a host of friends have contributed. At the University of Utah Floyd O'Niell and Gregory Thompson made available valuable materials relating to the Utes in southeastern Utah. Librarians have been openhanded and pleasant in their dealings as have people at the Historical Department of the Church and the Utah State Archives. The library staff at the Utah State Historical Society has given me free rein in the society's library. Beyond Utah's borders, the Denver Public Library, the Denver Regional Records Center, and the National Archives have made repeated contributions to my effort. As always, my wife, Betty, has shouldered the single most important effort in checking writing style, editing, typing, and in research and in contributions to the general direction the study has taken. My daughter and son, Colette and Joe, have willingly cut their editorial milk teeth on this study, doing much proofreading.

Introduction

The work that follows is a history of the La Sal National Forest in its regional perspective. In the narrow sense it deals with the La Sal Mountains and the Blue Mountains-Elk Plateau country that comprises the La Sal Forest. In the broader geographic context the area of this work lies in two states—Utah and Colorado—and includes the country bounded on the west by the Green and Colorado rivers, on the north by the Roan Cliffs, on the east by the Dolores Valley, and on the south by the Four Corners area where Utah meets Colorado, New Mexico, and Arizona. The La Sal Forest, and indeed the entire region, is isolated from Utah by the canyons and deserts of the Colorado Plateau and by the rim of the Great Basin. In some respects it relates to western Colorado rather than to Utah, but state borders and Mormon influence constitute bonds that more than offset the geographic and economic forces that attract it to Colorado. Historically the region's isolation gave it a general unity. The timing of its settlement, its preoccupation with Indians, problems of space, and the arid nature of the country also have been unifying factors.

My purpose has been to study the La Sal Forest in its regional setting. Thus, while I have focused primarily upon the development of the Forest, I have been concerned also with the character of the society that depended upon the Forest, and have attempted to understand the interrelationships of society and forest.

My basic premise is that since its founding in 1906 the La Sal Forest has been an important part of a regional progression away from what I have termed frontier isolationism toward full integration into the mainstream of America's national life. This process was under way when the Forest became a part of southeastern Utah.

Settlement had been initiated in the region only three decades before. A little known hinterland, its rugged and drouth-wracked beauty was isolated by the political boundaries of the Four Corners states and by the awesome natural barriers that set the Colorado Plateau apart from the Great Basin and other physiographic provinces.

At the time of settlement the region had been the domain of explorers for a century and continued to be a refuge for Indians. Its first pioneers only partially understood the region's potentials and problems—a fact particularly apparent in the determined effort of the San Juan Mormons to establish a simple agricultural village society. With passing time, misapprehensions were overcome, adjustments were made, and the necessary individualism of the earliest frontier was partially supplanted by more public or government-oriented views.

Thus, by 1906 the region had passed through a number of important transitions. But understanding of the potential of planning and regulation, as contrasted to frontier opportunism, was still limited; the region therefore lacked much of the organization that characterizes modern society. A role of the La Sal National Forest during its first twenty-five years, was to prepare the region for an increase in public regulation and services. With one of the best bureaucratic systems and one of the most practical applications of the Progressive movement's method, the Forest Service became an important force in southeastern Utah's movement to full integration with modern America following the Great Depression and World War II.

To portray this transition from frontier to mainstream America I have concentrated upon the processes by which early settlement was accomplished and, in the period after the advent of the National Forest, upon the role of the Forest and its influence on the region.

Part One

Last Frontier: Settlement to 1906

Chapter I

Exploration to 1880

The history of southeastern Utah prior to 1880 was in large measure the history of exploration. Remote and uninviting, the area attracted few settlers. But for various reasons travelers and explorers of three nations—Spain, Mexico, and the United States—took its measure between 1760 and 1880. For some it was a passageway, for some it was an access to furs; for others it was an Indian mission and a strategic approach to Zion; for yet others it was a region for railway exploration, for river adventure, or for topographical survey.

The first explorers in this area, as elsewhere in the West, were undoubtedly Indians. Oncoming whites found natives scattered throughout the entire region and depended upon them for directions and for knowledge of water and campsites. There is little way of knowing to what degree Indians knew the country, but by the early 1800s both the Utes and Navajos had horses, enabling them to roam widely.

The Escalante expedition obtained a guide to the Utah Lake country, as far away as the Uncompahgre River in Colorado. However, the long looping route they followed indicates that their guide was not well versed in geography and that the Indians generally did not have a knowledge of the broad sweep of country in 1776. Later, after the arrival of Anglo-American settlers, there were well-established Indian trails between the northern valleys of Utah and the Hopi villages and, more important in this connection, over the Wasatch Plateau and across the Green and Colorado rivers to Navajo country in what is now known as the Four Corners area.

Spanish Explorers and the Old Spanish Trail

The Spanish were the first white explorers of the La Sal Forest region. Beginning with halting entradas in the 1760s, they worked

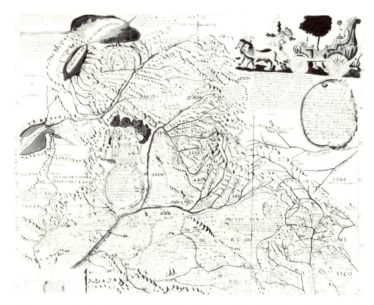

"Miera Map" of the country explored by the Escalante Expedition.
By permission of the Utah Historical Society.

out much of the avenue between Santa Fe and California, which
came to be known as the Old Spanish Trail. Perhaps the most important transmountain route for a decade or so early in the nineteenth century, the Spanish Trail made the La Sal Forest area one
of Utah's most traveled and best known regions. The mountains
that comprise the Forest were essential to the success of the route
as they have been to more recent utilization.

The Escalante-Dominguez expedition, with its passage through
much of Utah in 1776, is at once the most spectacular and the best
recorded of the Spanish penetrations of our region. However, it
does not appear to have been the first. This is evident in the fact
that Escalante and the expedition's map maker, Don Bernardo
Miera y Pacheco, referred to many important physical features by
names they still bear. There is no certainty as to when Spanish
names were first applied, but it must have been no later than the
1760s when the first recorded visits took place. One such expedition was made in 1765 (by some accounts 1761) by Juan Maria de
Rivera, who penetrated to a spot on the Gunnison River not far
from the east foot of the La Sal Mountains. During the next decade
Spanish traders traveled the same route, extending the trail and
very likely establishing some knowledge of the La Sal and Abajo

(Blue) mountains.[1] Typical of these travelers were Pedro Mora, Gregorio Sandoval, and Andres Muniz, who had been with Rivera in his earlier trip.[2]

The Escalante-Dominguez expedition of 1776 provided a thoroughly documented account of a trip through Utah. Launched for the primary purposes of making contact with the natives of the area and seeking out a passageway between the provinces of New Mexico and California, the expedition was under the direction of Fray Francisco Atanasio Dominguez. As official recorder of the journey, Friar Silvestre Velez de Escalante both distinguished himself and claims our attention as the chief figure connected with the expedition. The map maker Miera, referred to above, also was of considerable importance.

Leaving Santa Fe on July 29 (the scheduled date was July 4), the expedition traveled a known route to the Gunnison River. Among the other items noted are references to both the Sierra Abajo and the Sierra La Sal. Of the latter, Escalante wrote: "Near here is the small range which they call Sierra de la Sal because close to it there are salt flats where, according to what we were told, the Yutas who live hereabouts get their salt."[3] As he wrote, Escalante was only a few miles east of the La Sals. The expedition toiled on to the northeast for many miles before turning west into the Uinta Basin and thence to Strawberry Valley, Spanish Fork Canyon, Utah Valley, and south on a course approximating that of Highway 91 before abandoning the attempt to reach California. The explorers returned to Santa Fe by way of the Crossing of the Fathers on the Colorado River and the Hopi villages.

Little official attention was paid the area of Escalante's exploration during the remaining years of Spanish control, which ended in 1821. But Indian traders apparently continued to come and go. Unfortunately, they left little documentary evidence of their doings. However, incidental reference indicates they were in the area. For example, a governor of New Mexico writing in 1805 referred to Manuel Mestas, "who for approximately fifty years has served as Yuta interpreter . . . the one who reduced them to peace."[4] Mestas ranged as far north as Utah Lake to reclaim horses that had been taken by the Indians and undoubtedly had more than a passing knowledge of the La Sal Forest region.

---

1. Officially and historically designated the Abajo Mountains, this small range is called the Blue Mountains in southeastern Utah. I have used the two names interchangeably according to the context of my references.

2. Joseph J. Hill, "Spanish and Mexican Exploration and Trade Northwest from New Mexico into the Great Basin, 1765-1863," *Utah Historical Quarterly,* 3 (1930): 3-6.

3. Herbert E. Bolton, *Pageant in the Wilderness* (Salt Lake City: Utah State Historical Society, 1950), p. 148.

4. Hill, p. 16.

In 1813 Mauricio Arze and Lagos Garcia led a trading expedition that made contact with Indians at Utah Lake and points south along the Sevier River. As far as routes and distances go, the record is casual, suggesting that the Arze-Garcia party was not only well acquainted with the way but assumed their readers would have some familiarity with it as well. The attitude of the Indians with reference to trading in slaves also suggests previous contact, as does the comment of comparison that the 109 pelts acquired were "but a few."[5]

In the decades that followed, the route was extended to California and became known as the Old Spanish Trail. In the main the traffic that moved over it was that of commercial people and homeseekers. During the earliest years, commerce was dominated by Mexican traders between Santa Fe and Los Angeles. Later on, Americans, many of them trappers forced into new pursuits by the simultaneous collapse of the fur sources and fur markets, carried trade goods over the Spanish Trail, or made their way to California to live. Taking a characteristic Spanish approach, large caravans made annual expeditions over the Spanish Trail. Sometimes involving as many as 200 to 300 men and commensurate numbers of pack mules, westbound traffic transported blankets and other products from Santa Fe. Eastbound trade customarily brought great herds of horses and mules, which California was producing in untold thousands by this time.

Numerous variants of the trail existed. Most of these have been swallowed up by the forces of nature, but the location of water and the character of the terrain enables us to follow the general course of the trail with considerable confidence. A good guess would bring the trail into Utah in the neighborhood of Paiute Spring, directly east of Monticello. Proceeding by way of Three-Step Hill through Lisbon Valley, and taking advantage of springs in both the East and West Coyote drainages, it passed over the southwest spur of the La Sal Mountains to Spanish Valley and the Colorado River crossing at Moab. Continuing either by way of Moab Canyon or Court House Wash, traffic probably held to the face of the redrock cliffs that swing left, or west, near the point where Highway 50-6 leaves Moab Canyon, utilizing springs found along the cliff front. Crossing the Green River at what came to be called the Gunnison Crossing, the main trail proceeded up Saleratus Wash, then through one of the region's multitudinous cottonwood washes to Buckhorn Flat and west across it before turning south and following down the east bench of the Wasatch Plateau to Wahsatch or, as we now know it, Salina Pass. Other breaks in the face of the Wasatch Plateau doubtless received occasional use. By the same token, travelers likely found good reason to make variant paths as they pushed west from the

5. LeRoy R. Hafen and Ann W. Hafen, *Old Spanish Trail, Santa Fe to Los Angeles* . . . (Glendale, Calif.: A. H. Clark Co., 1954), p. 186.

Gunnison's Butte at crossing of the Green River. Butte was named for John W. Gunnison.

Green River, finding the few passageways through the San Rafael Swell.

The Fur Trade and Knowledge of Southeastern Utah

The La Sal and Blue (Abajo) mountains, with their supplies of beaver and other fur-bearing animals, attracted some attention from fur trappers. The area lay between Taos, New Mexico, an early center for wintering trappers, and the so-called Snake country in northern Utah and southern Idaho and Wyoming. The list of trappers making expeditions into or through the area of our interest is large. However, only passing note of a number of the more important men will be made here. As early as 1824 three Taos groups are reported to have made trapping tours that carried them into southeastern Utah. William Wolfskill and Ewing Young worked the San Juan and other tributaries of the Colorado; Etienne Provost trapped the Colorado and Green rivers; and Antoine Robidoux led a brigade to the Green River. The first reference to an approach from the north or west is in William Henry Ashley's exploration of the Green River in 1825. Putting into the river in the neighborhood of South Pass, his party floated down to the mouth of the Duchesne River. According to his diary, he left most of his men and paddled onward twenty-five miles to about the mouth of Minnie-Maud Creek. However, in a letter to General Henry Atkinson he reported he had drifted down-stream some fifty miles. It is historian Dale Morgan's opinion that the Minnie-Maud report is more nearly accurate. But if the Atkinson letter were countenanced, Ashley may have reached the mouth of Rock Creek, which placed him directly east of Sunnyside and some-what north of the Old Spanish Trail.[6]

In 1827 trapper Daniel T. Potts worked the Sevier River, passing east from it over what he termed "a large snowy mountain which divides" Utah Lake from "the Leichadu (Green River)" before being turned back by hostile natives.[7]

Three years later the William Wolfskill-George C. Yount expedi-tion made a trek through southeastern Utah en route to California. Leaving New Mexico in the fall of 1830, they crossed the Colorado and, when an early winter struck, forced their way through snows two or three feet deep to reach "a stream called Pooneca," now believed to be the Sevier River.[8] Yount later reported that the area of our interest "was an extremity of mountainous and barren territory."[9]

During the years following his first visit to Green River country, Antoine Robidoux established two trading posts in areas adjacent to the La Sal National Forest. The first of these was Fort Uncom-pahgre on the Gunnison River near present Delta, Colorado. Extend-ing from this base, his operations penetrated into Utah by way of the Colorado and Green rivers and on via the White, or what is presently known as Price River. By the late 1830s Robidoux's interests in Utah merited the founding of Fort Robidoux in present-day Uintah County. While he knew the Spanish Trail, his main route of travel between Fort Uncompahgre and the new outpost cut off many miles by turning north up Westwater Canyon, climbing the Roan Cliffs, and proceeding northwest to the Green River near Ouray.[10]

Another figure, who even more than the foregoing is obscured by the years that have intervened, is Denis Julien. While Julien left little in the way of ordinary documentation, he literally left his mark upon the country, chiseling his name and the year of his passing on rocks along his route. In 1831 he cut his inscription near White Rocks on the Uinta River. During the next five or six years he left his "calling card" at several sites along the Green and Colorado rivers, where the Powell expedition of 1871 found at least five of them. Frederick

6. Dale L. Morgan, *Jedediah Smith and the Opening of the West* (Indi-anapolis: Bobbs-Merrill, 1953), pp. 164-68.

7. Donald M. Frost, *Notes on General Ashley, the Overland Trail, and South Pass* (Worcester, Mass.: Proceedings of the American Antiquarian Society, 1945), pp. 66-67.

8. F. H. Day, "Sketches of the Early Settlers of California: Ziba Branch," *Hesperian* 3 (1859): 337-39.

9. Memoirs of George C. Yount, typescript, Bancroft Library.

10. Charles Kelly, "Antoine Robidoux," *Utah Historical Quarterly* 6 (1933): 115-16.

S. Dellenbaugh, historian of Powell's second trip, noted the Julien marks and, unable to find any information about him, referred to him as the "mysterious D. Julien." It has been learned subsequently that Julien was a small trader working out of St. Louis and that he was in the general area of the Green River. It is thought that he was a victim of the treacherous rapids of Cataract Canyon.[11]

The Elk Mountain Mission

The first recorded Mormon exploration of southeastern Utah was in 1854. But Mormons had manifested an interest in the region long before that time. Indeed their first note of the Navajos who inhabited the Four Corners area predated their arrival in Utah by sixteen years. During Oliver Cowdery's first mission to Missouri in 1831, he wrote Joseph Smith telling of a large tribe of Indians who lived some 300 miles west of Santa Fe, ran sheep, did considerable weaving, and were called the "Navashoes."[12] The years after the Mormon arrival in the West saw the Church expand, establishing settlements throughout the Great Basin. Part of its thrust was southward. While the main drive of the southward movement tended west to develop a seaport in southern California, a minor effort stressed the need to serve and control the Indians who inhabited the southeastern part of the territory.

Pursuing this latter interest, the Latter-day Saints early made contact with Walker, chief of the Utes. Bound by no narrow concept of territoriality, Walker raided in California, traded in northern Arizona, and utilized the Old Spanish Trail as an escape avenue during the Walker War of 1853.[13] Hearing of his trading trips to the Moquis (later known as Hopis), Mormons followed his path across Ute Crossing (Crossing of the Fathers) on the Colorado River to make repeated visits to the mesa dwellers.[14] By a somewhat different token, Walker's knowledge of the Old Spanish Trail appears to have helped turn Mormon interest to southeastern Utah in the mid-1850s. Supporting this view was Lieutenant John W. Gunnison's report of an 1853 meeting with Utes west of the Green River crossing which indicated that Walker was in "New Mexico to dispose of a herd of cattle which he had stolen" from the Mormon settlements.[15]

---

11.   Charles Kelly, "The Mysterious 'D. Julien,'" *Utah Historical Quarterly* 6 (1933): 83-88.

12.   Joseph Smith, *History of the Church of Jesus Christ of Latter-day Saints,* 2d ed. rev. 1 (Salt Lake City: Deseret Book Co., 1948): 182.

13.   Thomas J. Farnham, *Life, Adventures and Travels in California* (New York: Nafis and Cornish, 1849), p. 374.

14.   Charles S. Peterson, "The Hopis and the Mormons, 1858-1873," *Utah Historical Quarterly* 39 (1971): 179-94.

15.   Lieutenant E. G. Beckwith, "Report of Exploration of a Route for the Pacific Railroad Near the 38th and 39th Parallels of Latitude," *House Document* 129 (1855), p. 67. For an excellent treatment of Army explorations cited here

The Mormons dispatched an exploration under William Huntington during the summer of 1854. Proceeding south via the Spanish Trail, Huntington lowered his wagons down a steep drop in Moab Canyon just west of the present headquarters for the Arches National Park, crossed the Colorado River, and rolled on to the head of Spanish Valley before being forced to abandon his wagons. Caching his equipment, he continued south, making one of the great prehistory finds of the entire western experience when he came on the Hovenweep ruins near the present border of Colorado.[16] Turning home, he left at least part of his wagons and equipment, including items that suggested an intent to settle.

William Huntington's 1854 sortie was followed by a more ambitious Mormon effort in 1855. This so-called Elk Mountain Mission was part of a general move to control the approaches to Utah.[17] An important element in control was, of course, occupation. Another was establishing friendly relations with Indians.

With this in view, in April, 1855, Mormon leaders called Alfred N. Billings and forty other men to establish an outpost at the foot of the La Sal Mountains, then called the Elk Mountains. Outfitting at Manti, the party took the trail on May 21 with fifteen wagons, sixty-five oxen, thirteen horses, and a small stock of trade goods and equipment with which to settle. For the first thirty miles, to Salt Creek in Salina Canyon, they followed a road used by the Sanpete settlements to procure salt. From Salt Creek they took Gunnison's route over the Wasatch Pass and north through Castle Valley to just beyond the present location of Castle Dale. Advised by Indians that a shortcut existed (in reality the main line of the Spanish Trail), they left Gunnison's trace, which looped north, to avoid the rough dry stretch north of the San Rafael River.[18] Running east five miles from where it left the Gunnison trace near Huntington Creek through a sandy and broken terrain, the trail came to "an open country," or the Buckhorn Flats. Pulling through Buckhorn Flats for about ten miles, the missionaries found water in a hole which required "8 or 10 men to get water up to the cattle" by lifting it about 150 feet with their lariats. Having exhausted the supply, they rested until 9:30 p.m. and then drove until 4:00 a.m. before finding water again. From this

as well as in the west generally, see William H. Goetzmann, *Army Exploration in the American West, 1803-1863* (New Haven: Yale University Press, 1965).

16.   *Millennial Star* (Liverpool, England) 27 (1855): 233.

17.   This phase of Mormon expansion has been treated in various places. Among the best are Milton R. Hunter, *Brigham Young, the Colonizer*, 3rd ed. (Independence, Mo.: Zion's Printing and Publishing Co., 1945), pp. 63-85 and A. L. Neff, *History of Utah*, L. H. Creer, ed., (Salt Lake City: Deseret News Press, 1940), pp. 218-23. A prizewinning article by Eugene Campbell has challenged this concept, but as far as the Elk Mountain Mission is concerned it is unconvincing and in my opinion does not prove that control of the approaches generally was not a major factor in the colonizing efforts of the 1850s.

18.   Beckwith, p. 71.

Casa Colorado and La Sal Mountains. From J. N. Macomb, *Exploring Expedition.*

point it was five miles to the intersection with Gunnison's route in Saleratus Wash, which they followed, arriving at the Green River on June 2. Pausing first to preach to and confer with Indians camped at the river, they began crossing—a process that consumed seven full days. Once east of the river, they pushed on rapidly, arriving at the Colorado on June 10.

By June 15 the missionaries had completed the Colorado crossing and had chosen a site on the southwest side of the valley upon which to build a fort. More thorough consideration resulted in their changing the fort site to a position on the east of the valley about one mile from the river crossing. Clearing land and planting a small farm, they built a corral of upright logs six feet high. Water was brought out and the job of maintaining dams and ditches begun. After they completed these first critical duties, they built a fort. It was sixty-four feet square with rock walls tapering up twelve feet from a four-foot base to one and one-half feet in thickness at the top.

Indians were numerous and interested. While they manifested little overt hostility at first, they warned the missionaries not to bring additional people. Begging and some theft were reported and a good deal of trading went on. This was directed by Levi G. Metcalf, who, along with Lot Huntington, had been to the Elk mountains before— likely with the William Huntington expedition of the previous year.

The Indians apparently dealt in buckskins and horses. The briskness of trade in horseflesh is evidenced by the fact that a company with no more than thirteen head of horses when it left Manti in May, sent home sixteen head on July 19, thirty-five on August 20, and eighteen more on September 19, and the pioneers could still mount the entire party when they found it necessary to retreat later in September.[19]

It is not clear what the whites used as trade goods. Although it is difficult to understand why they would traffic in munitions, the fact that their supplies included "200 pounds of lead, 99 pounds of powder and 37,800 gun caps" hints that they did.[20] That they traded gun caps, along with a gun and buckskins, to the Navajos, also suggests that there was some traffic in arms.[21] Whatever the trade goods, barter was an important element in the short life of the Elk Mountain Mission.

Upon arrival in the area, the party immediately began to explore the surrounding country. On June 12—two days after they reached the north bank—Billings took five colleagues and explored both Mill Creek and Pack Creek. Pushing up Pack Creek, the men found William Huntington's cache some eighteen miles from the river. They also conducted exploration up the west slope of the La Sals.

But their exploration was not limited to short junkets. Still manifesting a sharp interest in the Navajos, the missionaries made a long trip into Navajo land. This expedition grew out of a visit from the Ute Chieftain Arrapeen, who arrived at the mission on July 14 enroute to trade with the Navajos south of the San Juan River. After haranguing the local natives about accepting the Latter-day Saints as neighbors, he went on south "to trade Piede children for horses."[22] Tension among the Indians was apparent when Arrapeen returned, bringing with him four prominent Navajos who came threatening war if horses stolen by the Elk Mountain Utes were not returned forthwith. After some grumbling on the part of Elk Mountain Indians, a preliminary settlement was reached when the Utes agreed to return any stolen horses that could be found among their people. It was also concluded that Ute representatives should be sent south to negotiate a broader agreement.

Evidently extending their good offices, Billings and a handful of missionaries headed south on August 30. Passing two forks leading to Santa Fe, they followed a trail across Dry Valley, skirted the foot of the Blue Mountains, and followed Comb Wash to the San Juan River. South of the river they proceeded "near 40 miles" to an important

19. Memorandum, Account Book and Diary of Alfred N. Billings, typescript, Utah State Historical Society.

20. "Personal Diary of Oliver Huntington," as quoted in Faun McConkie Tanner, *A History of Moab, Utah* (Moab: Times-Independent Press, 1937), p. 16.

21. Diary of Alfred N. Billings, p. 16.

22. Ibid., p. 8.

"settlement" of Navajos.[23] Although there was some tension as the Ute delegation approached the village, negotiations apparently went well, and trading was friendly and brisk.

Billings and his explorers arrived back at the fort on September 12. The next days were spent in getting another party ready to return to Salt Lake City, and on the 19th six of the missionaries left, leaving a weakened garrison of no more than seventeen or eighteen men. In less than a week all of these except three killed by the Indians beat a hasty and disorderly retreat.

The Elk Mountain Mission was permanently abandoned. The effort was, of course, not a total loss. Utahns for the first time became acquainted with the region that encompassed more than one-third of the territory. They recognized at least two major routes—those by which Highway 50-6 and Interstate 70 gain access to the Colorado Plateau—as the connecting links to the rest of the territory. They also acquired an understanding of some of the problems and prospects of the La Sal National Forest's region.

Mormon penetration of southeastern Utah during the next two decades was sharply limited. In no small part this was the result of Indian hostilities in the Black Hawk War.[24] Because of the on-going controversy between the Church and the federal government, the United States Army did not play the same role in pacifying hostile tribes in Utah that it did elsewhere in the West. One result was that the region east of the Sanpete and Sevier valleys long remained under Indian control.

Military and Other Official Explorations, 1850-1880

To this point our consideration of the exploration of the La Sal Forest and its environs has been primarily concerned with frontiersmen. Some were churchmen, some traders, and some Indian fighters, but for the most part they followed biddings other than official as they approached this area. Official explorers were also important. Southeastern Utah was one of the last areas in the continental United States to attract government explorers. In part this was the product of strained relationships between the Mormons and the federal government; in part it reflected the barrier reared by the region's remoteness and the hostility of the natives. But while government explorers came late, they did come; once involved they did more to lay bare the secrets of the canyonlands and their adjacent mountains than all earlier explorers. The following pages will briefly trace their impact and that of one unofficial but related exploration.

---

23. *Ibid.*, pp. 14-17. *See also* "Diary of Ethan Pettit," typescript, Utah State Historical Society.

24. For the best account of the Black Hawk War, see Peter Gottfredson, *History of Indian Depredations in Utah* (Salt Lake City: Skelton Publishing Co., 1919). *See also* Carlton Culmsee, *Utah's Black Hawk War* (Logan: Utah State University, 1973).

In the early 1850s no events held greater fascination to Americans than the discovery of gold at Sutter's Mill and California's subsequent admission as a state. Their imaginations fired by visions of a continental destiny, Americans in the early 1850s looked forward to a transcontinental link binding California to the motherland. The five great railroad surveys of 1853 were direct products of this excitement. One, the 39th Parallel Survey, passed through southeastern Utah.

This expedition was conducted under the leadership of Captain John W. Gunnison of the topographical engineers. With a party consisting of about seventy men, including a military escort, teamsters, and a small corps of scientists, he began his march from Fort Leavenworth in Kansas on June 23, 1853. His train consisted of eighteen six-mule wagons and sufficient livestock to draw them, as well as a number of drovers trailing sheep and cattle to California. He had chosen wagons as the mode of travel for two reasons: first, to test the practicality of the 39th Parallel's route for a wagon road and second, to better assess its suitability for a railroad.[25] Proceeding up the Arkansas River, Gunnison crossed through the Sangre de Cristo Pass into the San Luis Valley of Colorado, which he left by way of Cochetopa Pass, and, following what has since been known as the Gunnison River, descended to the Grand River at present-day Grand Junction. From about Cochetopa Pass, Gunnison's train was guided by Antoine Leroux, an experienced guide whose services were in frequent demand throughout the Southwest. Because of prior commitments, Leroux remained with Gunnison only long enough to get him down the long stretch of the Gunnison River and point him through the passageway that ran west between the Colorado River and the Roan Cliffs toward the Spanish Trail.

Included in the information Leroux transmitted was an account of how the Abajo Mountains came to be named. Looking out over southeastern Utah from a lofty eminence along the Gunnison River, he pointed to the highest peak in the small range and noted that it was near the "junction of Grand and Green Rivers, considerably below the fords for this trail, or. . . below any ford on Grand river known to the New Mexicans, and hence its name."[26]

Enabled by late summer rains to leave the serrated banks of the river, Gunnison made good time, striking the Spanish Trail about twenty miles southeast of the Green River crossing on September 29. To Gunnison's eye—pleased by past weeks of grand scenery in the Rockies—the surroundings presented a sorry spectacle. He reported that it was disheartening in the extreme:

Except [for] three or four small cotton-wood trees in the ravine near us, there is not a tree to be seen. The plain lying between us and the Wahsatch range, a hundred miles to the west, is a series of rocks, parallel

---

25. Beckwith, p. 5.
26. Ibid., p. 57.

chasms, and fantastic sandstone ridges. On the north, Roan mountain, ten miles from us, presents bare masses of sandstone, and on the higher ridges, twenty miles back, a few scattering cedars may be distinguished by the glass; Salt Mountain [the La Sals] to the east, is covered half down its sides with snow; and to the south, mass after mass of coarse conglomerate is broken in fragments, or piled in turret-shaped heaps, colored by ferruginous cement from a dark black to a brilliant red, whilst in some rocks there are argilaceous layers, varying to gray or glistening white. The surface around us is whitened with fields of alkali, precisely resembling fields of snow.[27]

Southeastern Utah's deserts obviously had much the same appearance in 1853 as they do today. However, the California migrants that trailed their herds through this same desert in Gunnison's wake reported that their stock came through in good shape. As Lieutenant E. G. Beckwith, Gunnison's assistant, reported, this fact "bears directly upon the grass on this route."[28]

Arriving at the Green River on September 30, the Gunnison expedition crossed in one day, in contrast to the seven days that it would take the Elk Mountain Mission in the spring of 1855. On the west bank they found a group of "Green River Utahs" who, along with being the "merriest of their race," were uneasy about the war then under way between Chief Walker and the Mormons. In Castle Valley, west of the river, Gunnison continued to meet many Utes who had congregated along streams to take advantage of ripening buffalo berries. Like their tribesmen at the river crossing, they were initially afraid of the Gunnison party. However, once word had spread that the travelers were not Mormons, most of the natives were friendly but loath to be lured into any situation that would carry them nearer the settlements. Beginning at the Green River, the Gunnison party attempted to obtain an Indian guide. Just as it appeared that all overtures had been unsuccessful, one Indian more bold than the rest succumbed to the "display of . . . trinkets, cloths, paints, and blankets they so much covet" and offered his services. As it turned out he was both a good "judge of natural wagonroads" and prudent, for while they were still several days from the settlements of Sanpete Valley, he was smitten with remorse that he had left his family in "want for food" and, all protestations notwithstanding, took his leave.[29]

As indicated previously, Gunnison left the Spanish Trail on the second day out from the Green River. In a detour of seven days he advanced north along the Roan Cliffs to cross the White, or Price, River somewhat west of Woodside. Noting that the Price River "winds very much among high hills, frequently impinging against their bases, and at various points passing through narrow cañons," the com-

27. Ibid., p. 66.
28. Ibid., p. 75.
29. Ibid., pp. 68, 75.

pany judged it impractical as a course of travel and pressed on, likely turning west a bit north of where the river cuts through the point of Cedar Mountain. From here their course held south by southwest for several days before striking the Spanish Trail again in the neighborhood of Castle Dale. Signs of the old trail were so distinctly apparent in this area that the Gunnison chronicler noted on October 11:

> The Spanish Trail, though but seldom used of late years is still very distinct where the soil washes but slightly. On some such spaces to-day we counted from fourteen to twenty parallel trails, of the ordinary size of Indian trails or horse-paths, on a way of barely fifty feet in width.[30]

Unfortunately, time and traffic have obliterated almost every vestige of the Old Spanish Trail through southeastern Utah.

The explorers ascended Wahsatch, or Salina, Pass quickly and easily, taking no more than one day. The descent was another matter. It took them several trying days and much work to clear timber and to move rocks in order to reach the Sevier River.

Gunnison was killed by Indians a few days later near present Delta, Utah. The route he had explored was adjudged unsuited for transcontinental railroading. On the other hand, a more southerly emigrant road to California had been opened and the military had been given access to "and command of," the Utah country.[31] Southeastern Utah also had been opened to wagon traffic. As we have seen, Mormons passed over Gunnison's road during the next two years in their effort to establish the Elk Mountain Mission. The road's opening was directly responsible for the timing of that enterprise.

The transcontinental railroad surveys of 1853 also spawned a freelance exploration which passed through southeastern Utah. Led by John C. Frémont, this expedition showed little of the competence apparent in the conduct of the Gunnison survey. In a sense, Frémont's was a spite trip because he had not been awarded one of the official surveys. In another sense it was an act of archaic chivalry quite as anachronistic as Don Quixote's had been. In still another, it was merely another adventure in Frémont's ongoing political joust.

Organizing in August of 1853, Frémont left St. Louis late in the season, hoping to upstage any achievement of the official survey by making a winter crossing of the Rocky Mountains. With ten Delaware Indians and a retinue of scientists and comrades that read like a Who's Who of the international set, but without a guide, he plunged into the mountains of southern Colorado as a hard winter struck. Following the Grand River (as the Colorado above its confluence with the Green was known), the party was reduced to eating horseflesh. With a show of gallantry and an eye to a publications achievement even more spectacular than the reports of his earlier explorations, Frémont pressed through deepening snows, crossing the Green River

---

30. Ibid., p. 71.
31. Ibid., p. 77.

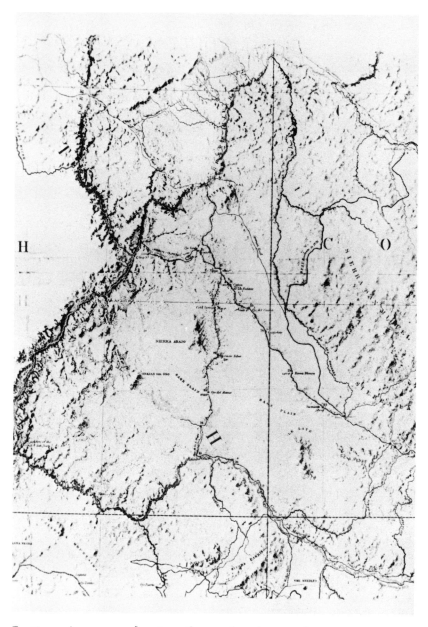

Portion of a map showing the explorations and surveys in New Mexico and Utah made under direction of the secretary of war by Captain J. N. Macomb, assisted by C. H. Dimmock. Adapted from Macomb, *Exploring Expedition.*

and floundering across Castle Valley—in this particular year a barren expanse of deep snow, terribly cold and devoid of either provender for stock or of game for human nourishment. Ignoring or missing Gunnison's Salina Pass route, he took what has come to be known as Frémont's Junction into Rabbit Valley, where a stream and village were subsequently named for him. Desperate in the face of mounting hunger, he cached his paraphernalia and turned west, traveling by way of Grass Valley and the Sevier River to Parowan.

Reflecting little credit on Frémont, the expedition was never officially committed to writing. Priceless daguerreotypes taken by S. N. Carvalho were lost or burned, as were Frémont's notes. A confused tradition, the essence of which emphasized man's puniness in the face of desert wilderness, was its main product.[32]

The occupation of Utah by federal troops during the so-called Mormon War led to a less colorful but more important exploration in 1859. Intent on establishing alternate routes into the Great Basin, the government ordered Captain John N. Macomb, chief topographical officer in New Mexico, to check the possibilities of the Old Spanish Trail. With an appropriation of $20,000, Macomb was able to take John Strong Newberry, America's foremost geologist, and a military escort under Lieutenant Milton Cogswell, as well as to obtain the services of Albert H. Pfieffer, a well-known and effective agent to the Utes in northern New Mexico and southern Colorado.[33]

Macomb left Santa Fe in mid-July, 1859, calling his exploration the San Juan Expedition. Taking the Old Spanish Trail, he followed the Rio Chama and the southern base of the La Plata Mountains to the Colorado Plateau. He gave the vast sweep of country that lay ahead the apt name of the Great Sage Plain, and continued on into Utah, touching at well-used watering places named Guajelotes—after its water dogs—and Ojo del Cuerbo. Macomb's Ojo del Cuerbo may well be Paiute Spring, which lies directly east of Monticello just inside the Utah border. If not Paiute Spring, it was some other spring in the

32. Sources for Frémont are Solomon Nunes Carvalho, *Incidents of Travel and Adventure in the Far West,* ed. Bertram W. Korn (Philadelphia: Jewish Publication Society of America, 1954); Leland Hargrave Creer, *The Founding of an Empire* (Salt Lake City: Bookcraft, 1947), pp. 121-23; and Jacob H. Schiel, *Journey Through the Rocky Mountains and the Humboldt Mountains to the Pacific Ocean,* trans. and ed. Thomas N. Bonner (Norman: University of Oklahoma Press, 1959).

33. John N. Macomb, *Report of the Exploring Expedition from Santa Fe, New Mexico to the Junction of the Grand and Green Rivers . . . 1859* (Washington, D.C.: U.S. Government Printing Office, 1876). *See also* A. B. Bender, "Government Exploration in the Territory of New Mexico, 1846-1859," *New Mexico Historical Review* 11 (1934): 26; A. A. Humphreys to J. N. Macomb, 6 April 1859, *Senate Executive Document 1,* 36th Cong., 2d Sess., 1859-1860, 146; and Scott L. Greenwell, "A History of the United States Army Corps of Topographical Engineers in Utah, 1843-1859" (Master's thesis, Utah State University, 1972), pp. 197-204.

Spanish Bottoms of the Colorado River at the mouth of Lockhart Draw.

same neighborhood, since Newberry suggested a rough triangulation that permits location with a fair degree of accuracy: "We have approached comparatively near to the Sierras Abajo and La Sal, the one being twenty, the other forty miles distant."[34]

At a point fifteen miles northeast of "the Sierra Abajo," Macomb followed a lateral canyon into the great depression (Dry Valley) that spreads between the two mountains. From there his expedition continued through what they termed Cañon Pintado to "Saurian camp," where they found petrified dinosaur bones, before going on to deep tanks in the sandstone which had "become an important watering-place on the Spanish Trail" and thence to Ojo Verde, "a copious spring in a cañon cut out of the red sandstone."[35] Leaving most of the party, Macomb and Newberry then struck southwest from the Spanish Trail following a long canyon to the heart of present Canyonlands National Park, where they became the first known Anglo-Americans to see the confluence of the Green and Colorado rivers.[36]

In traveling to Utah they had taken the Spanish Trail the entire distance. In this they had accomplished one of their purposes. Another objective was to chart the trail's course. According to the map that accompanies Macomb's report, their course after entering Utah

34. Macomb, p. 90.
35. Ibid., p. 93.
36. Ibid., p. 97.

coincided with the western variant of the Spanish Trail to a point a few miles east of their camp at Ojo Verde. Beyond that point their map projected the main trunk of the Spanish Trail across Dry Valley in a northerly direction to Kane Spring and drops through Spanish Valley to cross the Colorado River just north of modern Moab. An eastern variant of the trail is shown as approximating Father Escalante's route from the big bend of the Dolores River for a number of miles before bearing off to the left, evidently through Paradox Valley, and from there over the east point of the La Sal Mountains.

Having satisfied Newberry's interest in the geology of the Colorado River, the explorers returned to Ojo Verde, where Newberry recorded the following description of the La Sal Mountains:

> The La Sal Mountain shows very finely from this point, distant twenty miles. It is seen to be composed of several short ranges, separated by narrow valleys; having a trend several degrees north of east, but these are set somewhat *en echelon,* and the direction of the longest diameter of the mountain mass is north-northwest and south-southeast; such, at least, seems to be the structure of this sierra as seen from a distance.[37]

Heading almost due south they left Dry Valley by what must have been Peter's Hill, crossing the east bench of the Abajo Mountains and making their camps at springs in the vicinities of what later came to be Carlisle Ranch, Monticello, and Verdure. Interestingly, they called one of the springs on the east slope of the Abajos (in the immediate neighborhood of Monticello) Mormon Spring. No explanation of where the name came from is given, but there can be no doubt that it is a clear recognition that Mormon travelers had passed that way. It is impossible to know surely whether it reflected the passing of groups subsequent to the Elk Mountain Navajo expedition. However, given man's tendency to roam and the obvious interest of the Navajos in trade, one is tempted to suspect that other Mormons had also camped there. While at Mormon Spring, Newberry gave America its first word picture of the Sierra Abajo:

> Within the last few weeks we have been on three sides of this sierra, and have learned its structure quite definitely. It is a mountain group of no great elevation, its highest point rising some 2,000 feet above the Sage-plain, or perhaps 9,000 feet above the sea. It is composed of several distinct ranges, of which the most westerly one is quite detached from the others. All these ranges, of which there are apparently four, have a trend of about 25° east of north, but being arranged somewhat *en echelon,* the most westerly range reaching farthest north, the principal axis of the group has a northwest and southeast direction.[38]

The explorers then traveled south, possibly by way of Recapture Wash, to strike "the San Juan River, in latitude 37° 16′ 27″ and longitude 109° 24′ 43″, on the 2d September, 1859." Finding the bottom-

---

37. Ibid., p. 93.
38. Ibid., p. 100.

land of the river to be "a light and loose soil, into which the feet of the mules would frequently sink for some 18 inches," they worked up the north bank of the river for about 120 miles before crossing and heading back to Santa Fe via Cañon Largo.[39]

As Macomb made his way homeward in the fall of 1859, America was entering the period of the Civil War. The Old Spanish Trail was forgotten for the time being, but from the war itself and from the generation it spawned came the last great explorers of the American West and the first great managers of the public domain. Among these were John Wesley Powell and Ferdinand V. Hayden.

Preoccupation with the war was such that it was 1869 before official explorers began to find their way into the country again. In that year Powell floated down the Green and Colorado rivers. Canyon-locked most of his downstream trip, he saw little enough of the mountains adjacent to the river, but at those points where walls broke or he climbed to some eminence, Powell doubtless saw the La Sal and Abajo ranges. Furthermore, as he made his second canyon journey in 1871 and later surveyed and explored the plateau country west of the river, he came to understand the balance between mountain and moisture on the one hand and desert and canyon on the other. Clear to him also was the importance of grazing to the successful exploitation of such a country. In his mind emerged a sense of the relationship of frontier society and control of natural resources that this work traces in the La Sal National Forest area.[40]

To the east of the Colorado River the plateau country lay in the domain of another of the west's great surveyors, Ferdinand V. Hayden. Although most of his attention focused on areas beyond Utah's borders, his surveys did extend into its extreme southeast, beginning with an expedition to the La Sal Mountains in 1875. Actually, two Hayden parties—one under James L. Gardner, geographer and first assistant of the Hayden Survey, and one under Henry Gannet, later head of the United States Geological Survey—joined in the La Sal reconnaissance. They met somewhere in the field east of the La Sals and proceeded together. Numbering thirteen men and eighteen pack animals, the combined group passed west from the Gunnison River to the Dolores via Unaweep Canyon, a fine natural passageway later known as the Gateway Trail. Crossing the Dolores, they found the east spur of the La Sals immediately ahead. Mounting this, they worked from a base camp well up the mountain's east side for about two weeks, during which time they must have obtained a good idea

---

39. Ibid., p. 6.
40. See John Wesley Powell, *Report on the Lands of the Arid Region of the United States, With a More Detailed Account of the Lands of Utah*, 2d ed. (Washington, D.C.: U.S. Government Printing Office, 1879). *See also* William Culp Darrah, *Powell of the Colorado* (Princeton: Princeton University Press, 1951); and Wallace Stegner, *Beyond the Hundredth Meridian: John Wesley Powell and the Second Opening of the West* (Boston: Houghton Mifflin, 1954).

of the general layout of the mountain. To the Hayden explorers fell the honor of naming many of the La Sal peaks, including Mount Peale and Mount Tukuhnikivatz. They also charted the mountain's major drainages with considerable fidelity.[41]

Having completed their work on the La Sals, the Gardner-Gannett party headed southwest across Dry Valley to conduct a similar reconnaissance of the Sierra Abajo. At this point, however, Indians intervened, and the Hayden surveyors fled, abandoning their plans to survey the Blues. Unfortunately, they were forced to dump their scientific equipment and records of the La Sal survey to hasten their retreat.

The same month another Hayden party crossed from the Hopi village of Tewa to the Mancos River. Included was William Henry Jackson, one of the West's great photographers, who recorded that the party had a brush with Indians somewhere along Montezuma Creek that culminated in little loss except to the dignity of the explorers.[42] But the two episodes cooled the ardor of Hayden's men, and the Abajos were not surveyed that season. Indeed, the Hayden reports indicate that the latter mountains were never the object of the kind of attention given the La Sals in 1875.

However, two additional explorations of the La Sal Forest area were conducted by Hayden surveys in 1876. The first of these was under the direction of W. H. Holmes and a Mr. Wilson. The object of their expedition was the Sierra Abajo "or Low Mountains of Southeast Utah."[43] Approaching the Abajos from the east along the Old Spanish Trail in mid-September, they were delayed for several days by unseasonable storms. Behind schedule, they did no more than ascend the main summit, which they were able to gain on horseback by means of "a steep ridge" projecting four or five miles "to the east from the main crest."[44] Wilson established "the desired primary triangulation station," which seems to suggest that some more or less consistent survey of the region was contemplated. But for the moment they did nothing more than look, make a few sketches—some of which are of excellent quality—and record a few impressions. Of significance here is that Holmes recognized the Elk Plateau for what it is but interestingly called it by a name that reflected one of its most dominant features—Bear's Ears Plateau. After this cursory glimpse, Holmes turned east, following a footpath he hoped would lead him directly to western Colorado's Lone Cone, which at eighty miles distance was

41. Ferdinand V. Hayden, *Ninth Annual Report of the United States Geological and Geographical Survey* (Washington, D.C.: U.S. Government Printing Office, 1876); and *New York Times*, 5, 9, and 25 September 1875.
42. William Henry Jackson, *Time Exposure* (New York: G. P. Putnam's Sons, 1940), pp. 240-41.
43. Ferdinand V. Hayden, *United States Geological and Geographical Survey of the Territories* 10 (Washington, D.C.: U.S. Government Printing Office, 1878): 189.
44. Ibid.

plainly visible then as it is today. Holmes was disappointed in his hope that a direct route existed between the two mountains when he came on a canyon 2,000 feet in depth that forced him to detour north twenty miles to an access point where he had crossed the previous year.[45] While Wilson paused to establish a triangulation station on the Lone Cone, Holmes rushed on to the "Central or Dolores group of the San Miguel" where he conducted another hurried reconnaissance. He had, as he put it, completed "within a period of 84 hours the examination of two important mountain groups, distant from each other fully 100 miles. This great haste was necessitated by circumstances over which we had not control."[46] Those of us interested in the history of southeastern Utah may well lament that "circumstances" resulted in a limited record for the area.

Henry Gannett apparently also made a reconnaissance that enabled him to discuss the drainage areas of the Grand and San Juan rivers. But in both cases his efforts were concentrated primarily in Colorado, producing little information of importance to the study here presented. William H. Jackson and W. H. Holmes also worked on prehistoric remnants in the area. The course of each crossed in and out of Utah, but their reports reflect little information on the forest region.

Lower San Juan. From J. N. Macomb, *Exploring Expedition.*

45. Ibid., p. 193.
46. Ibid.

General Land Office surveys had penetrated the San Juan country by 1880. That year Mormon settlers found a blazed tree marked by a "Ferdinand Decker" (actually his name was Ferdinand Dickert), noting the elevation and the number of miles from Salt Lake City. An examination of the land office records at the Bureau of Land Management office in Salt Lake City also reveals that R. J. Reeves surveyed Township 33S 26E near the Colorado border in July 1878; the next month Ferdinand Dickert surveyed four noncontiguous townships. Others followed until by the time settlers arrived at Bluff in 1880, at least four, and possibly more, land office surveyors had worked the country.

The history of southeastern Utah during the century that ended in 1880 was largely the history of its exploration. In the main it was an uncoordinated effort. No fewer than three nations took part, and at least four groups were involved—the Spanish, mountain men, Mormons, and official explorers. A progressive development is discernible as trails and camps opened by one group were utilized by the next, and some cause and effect relationship is apparent in their various approaches to the area. Yet the exploration of each group was largely independent of the others and was prompted by quite different objectives. Spanish and Mexican traffic over the Old Spanish Trail made the region part of a transmontane thoroughfare by the early 1830s— better known than most areas in the West. After the Mexican War the region received little attention for several decades. Fur trappers and other travelers passed that way less frequently than before. The entire eastern part of Utah was an "outback" to the Mormons, and, with the exception of the Elk Mountain Mission and a few random penetrations, they knew little of it. Government explorers—from Gunnison to Powell and Hayden—did most to make the region known. They took its awesome measure, recognized some of its characteristics, sensed its enchantment, and began to assess its prospects. By 1880 settlement was only beginning, but the groundwork was laid. Much of the area was known. In the years that followed, a sparse population moved in, dividing itself into two identifiable elements. One was the Mormon-mission colony along the San Juan River and the other a more individualistic settlement in the neighborhood of the La Sal Mountains.

Chapter II

Settlement around the La Sal Mountains 1875-1885

Converging Forces

The process of colonization was launched early in the Great Basin portion of Utah. Beginning with the founding of Salt Lake City in 1847, Mormon colonies extended north and south during the next three decades until virtually every habitable oasis was taken up. By contrast the Colorado Plateau long lay beyond the pale of Utah settlement. For all practical purposes it remained unheralded, unprized, and uninhabited until the latter part of the 1870s.

Elsewhere in the Four Corners region, settlement forged ahead of this last wilderness area. Statehood came for Colorado in 1876, by which time mines, railroads, and livestock were converging on its southwest corner. Known to generations of Hispanic frontiersmen, northern New Mexico and Arizona were occupied by scattered forts and Indian agencies during the decades after the Treaty of Guadalupe Hidalgo. And Mormon colonizers, ranchers, miners, and traders began to move into the region in appreciable numbers in the years immediately prior to settlement of Utah's far southeast.[1]

With the Mormon settlements beyond the rim of the Great Basin to the northwest, the burgeoning state of Colorado to the east, and nascent communities in northern Arizona and New Mexico, the arid and rugged distances of southeastern Utah finally began to yield to encroaching civilization. Hardy cowboys with no strong need for close neighbors appeared first, arriving at least as early as 1877. Miners may well have preceded them but left a mark so

---

1. For Mormon settlement of northern Arizona and New Mexico, see Charles S. Peterson, *Take Up Your Mission: Mormon Colonizing Along the Little Colorado River, 1870-1900* (Tucson: University of Arizona Press, 1973).

fleeting that their doings are impossible to reconstruct. Close on the heels of the first small stockmen (and in some cases included among them) came the Mormons. First Fort Montezuma, then Bluff, and, as the years turned, a handful of other villages were established, along with a number of false beginnings that could not stave off drought, distance, and poverty long enough to become towns. The great livestock men came almost simultaneously with the Mormons. Following the lead of the first small ranchers, men with money founded a half-dozen large cattle outfits. Before long a pressing procession of miners added their influence. Beginning in the mid-1880s, the miners sweated and choked in canyon infernos along the San Juan River or, according to the season, reveled or shivered in camps high in the Blue Mountains and the La Sals. Planning and talking, they dreamed of jerry-built mining towns, mills and smelters, roads and railroads, and most of all, of breathtaking wealth.

Thus, when it did take place, settlement in southeastern Utah was the result of numerous wakening forces. While it oversimplifies, the complexity of these forces may be reduced by regarding settlement in terms of Mormon and gentile. The processes employed by the Mormons in occupying a country tended to the unique and restricted, the gentiles to the general and characteristic. Too much may be made of Mormon cohesiveness, as it may be of gentile individualism. Yet there was a cooperative Mormon mode to which enough Latter-day Saints adhered to make it clearly distinguishable from the more economically, promotionally, and individualistically oriented style of the gentiles. In addition to this social division, something of a geographic axis existed as well, with the Mormon influence strongest in the south, or San Juan area, and the gentile in the north around the La Sal Mountains. Neither influence monopolized its sphere, but each clearly marked its area. In the settlement of the San Juan country the mission form was dominant; at Moab, Castleton, and La Sal, the individual was more important. Another way of characterizing the distinction between the two communities is to note that the Moab area was settled; the San Juan area was colonized. To the one, settlers came seeking their own fortunes; to the other, a colony was sent, directed by the central leadership of the Church.

Ranches at Moab and La Sal

Since this was true, the first settlements of the Little Grand Valley (Moab) and La Sal areas developed without benefit of the extensive records that so often characterized Mormon colonization. Consequently, beginnings there are sometimes vague and difficult to trace. There is one important exception, however, and that is the Elk Mountain Mission which has been considered in another con-

Pioneer road north from Moab. U.S. Forest Service photo.

nection.[2] With the failure of the Elk Mountain Mission, the area passed from view, although part of Johnston's Army made its way from Utah via the Old Spanish Trail and must certainly have crossed at what is now Moab. The Black Hawk Indian War—finally settled in 1869—along with the formidable canyons of the Colorado, were effective barriers for many years. But with the growth of the livestock industry and continuing quests for new mining frontiers, Little Grand Valley and the La Sal Mountains began again to assume importance during the 1870s. The first shadowy entrants emerge in a confusing chronology during the latter half of the 1870s.

According to Faun M. Tanner, Moab historian, two cowboys, George and Silas Green, wintered about four hundred cattle in this area in 1874-75.[3] Other sources place this date in some question, and the winter they spent there may have been the next or even

2. According to L. D. Heywood, formerly La Sal Forest Supervisor, the irrigation ditch by which the missionaries took water from Mill Creek was left open and water continued to run in it, cutting an "arroyo through town which was still clearly visible in 1940." See "Historical Information, La Sal National Forest" (1940), Manti-La Sal National Forest Historical Files, Price, Utah, p. 32.

3. Faun McConkie Tanner, *A History of Moab, Utah* (Moab: Times-Independent Press, 1937), p. 27.

the following year. By 1877 a somewhat more evident set of events may be seen. At that time a number of families from the "Utah settlements" pushed into the area. The newcomers found a Negro, William Granstaff, and a French-Canadian trapper living at the old Elk Mountain Fort. These two men had come into the valley prospecting and stayed to raise a few vegetables and gather some of the remaining Green cattle. Each claimed half of the old fort and substantial areas in the valley. They had sufficiently laid their imprint on the region for a major La Sal Mountain drainage, where Granstaff ran his share of the Green cattle, to be called Nigger Bill Canyon. During 1877 additional settlers arrived. According to Frank Silvey, pioneer historian of the La Sal locality, the family of Tom Ray arrived in the spring, going through Little Grand Valley to what is now Old La Sal, where they established a ranch and ran a fine herd of Milking Shorthorns.[4] Coming from Tennessee by way of California and then Mount Pleasant, the Rays had intermarried with and become friends to the Maxwells (Cornelius, Philander, and Tom), Neals Olson, and Billie McCarty and his family, all of whom followed the Rays to the south slope of the La Sal Mountains, settling at Coyote or present La Sal during the autumn of 1877. Arthur Barney of Sevier County was hired by McCarty to help him make the move. The account of Barney's trip into the remote and primitive "Lasalle mountain in Colorado" is both interesting and instructive:

> That fall a Mr. Billie Mccary [McCarty] come along and wanted 2 or 3 teams to go the Lasalle mountain in Colorado with provisions for his ranch which was about 50 miles southeast of the Le Grande river. I got Uncle Walter and his son John to take a load and to go with me, we loaded up and went to Salina creek to where Gooseberry empties into Salina creek. Then up Gooseberry creek and over the Taylor mountain, up Meadow gulch into Castle valley, through Castle valley, through Buckhorn Flat, past the points of Cedar mountain, down a long gulch to Green river, where Green river city is now located. But at that time it was a wild unsettled country from Salina, except 3 or 4 families on Grand river. . . . By the time we got to the Grand river our stock was gaunt and hungry and no feed or grass on the west side of the river. And on the east [west?] side of the river was a notice, "No Camping Allowed." That looked kind of suspicious to me so I went and read the notice again, then I took it down and threw it out in the river as far as I could. Then John and I took two of the horses to test the ford and to see what was on the other side of the river. When we got on the other side we found the whole country covered with grass about a foot high. We looked up the valley about a half mile and seen a house, so we headed for the house. When we got to it a woman came out. We passed the

4. Frank Silvey, *History and Settlement of Northern San Juan County* (n.p., n.d.), p. 2. According to A. N. Ray, a son of Tom Ray, the Ray party arrived in Moab during October 1877, and proceeded to La Sal Creek on 1 January 1878. The Maxwells and McCartys are said to have taken up their ranches at Coyote at the same time. *See* A. N. Ray, La Sal National Forest Historical Document (1936), Manti-La Sal National Forest Historical Files.

time of day with her, and as she seemed to be in a talking mood, I asked her how it was that there was no camping allowed on this side of the river, she said "This is a free country and you can camp where you please." So I told her about the notice on the other side of the river. You ought to have throwed the notice into the river, which seemed to ease her a little. When we started back she hollowed [sic] after us and told us to come over and stay just as long as we wanted to. So we re-crossed the Grand river and started over with our wagons. This was on a riffle and if you got too far down you went into swimming water, the ford was crooked so I took lead and when we had got about half way across I looked back and could see that Uncle was gitting to low down so I yelled at him to pull up the river which he did. . . .

Now we are on the east side of the Grand river where we camped with plenty of grass and fire wood, we stayed here until next morning when we started on up a long narrow valley. Our next water was Kane

Stock's Ranch near Moab about 1915. U.S. Forest Service photo.

springs where we camped over night. That day we were in Montie valley, plenty of grass and lots of cedars at night were at the Mc-Carty ranch at the foot of the La Salle mountains in Colorado, so we unloaded. Next morning we started back on our lonesome road. When we got back to Monroe our horses were pretty well jaded and looked like the last rose of hard times and starvation.[5]

Reading Barney's account one wonders if even at that early date an influx of people had not aroused hostility and opposition. It is easy to believe that Bill Granstaff or his French cohort—or whoever may have inscribed the sign Barney so expeditiously took care of—meant to resist even 1877's trickle of migration. Whether or not the Frenchman had protested against emigrants pasturing stock on country he considered to be his own, it was only a short time before he withdrew in the face of encroaching civilization and is said to have floated on down the Colorado River in quest of trapping opportunities.[6] Granstaff also soon passed from view.

Paradox Valley, just beyond the east slope of the La Sal Mountains on the Dolores River, was first settled in 1879. According to some accounts, the initial settler was Bill Hamilton, who established a ranch just below the present site of Paradox. The following years the Galloways and Goshorns moved onto ranches in the upper valley, Tom Swain came in 1881, and the Talbert and Waggoner families arrived soon after from Nevada. The Taylor brothers, who came in 1877, trailed cattle into the northeast slopes of the La Sals looking for a trail the Indians had told them about and located the fine grazing country later known as Taylor Flats and Taylor Creek. Somewhat later John Brown, Philander Maxwell, and Irving D. Ames settled in Sinbad Valley north of Paradox. Ames was particularly active in his efforts to develop the area, building a ditch from Taylor Creek to Sinbad Valley.

The Emergence of Towns

During the next three or four years settlers continued to come into the area, establishing communities in Little Grand (Moab) Valley, Little Castle Valley, and on the south side of the La Sals.[7] Coming for the most part in small family groups, settlers were usually cattlemen looking for new ranges, but some came to homestead and develop farms and orchards. The stockmen apparently

5.   Journal of Arthur Barney, typescript, Brigham Young University, pp. 36-38.
6.   Tanner, p. 30.
7.   In 1880 Richardson was established by a Professor Richardson, a teacher, who ran a post office, giving the town its name. Professor Valley and Professor Creek were also named for him. Dewey, located in the same general locality, was named after Admiral George Dewey following his victory over the Spanish fleet in Manilla Harbor in 1898. See H. S. Rutledge, La Sal National Forest Historical Document (1936), p. 7. For other Grand County settlements see Phyllis Cortes, comp., *Grand Memories*, (Salt Lake City, 1972).

entered into farming to the degree their interest in livestock permitted, and rudimentary irrigation systems soon were developed at Moab and Bueno and perhaps elsewhere.

Such evidence as exists points to the Mormon settlements as the most important places of origin for this influx. However, very few Mormons appear to have felt they were called and sent to the country as missionaries. Apparently the only one who was clearly directed by Church call was Randolph H. Stewart from Huntington, who was assigned as bishop of Moab in 1881. Others, like polygamist John H. Standiford, who took sanctuary in Moab during the mid-1880s, may have been counseled by the Church to repair to this remote quarter but were not called in the strict sense of the term. This same period saw the first settlement of what is now Emery County. While the Church officially sanctioned movement from Sanpete to Emery County's Castle Valley, it did not employ the formal mission call as it did in the colonization of northern Arizona and the San Juan. In one sense, settlement around Moab was an extension of this general movement east from Sanpete and Sevier counties, and many of its first settlers originated in those counties. On the other hand, settlements in the locality were characterized by larger numbers of non-Mormons, and a spirit of free enterprise and independence existed that was alien to the Emery County towns and, as we shall see, to the settlers of southeastern Utah's San Juan.

With its strategic location near the river crossing, Moab had natural advantages that quickly made it the most important of the new towns. Called first Mormon Fort and then Grand Valley, it was named Moab probably as early as 1881 by a committee appointed for that purpose. The choice stemmed, according to a tradition cited by Faun M. Tanner in her *History of Moab*, from a Bible-reading settler named W. A. Peirce who saw in the region's remoteness and flat-topped plateaus a similarity to the biblical Moab known as the "Far Country" and as a land of flat-topped mountains.[8] Moab's supremacy notwithstanding, Little Grand Valley's first post office was located a few miles up Spanish Valley at Bueno, or Poverty Flats, under the name of Plainfield. The dominance of the town nearer the river, however, soon resulted in a shift, placing the post office in Moab. By 1880 Coyote (present La Sal) and La Sal (Old La Sal) both had villages of a half-dozen families who banded together for protection from the Indians. Like Moab, they lay on a mail route that ran from Salina to Ouray, Colorado, through 350 miles of the roughest and wildest country in the American West. After 1879 La Sal boasted a post office, with Mrs. Tom Ray designated as postmistress. La Sal and Coyote were located at strategic spots that made possible their control of both water and grazing on the south slope of the La Sals; but life does not appear

8. Tanner, p. 32.

to have been easy. In addition to Indian problems, distance and climate made operations marginal, and the original families were soon scattered to various climes and activities, including the outlaw life of Bill McCarty's sons.[9]

While most early settlers came from the Utah settlements, there can be no question that some came from Colorado. Two important elements in this westward movement were mining and cattle ranching, both of which had their origins in Colorado. Indeed, southeastern Utah mining and big ranching were originally little more than extensions from Colorado. Names such as Tom Goshorn, Billy, or "Race Horse," Johnson, the May brothers, and the Talberts all leave clear trails back to Colorado.

Not entirely typical of this class of settler, but useful because the story of their coming to Utah has been told in some detail, was the family of John Silvey. Originating in Zanesville, Ohio, the elder Silvey had come west by stages, migrating to Missouri in 1867, to Iowa in 1874, then back to Missouri in 1878. Still restless, he pushed as far west as Leadville in the spring of 1882. Either dissatisfied with prospects there or not oriented to mining, he moved on and in the company of two sons, Jack and William, headed west by wagon. Making their way down the long drainage of the Gunnison River, they passed Grand Junction, which, in a terse remark that hints he might have planned to stop there, Mr. Silvey characterized as being fit only ". . . for the boys to play marbles on."[10] Over much of the route their course paralleled the grade of the Denver and Rio Grande Western Railway, which was then building into Utah. Leaving the line of the railway at Thompson, they arrived in Moab sometime in June, where they found twenty settlers and a post office. Frank Silvey, another son who has left an interesting account of settlement at La Sal, notes that there was no store at the time but fails to indicate whether the town boasted a school or a church. Moving on to La Sal, they found Tom Ray comfortably situated, and they established themselves in his neighborhood. In August, Mrs. Silvey and Frank came by train to Durango, where the elder Silvey met them and brought them back to their new home, passing through Mancos Valley, the Big Bend of the Dolores, and through Cross Canyon into Utah. By way of Three Step Hill, they came down Lisbon Valley where they were directed to water by means of a charcoal drawing of "a burro with its ears pitched forward, towards the water hole, with the words, 'See, See Water, Underneath.' "[11]

Pausing briefly at Coyote, they arrived in La Sal, where they

9. Charles Kelly, *The Outlaw Trail: A History of Butch Cassidy and His Wild Bunch* (New York: Bonanza Books, 1938), p. 16 ff.
10. Silvey, p. 24.
11. Ibid., p. 27.

immediately took up the work of improving squatter's claims they purchased from previous claimants. The primitive character of their lives was evident in the fact that they whipsawed lumber at the rate of two to three hundred feet per day to floor and roof the cabins into which they moved.[12]

Before turning from the settlement of the north end of the La Sal Division, reference should be made to Bueno and Castleton, both of which were established by the early 1880s. While he fails to address himself directly to the subject, Frank Silvey indicates that a prospector named Doby Brown, who had first located near Coyote, moved to the head of Castle Creek near where the Castleton post office was later established in 1882. Not long thereafter, the Pace family moved into the area, where they carried on a flourishing

Moab street, early twentieth century. U.S. Forest Service photo.

12.   Ibid.

livestock enterprise. Later, Castleton became a point of supply—albeit a most remote one since roads were late in being developed—for the mining districts that briefly appeared on the northwest slope of the La Sal Mountains. Little Castle Valley's proximity to the mines and to the river (the only possible mode of transportation) led to the development of sawmilling there at an early time. The Branson family, particularly, were active in the sawmilling business, floating down the river rafts that sometimes carried 10,000 feet of lumber.[13]

Located some six miles above Moab, Bueno—known first as Plainfield and more recently as Poverty Flats—was first settled during the late 1870s. While the division between settlers at Bueno and what might properly be referred to as early Moab is not entirely clear, it appears that J. H. Shafer, Fred Powell, and the family of A. G. Wilson had located in the southeastern part of Spanish Valley by 1879. During that year, settlers in the upper valley were sufficiently aggressive to establish the area's post office under the name of Plainfield, with C. M. Van Buren as postmaster. Comprised of a shifting ranch population, Bueno apparently became something of a ghost town with few, and perhaps no, settlers living in anything that might be termed a townsite during 1882-83. By 1885, however, Bueno had been injected with new life. Passing that way in November, F. A. Hammond, who was en route to San Juan County to take over the leadership of the Mormon community there, found five families "at Brother McConkie's." He described their circumstances: "They have raised one crop, have a nice location here for a town." Before heading on, Hammond took a turn up Pack Creek and around Spanish Valley, sizing up prospects for other townsites. Pleased with what he saw, he recorded: "Found good site 1½ miles east from where located [Bueno]—some 8000 acres of good land."[14] Although Hammond was an aggressive colonizer, little came of his plans to plant a sister town near Bueno. Unlike Moab, the upper end of Spanish Valley fell within the bounds of San Juan County when the Territorial Legislature established it in preparation for the San Juan Mission in 1880. Isolated from the south San Juan community, Bueno was more oriented to Moab during its first years. Later, Erastus Bingham, G. W. McConkie, and other public-minded citizens worked to get San Juan County to establish a school there and to give their area the attention it deserved with regard to roads.[15] Meantime a concurrent but quite different set of events led to the development of San Juan County.

---

13. *Grand Valley Times* (Moab, Utah), 1 October 1897.

14. Francis A. Hammond Journal, 21-24 November 1884, original, Historical Department of The Church of Jesus Christ of Latter-day Saints, Salt Lake City, Utah.

15. Minutes of San Juan County Court, 1880-1900, xerox, Utah State Historical Society, p. 32.

Chapter III

Colonization of San Juan

The San Juan Mission

If the record of early settlement in the Moab area is limited, the record of colonization on the San Juan River is definite and extensive. More precisely, it is the record of the Mormon Church's San Juan mission that is definite and extensive. Beginning with exploration in 1879, Mormon colonizing extended well into the twentieth century. Unlike the communities that clustered around the base of the La Sal Mountains, the San Juan was colonized under the auspices of the Mormon Church. It was designated as an area of colonization by the Church, and its population was originally established by mission call and in large measure maintained during its formative years by the same method. It was a united effort. Cooperation characterized its process. Laudable as these qualities may be, the San Juan Mission did not avoid trouble and even defeat. Indeed, the history of the mission with its heroic but, as it proved in the long run, hopeless effort to find passageway via the Hole-in-the-Rock suggests that cooperation and common goals were not only insufficient at times but also contributed to human suffering. Individuals, lacking the organization and confidence provided by the causes and the leadership of the Church, probably would not have conceived of the undertaking, or if they had, would have recoiled from its threats, thus avoiding its costs.[1]

It is important to note that by 1880 the colonizing mission was a passing phenomenon in the Church. More individualistic methods were coming to predominate. But for the hardy handful who were

---

1. For the definitive treatment of the Hole-in-the-Rock experience, see David E. Miller, *Hole-in-the-Rock: An Epic in the Colonization of the Great American West* (Salt Lake City: 1959).

true to their call, the San Juan Mission was of transcendent importance. By a thousand repetitions, they confirmed that they were especially chosen to control renegade Indians and whites who, if left to their own designs, would menace the Mormon community at large. As Albert R. Lyman, historian of San Juan, puts it, the mission was a buffer, planted "in the very heart of all this incipient danger. . . ."[2] Or as the son of a member of the original party elaborated:

> . . . They were an established outpost, detracting marauding Indians from interior southern settlements of Utah Territory as well as being a point of interception of bank robbers, horse thieves, cattle rustlers. . . . These people were to be the shock absorbers of premeditated plots of Caucasian outlaws and Indian renegades. . . .[3]

However, among some of them there was a marked ambivalence as to the wisdom and even the propriety of the mission. As the rigors of colonization were confronted, this ambivalence was manifest in vacillation and difference of opinion, both on the part of the San Juan missionaries and the Church leaders upon whom the former depended for assurance that their sacrifices were meaningful. Indeed, it may be said that the first five years on the San Juan were spent in an agonized discussion about the merits of continuing the mission. Division among the settlers was apparent from the time of their arrival, continuing in dissension and in many cases despair and withdrawal.

Doubt that the mission's gain to the Church was worth its human costs appeared at the highest level as early as 1881. After hearing that danger from Indians was great and that a livelihood could be had only by working away from home, President John Taylor declared that the Presidency of the Church did not require the missionaries to stay if it were not a good place to live.[4] Taylor's feeling that the Church's design upon the country was not such as to require people to remain against their will was not shared by everyone. Edward Dalton of Parowan, who was dispatched to Bluff as Taylor's representative, appears to have directed the missionaries to persist. After his visit they tightened their belts and rebaptized each other, hoping thus to purge division and frustration.[5] In October of 1883, Platte D. Lyman, who was president of the San Juan Stake, visited Salt Lake City. He found Church leaders there divided "with regard to the

---

2. Albert R. Lyman, "The Fort on the Firing Line," *Improvement Era*, 51 (1848): 797. *See also* "The Writings of Kumen Jones," typescript, Brigham Young University, Provo, Utah, preface.

3. Morgan Amasa Barton, "Back Door to San Juan," p. 9, as quoted in Miller, pp. 41-42.

4. Diary of L. John Nuttall, 3-5 November 1881, typescript, Brigham Young University, Provo, Utah, pp. 406-9. Nuttall was Taylor's secretary and for several years kept excellent notes on the inner councils of the presidency.

5. Journal of Platte D. Lyman, 3-10 December 1881, typescript, Utah State Historical Society, pp. 45-46.

wisdom of continuing" the mission.[6] Returning to Bluff, he found "some of the people considerably exercised over a report of the probality [*sic*] of the abandonment of this mission, which however strikes many of the people quite favorably." A public letter followed in which Apostle Erastus Snow charged Lyman with being "destitute of faith" because he felt the costs of "securing the region" outweighed its worth.[7] A heated discussion ensued, during the course of which a majority expressed themselves as favoring at least one more season. The question remained open, with leaders and missionaries divided in opinion, until 1885. The cost of doubt was high in terms of anxiety and intransigence, but, like other problems, it was dealt with by the group and the sense of destiny and peculiar cooperativeness of the mission were fixed on the country.

The San Juan District: Terra Incognita

Because of this emphasis on the mission, folklore, Church records, and history books alike give the impression that San Juan began with the mission's advent. Indeed the tradition that the country was absolutely raw exists in something of a contradiction to the idea that it was a haven for cowboys and outlaws, the control of whom required the establishment of a buffer community. An examination of the early record reveals that in reality the country had been the object of some attention before 1879. However, since evidence of earlier penetration was not obvious, the tendency of the San Juan Mission to regard the country as pristine at the time of its entry is understandable. Characteristic was the reaction of one member of the Hayden Survey who had written in 1875: "If a wilderness be a region which has no place on the maps and no sign of civilized habitation, then the Sierra La Sal is certainly a wilderness. . . ." He informed readers that there was no record of any penetration and that before the Hayden Survey there was "no sign that prospectors had wandered there" and no settlements "North, South, East, or West" nearer than 200 miles. It was, he concluded, "emphatically the *terra incognita* of the country."[8]

Terra incognita it was. But, as indicated in our chapter on exploration, it had been the object of numerous visits. Explorers and miners had learned much about the country, and an indefinite number of prospectors appear to have worked it. John D. Lee, of Mountain Meadows Massacre notoriety, looked at the San Juan as a possible haven for himself during the early 1870s and recorded numerous references to miners—some of them with wagons and families—passing

---

6. Ibid., p. 66.

7. Ibid., p. 68. *See also* Erastus Snow to John Taylor and the Council of the Twelve, 6 November 1879, Erastus Snow Letters, Historical Department of the Church.

8. *New York Times,* 9 September 1875.

his cabins at Lee's Ferry and Moenave (near Moenkopi, Arizona), bound for the San Juan. From them he acquired extensive and accurate data as to trails, distances, and the location of important landmarks such as Monument Valley and Blue Mountain.[9] Other early Mormons worked out the approaches to the region. Important among these was James S. Brown, who led a mission to Moenkopi in 1875. Brown and his followers, particularly Thales H. Haskell and Seth B. Tanner, became well acquainted with the desert country south of the San Juan River. Brown, who had lost a leg in a hunting accident, traversed the entire region in a carriage prior to 1878. Haskell had been as far as Moenkopi and Oraibi before 1860 and was among missionaries called to Arizona in the mid-1870s. Something of a recluse, Tanner had ignored the communal character of Mormon settlement, living first at a lonely site where the wagon road from Utah struck the Little Colorado and establishing a trading post at the mouth of Montezuma Wash at an early date—perhaps prior to 1879. As David A. Miller, historian of the Hole-in-the-Rock, notes: "He was probably as well informed as any man regarding the nature of the country."[10]

Another Mormon of equally enigmatic reputation—Peter Shirts—was also in the San Juan before 1879. Like Tanner, he was a loner and had preceded the main line of the frontier, arriving at Montezuma Wash in 1877.[11] The "San Juan Stake History" attributes the name Montezuma to Peter Shirts, but W. H. Holmes of the Hayden Survey refers to Montezuma Canyon in his 1876 report in a way that indicates it was well known by that name prior to Shirts's settlement there.[12]

Three Mormon families by the name of Harris also preceded the San Juan Mission into the country. Without explanation of how they came to be there, Platte Lyman recorded that they were living at the site of Bluff when the road-weary Hole-in-the-Rock pioneers arrived on April 5, 1880. They had, he wrote, "been here all winter." While Lyman gave no certain evidence that the Harrises were Mormon, he did refer to receiving letters "by the hand of Dan Harris," implying that Harris had come from the Utah settlements and was well known to Lyman.[13] George B. Hobbs leaves no doubt of their identity in his "Account of an Exploration from the Hole-in-the-Rock to Montezuma and Return." After struggling through the canyons east of the Colorado River for several days, Hobbs and his companions came upon a camp "occupied by white people. It proved to be a Bro.

9.   Robert Glass Cleland and Juanita Brooks, eds., *A Mormon Chronicle: The Diaries of John D. Lee, 1848-1876* (San Marino: Huntington Library, 1955), pp. 192-97, 272, 314-27, and 336-37.
10.   Miller, p. 39. Miller is in error in his statement that Tanner was not a Mormon.
11.   Ibid., p. 33.
12.   Hayden, *Ninth Annual Report*, p. 189.
13.   Journal of Platte D. Lyman, pp. 12, 18.

Harris, with his sons Geo. and Dan who had come from Colorado and settled just south of where Bluff City is now situated. These were settlers that we had not looked for as they had come in since Silas Smith's company had left Montezuma the previous August."[14] Elsewhere Hobbs tells that there were ten adults and five children in the Harris party.[15] When all fifty-nine men of the mission decided to draw lots dividing the meager land resource at Bluff, the spot evidently lost some of its attraction to George Harris. He became one of the first to dispose of his claims, selling his "log house, 10 acres of land, a cook stove, table, 3 gals of coal oil, and some work on the ditch, and one town lot, for 1 horse & cows & calves."[16] The items Harris disposed of suggest he had given up San Juan's frontier permanently and had retired to an area where these items could be easily replaced.

The Exploring Expedition of 1879

As noted previously, the Church had begun a move into the general region of which the San Juan was part in the mid-1870s. To begin with, San Juan was ignored, but the spread of Mormon settlers throughout northern Arizona and New Mexico brought it very much within the orbit of the Church, and in 1879 the colonizing process was initiated by the San Juan Exploring Expedition. Beginning about the first of the year, plans were laid and calls issued, and on April 14 twenty-six men and two women with a small number of children made their departure from Iron County under the leadership of Silas S. Smith.[17]

Heading south, the explorers took the line of Arizona migration, crossing the Colorado River at Lee's Ferry and passing along the Echo Cliffs (where Highway 89 now runs) before bearing east to Moenkopi. From Moenkopi they turned northeast and, making their own road, arrived at Montezuma on the San Juan on May 31. During the next ten weeks they explored, sized up prospects in Colorado, and took out a number of squatter's claims. Convinced that a colony could be established, they left several families to hold their claims and on August 13 started back by way of the "Silina-Colorado" road which they hoped would be a better route.[18] Leaving by way of Recapture Creek (later the main road north from Bluff), they passed

---

14. Miller, p. 90.

15. *Deseret News* (Salt Lake City), 29 December 1919.

16. Journal of Platte D. Lyman, pp. 12, 18.

17. Miller includes extracts from the explorers' official "Camp Records" which are part of the "San Juan Stake History," now in the Historical Department of the Church. Also included in Miller are two accounts by Nielson B. Dalley. Perkins, Nielson, and Jones, *Saga of San Juan* (Daughters of the Utah Pioneers, 1957), pp. 24-36, is also useful.

18. Kumen Jones, "The San Juan Mission to the Indians" (typescript, Brigham Young University, Provo, Utah), p. 10.

the Blue Mountains and crossed Dry Valley to strike the Old Spanish Trail. For the first time since leaving Moenkopi, they were back on a wagon road made by others than themselves. They traveled across the Grand and Green rivers, through Castle Valley, over the Wasatch Plateau into the Sevier Valley, and arrived back in Iron County on September 16.[19] They had traveled some 900 miles, about 275 of which were on roads of their own making.

The Hole-in-the-Rock

Silas S. Smith and his explorers, along with nearly two hundred other men, women, and children began immediately to prepare for the move to San Juan. Taking provisions for a six-week trip, they loaded mostly with the paraphernalia of homemaking. Time was of the essence. They were behind schedule because of the late return of the explorers. It was now doubly important to make a quick trip, allowing time for home building before spring came with its heavy work of breaking new land and controlling the San Juan River, which they had already learned would not be dealt with easily.

For this and other reasons, they took an unknown shortcut first called the Escalante Shortcut but known to history as the Hole-in-the-Rock route. Getting under way on October 22, 1879, the emigrants made good time to Escalante. Grazing was adequate and roads were good. No danger from Indians existed. A good deal of conviviality characterized their progress, with campfire meetings and receptions adding to the air of well-being. Pushing on to the desert east of Escalante, they followed a well-broken trail for ten miles and then a lone and meandering track of a cart which had been used to haul a small boat to the Colorado River. Intermittent camps were located along the approach to the river, explorations conducted by which the awesome difficulties they confronted became known, and winter settled in, closing all possibility of turning back to another route.

With little choice but to go on, they chiseled a road through a cleft to the river and out the other side by the latter part of January. Meantime, men, women, and children camped under uncomfortable if not dangerous conditions. Supplies both for roadbuilding and the sustenance of life continued to come in limited amounts. A handful of cowboys and other travelers who for one reason or another joined the expedition may have provided an additional increment in work force. A few men from Panguitch and elsewhere were also assigned to help, but in the main the San Juan Mission carried its own burden.[20]

19. Ibid., p. 11.
20. For a thorough treatment of this entire experience see Miller's excellent volume.

View of Hole-in-the-Rock and country beyond.

Under the direction of Church President John Taylor, the pioneers built a large boat and established a ferry. By January 26 the road was complete, and traffic began to move down it and across the river. With rough-locked wheels and dead trees, livestock, and other odds and ends used as ballast, wagons were dropped at a rate of eight feet to the rod for the first third of the way and five and one-half feet to the rod for the remainder. Once at the river, they ferried both wagons and livestock across safely.

While there was some sense of relief at having the Hole-in-the-Rock at their backs, the pioneers were under no misapprehension about the country ahead. It was rough, actually requiring more blasting and tedious effort than the Hole-in-the-Rock itself. They moved on up Cottonwood Hill by way of a V-shaped notch called the Little-Hole-in-the-Rock to Cheese Camp. At the latter site, they experienced the only serious altercation of the trip when certain parties, who David E. Miller records were "driving a large herd of horses, probably intended for trade with the Indians," proposed to hurry on. Fearing that the horse herders would take most of the feed, the wagoneers threatened to keep the herds back by force if necessary.[21] The dilemma was solved, in a minimum sense, when the horse herders agreed to push through at once, but to leave a maximum of feed for the emigrants. The company reached Comb Wash by the middle of March and slogged down its sandy bottom for ten miles to a spot near where it debouches into the San Juan. Discovering no roadway up the river bottom, the company found it necessary to pull over Comb Reef by way of San Juan Hill, cross Butler Wash, and move on to the site of Bluff, where they arrived on April 6, 1880. Teams were poor and humans exhausted. All in all it had been one of the West's great travel exploits.

Colonization

Although the three Harris families had located there during the previous fall and a few of the weary Hole-in-the-Rockers may have arrived the day before, April 6, 1880, is properly considered the date of Bluff's establishment. It was on that day that the bulk of the San Juan Mission's eighty-five wagons arrived. It was also on that day that the first steps were taken toward making it a habitable village. There is an air of the inevitable in the attitude of Bluff's first settlers. In a sense they had come that far and could or would go no farther. Bluff was home. While pioneers came and went and the little community passed through many hard days, it continued to be the center of San Juan's Mormon society for the twenty-five years that followed.

The town was born in recrimination and controversy. Nerves and tempers of the company had held with remarkable restraint for the

---

21. Miller, p. 127.

Bluff city, Utah, - Looking S.W. Nov 5th 1895. - No62.

The city of Bluff, about 1895. Courtesy of the Utah State Historical Society.

long trip. Now they seemed to have reached the breaking point. The related points of tension were land and the matter of how the company should distribute itself. A survey revealed that there were fewer acres than they had hoped for between the narrow bluffs of the river from which the town took its name. Limiting the breadth of streets and size of lots on the town site, the settlers decided that about twenty families would have to go on up the river to Fort Montezuma. Surprisingly, in a group that had acted in accord with what they took to be the good of the mission, no one was willing to go. Platte D. Lyman, presiding officer at this point and for several years thereafter, might have asserted his authority, sending whom he saw fit to Montezuma. But Lyman was not this kind of man. He had been either unwilling or unable to exercise assertive leadership on the trek; he did not exercise it now. His failure to do so later resulted in turmoil and in his own embittered withdrawal from the community.[22]

But in April of 1880 the want of strong leadership led the disputing settlers to draw lots for the privilege of remaining in Bluff. Inevitably, chance separated family and point-of-origin groups, and several stormy days ensued. Unhappy Montezuma selectees complained and even jumped claims allotted to those chosen to stay at Bluff. But finally those fortunate enough to have drawn for Bluff

22. *See* Journal of Platte D. Lyman, entries for 1884.

relented and accepted smaller plots of land, thus permitting the entire party to remain.[23]

The question of who was going to live at Bluff resolved—at least for the moment—the company went about the various functions of establishment. In the main these tasks were well known to them, for by 1880 Mormons had been in the business of founding agricultural villages for more than thirty years. Methods and techniques as well as human relations were part of a familiar tradition. They began building cabins, and more than forty were erected on town lots during the first summer. Prompted by a Church directive, settlers soon left their cabins, moving into a fort, where they lived for several years before gradually returning to the village lots.

Before the first month had passed, San Juan County was organized. In these first beginnings, secular government was as Mormon as the Church itself. The legislature had appointed Silas S. Smith, mission president, as county judge. He appointed Platte D. Lyman, Jens Nielson, and Zechariah B. Decker as selectmen and C. E. Walton as county clerk. They in turn designated Lemuel H. Redd as assessor and collector. Lyman was shortly appointed stake president, Nielson became the colony's most revered man as bishop of Bluff, and each of the other officers played important and continuing roles in the Church. During the next twenty years an unabashed effort was made to maintain Church control of the county.[24]

A Distinctive Life-Style

Roads were essential to life. Their construction became the major business of the county court (the territorial equivalent of the county commission). County officers handled construction and maintenance on a basis of assignment that was entirely in keeping with the communal character of the Mormon mission. Four long roads—of sorts— existed in 1880. Extending in each of the four directions, they were the community's effective lifeline. During the colony's first weeks, infusions of flour and other provisions flowed or, more properly, careened in over the east-west roads coming via both the Hole-in-the-Rock and southwestern Colorado.

A Mormon society had been planted and a Mormon stamp put on the country. Its life-style was clearly its own; it was not to be confused with communities across the border in Colorado or for that matter with Moab, La Sal, or the other villages that clustered around the base of the La Sal Mountains.

Since 1847 Mormon expansion had moved on the flux of the agricultural village. Growth and development of human virtue as well as economic opportunity were thought to be best served by the agrarian

---

23. Journal of Platte D. Lyman, pp. 12-15.
24. This is best seen in diaries, especially those of Platte D. Lyman and Francis A. Hammond. *See also* "The Minutes of the San Juan County Court."

village system. Mining and industry, on the other hand, were regarded to be negative and retrogressive in nature. The village was to be a place of homes, gardens, and farms. Later, when Bluff's settlers gained an understanding of how to handle the country, they turned from farming to livestock, but the village pattern and its emphasis on homes survived the shift. Unlike other stockmen, Bluff's cowboys did not become ranch dwellers but made the village the center of their operation. Finding a degree of affluence in livestock, they built great stone homes, many of which still stand, bearing lonely witness of the importance of the village concept upon the life-style of San Juan's missionaries.[25]

The village was a point of congregation and, in the broad sense, a place of worship. As people repaired to church for spiritual fortification, so they sustained one another in the confines of the community. Forced to western Colorado to find work, San Juan missionaries were offended by its strangeness and returned to home base with relief.[26] The village was a barrier to outsiders, and few who were not Mormon found it a congenial place. The term "outsider" had a twofold meaning; as the community took form, it applied to all newcomers—even the devout Latter-day Saints who had not shared in the ordeal of the Hole-in-the-Rock. But the term "outsider" laid a special brand upon those not members of the Church. Occasionally some non-Mormon did make his home in Bluff. Most of these left little mark upon the town's tradition. Albert Loper, later of Colorado River fame, is said to have built some of the stone buildings. There is no evidence that he was a Mormon. Charles Goodman, a gentile bachelor, lived at Bluff for years. He was regarded to be a worthy citizen, and his skill in photography added a much needed element of culture. But toleration for individuals notwithstanding, Bluff was a Mormon outpost, and any substantial invasion of outsiders would have been regarded a distinct threat.

The village provided minimum services. Tithing and other Church subsidies were distributed to the indigent on an organized basis, and a strong informal tendency to share resources also existed. The Cooperative Store was in business by 1882. Because much of its trade was in the form of barter, it was something of a clearinghouse, taking in surpluses and redistributing them or turning them into badly needed cash at outside markets. Midwives, first Mrs. Haskell and then Josephine C. Wood, ushered generations of babies into the world, usually without complication or loss. Platte D. Lyman reported that

---

25. *See* Lowry Nelson, "The Mormon Village: A Pattern and Technique of Land Settlement" (Salt Lake City, 1952); Feramorz Young Fox, "The Mormon Land System: A Study of the Settlement and Utilization of Land Under the Direction of the Mormon Church" (Ph.D. diss., Northwestern University, 1932), pp. 92-110; and Charles S. Peterson, *Take Up Your Mission*, pp. 154-64.

26. Journal of Platte D. Lyman, p. 41. Typical of their reaction was Platte D. Lyman's note that Durango was "the wickedest and most lawless town I ever was in."

three children were born one day in 1881 and that "13 children were born in this place" during the six months prior to January 1, 1883.[27] Midwives gave their time unstintingly in nursing and caring for the sick, and, along with anointing with oil by the priesthood of the Church, substituted for more formal medical care. In time of crisis, Bluff's citizens were quick with their help. In 1888 a Crosby boy, the son of the Elk Mountain Cattle Company foreman, accidentally shot himself. Fletcher Hammond left his ranching duties west of Comb Wash and brought the boy to Bluff. Already treated with prickly pear poultices, young Crosby was given further treatment and rushed on to Durango by the best team in town.[28] Bluff was no stranger to epidemic, and reports of sickness sweeping the entire community and of untimely death of the young are common. On such occasions others than the midwives lent their services. Interestingly, compensation was sometimes given for these services by the county. Such a case was that of Hanson Bayles, who in 1890 was allowed a bill of $37.50 by the county court "for services rendered by himself and others . . . [for] waiting on the sick in cases of diptheria."[29]

The village was also the major element in social and recreational activities. In these pursuits the church played the dominant role. Dances, usually off-limits to cowboys and other outsiders, were frequent. Some efforts at theatrical entertainment were also to be found but, to 1900 at least, were not an important aspect of life. The village was undoubtedly more important to the women and children as a means of diversion than to the men. The men had work which often took them outside and involved them in associations with a surprisingly broad spectrum of people.

In time the Mormons established villages at other sites in the county. As noted previously they struggled to maintain Montezuma for a few years. Later, a town called Holyoak appeared briefly along the river above Bluff. More important, because they were lasting, were Verdure and Monticello, which were established in 1887 as part of a strong Mormon move to reclaim the county from large cattle outfits which were expanding at the time. In 1885 F. A. Hammond had been called as stake president, specifically for the purpose of strengthening the area. After studying the situation for a year, he initiated a coordinated campaign in the winter of 1886-87 to forestall the cattle companies.[30] Cooperation was the major vehicle of colonization, as it had been in Bluff. Frederick I. Jones, Parley R. Butt, George A. Adams, Charles E. Walton, Sr., and others were chosen by Church council and sent to settle on North Montezuma Creek.

27. Ibid., pp. 35, 57.
28. Francis A. Hammond Journal, 3 May 1888.
29. Minutes of San Juan County Court, 1880-1900, 29 December 1890, p. 90.
30. Francis A. Hammond Journal, 1886-87.

Verdure and Monticello were the product. Joshua and Alma Stevens also were dispatched to obtain a town site at Indian Creek. This project soon lost impetus, probably because the Stevens brothers found it necessary to locate at a site even more remote than Indian Creek.

Also chosen as a town site in 1887 was White Mesa, later Blanding. Since the influx of Mormon settlers that F. A. Hammond anticipated did not materialize and possibly because the L C Cattle operation, based in the neighborhood, was still strong, nothing came of plans to settle there at that time. However, during the years that followed, a number of San Juan Mormons were attracted to White Mesa. Notable among them was Walter C. Lyman, who became president of the San Juan Stake and founding father of what was known first as Grayson and later Blanding. By the first years of the twentieth century, a few Mormon squatters were working ditches on Johnson Creek and making some effort to farm. Interest grew until by 1905 a community had formed of sufficient stability to merit the name of town. Of significance is the fact that Blanding in large measure became the heir of old Bluff, when most of the latter's settlers abandoned it by 1920.[31] The county seat had been transferred to Monticello in 1894, but even though Blanding's settlement lacked the clear-cut Mormon cooperativism that characterized the earlier villages, it inherited the Hole-in-the-Rock tradition and became the center of Mormon influence in the region.[32]

Having noted the spread of the village pattern, let us turn again to a consideration of the processes of colonization. While most of the following examples relate to Bluff, they were repeated with variation elsewhere in the county.

Mormon cooperativism was the basis of the approach to water development and hence to agriculture. A crew was put to ditch-making the day after the pioneers arrived at Bluff. Men could have been found involved in one way or another with water development almost any day throughout the next twenty-five years. Even under normal conditions the sandy soil through which the ditches ran cut out before crops could be watered. Or if the ditch carried an irrigating stream, floods did their damage, cutting away headgates, shifting the course of the stream away from ditches, and filling long stretches with sand. Ditch construction generally was winter work. Most of the community's men were out of the fields during the cold season, and large forces would be at the job. Recurrent washouts led to the digging of different ditches and in some cases to the lengthening of ditch lines as frontier engineers moved back up the river, seeking a place where water could be successfully taken out.[33] At no time during the early years was the water supply dependable enough to make farming truly successful.

31. See Albert R. Lyman, *History of Blanding, 1905-1955* (n.p., n.d.).
32. Minutes of San Juan County Court, 1880-1900, p. 168.
33. Journal of Platte D. Lyman, p. 51.

Damming the river proved to be beyond the capacity of the settlers. In 1879 the Exploring Expedition had joined Peter Shirts and the Mitchell family in building a diversion dam across the river. It was shortly swept away. Later efforts, which included complex and, considering the means at Bluff's command, rather sophisticated cribs, were also unsuccessful. Water wheels were tried. William Hyde, who had come to Montezuma from Salt Lake City, rigged up a wheel sixteen feet in diameter with a capacity of 23,000 gallons per hour during the spring of 1881. On March 29, Platte D. Lyman noted that the Hyde wheel began to "raise the water and pour it into the flume in a way that is all that could be desired."[34] This wheel was evidently used with some success for three seasons but appears to have been duplicated only once.[35]

Obviously, the cost of irrigation was high. Some idea of just how high may be had from Lyman's notation that on December 3, 1883, the Irrigation Company levied a new tax "of $29.00 per acre . . . to complete the ditch." This new levy brought water cost to a staggering $69.00 per acre, or a total of $48,300, for the 700 acres under the ditch. Since the entire effort for 1880 had been wiped from the books, these figures probably represent outlay for only two years.

Not surprisingly, the Bluff missionaries looked for other options. Platte D. Lyman and many others wanted to leave. However, late in 1883 they agreed to make one more attempt, letting their future be governed "by the success of the next season."[36] As they continued their struggle to form Bluff in the image of a hundred other Mormon settlements, changes were afoot that would enable Lyman and his colleagues to deliver themselves, in some degree at least, from the narrow confines of the agrarian village tradition. For San Juan Mormons, delivery lay in no small part in an understanding of their country's potential for livestock.

In 1884 the San Juan River contributed another strong lesson to their understanding. There is no evidence of abnormal snowfall that winter, but March rains brought the San Juan out of her channel, running a full seven feet above normal height, to sweep away ditches and to fill cuts. Cottonwood Wash also ran far more heavily than in any previous year, cutting a new course and dumping sheets of mud and water into the houses and outbuildings in the southwest part of town. Rains continued through April and May, joining with runoff from melting snow to wash away two water wheels and all vestiges of headgates and head ditches. Even more discouraging, the roaming course of the river cut heavily into the community's scanty bit of farmland. Furthermore, water from the river and from Cottonwood Wash continued to threaten the town itself. Interesting in this connection is the fact that the Bluff cemetery is located on a high bench that ap-

---

34. Ibid., p. 37.
35. Ibid., p. 75.
36. Ibid., p. 69.

proaches the great rock bluffs north of town. Fearing just such an eventuality as the floods of 1884, the founding fathers had placed it there where the dead could keep watch, safe in their lonely eminence.[37]

The floods of 1884 were enough for Platte D. Lyman and many others. They left Bluff, defeated in their attempt to make a farming town where agriculture had no prospects. With strong urgings from some Church leaders, others stayed on. Important to an understanding of why they stayed is knowledge of the role played by Bishop Jens Nielson. Revered to the point of adulation—especially by those who remained—Nielson was steadfast. Bluff was the sixth village the old pioneer had helped found. When people talked of leaving Bluff, he would point to the hilltop graveyard and remark that he would make only one more move and that would be "up on the Hill."[38] But the high waters of 1884 also marked a point of change for those who stayed. Thereafter the emphasis was increasingly withdrawn from farming and placed upon livestock. The shift indicated a growing understanding of the country which led in turn to the recognition that the agricultural tradition under which the San Juan Mission functioned during those first years had to be modified. This modification was essentially an adaptation of Mormon cooperativism to the individualism that characterized the livestock frontier, encroaching from Colorado and New Mexico.

Farming a failure, Bluff had been dependent upon the outside from the very first. This meant that supplies were hauled in from the Utah settlements. It often meant that men from Bluff spent the working seasons in the mines, on the freight roads, and on the railroad grades of Colorado, New Mexico, and even Arizona. As time passed, they worked livestock and still later found their way into the Forest Service as they sought to make a living in what by that time had come to be their country. In the early years as men and boys scattered in quest of work, Mormon cooperativism revealed itself in a board of trade which was calculated to secure the benefits of collective bargaining for the far-ranging work force. The board of trade provided some ecclesiastical contact for men otherwise removed from the influence of the Church, but it failed in its economic purposes.[39]

Conclusion

In conclusion, it is appropriate to develop the point that societies of distinctly different character occupied the north and south ends of the region. The village and cooperative pattern of settlement gave a distinct Mormon flavor to the San Juan area. The character of the Moab, La Sal, and Castleton district was more consistent with the

37. Interview with Arvilla E. Warren, Monticello, Utah, November 1970.

38. Interview with Albert R. Lyman, Blanding, Utah, 18 June 1970.

39. Peterson, *Take Up Your Mission*, pp. 131-35.

general frontier patterns of the West and less permeated with Mormon practices and values. It was not that the north end was without Mormons. Indeed, people who in some way or other recognized an affiliation with the Church constituted a majority of its population— probably a substantial majority. But taken with the other settlers they did not add up to a Mormon community in the way San Juan did. North end Mormons, with very few exceptions, had come unbidden, a freelance society prompted by their own ideas of opportunity. Their Mormonness was doubtless very apparent to their gentile neighbors, but it hardly emerges at all in the record of the community, much less being dominant.

Perhaps this boils down to the fact that an unabashed booster spirit characterized the economic activities of the north end society. By 1896 a newspaper was necessary. Under the able editorship of J. N. Corbin, the *Grand Valley Times* proclaimed not only the sterling merits of the region's mining and livestock potential but also, in the exaggerated tones of the day, plugged local business interests, communications, and transportation prospects. On the other hand, farming was kept in low profile. Actually, agriculture was probably more important to Grand Valley's economy than to San Juan's. However, it lacked the desperate emphasis so apparent in the early approach of the more southerly community; was quickly accepted, and rarely seen as a topic of promotion by the *Grand Valley Times*. The paper reflected the essential economic thrust of the locality and revealed a clear-cut community character—one that is still in evidence. A common identity existed—one growing from a sense that, as the country developed, prosperity for all would be the product. But this economic flux made for a loose union not given over to the problem of maintaining its internal associations but rather reflecting an assortment of interests loosely arrayed.

It will bear repeating that the north end community was not self-consciously involved with its own identity. This was true for two reasons. In the first place, it was not clear what the identity was. At times the dominant element appeared to be mining, at other times livestock, and at still others commerce and transportation. However, no single element placed an indelible stamp upon the country. And secondly, since it was under no general attack—though its various elements frequently suffered a wide variety of threats—it found no need to surround itself with defensive perimeters.

The Moab area had few heroes. Those it did have were probably successful businessmen or, in the realm of folk values, closely associated with the cowboy tradition. The cowboy—perhaps even the badman—occupied a prominent position in the area's mythology and continues to do so. It was easy for the McCarty boys to emerge from this social matrix. Of significance here is that Grand County chose prototypes from the general frontier for its heroes. Tom McCarty, homegrown outlaw that he was, was a figure around whom mythology arose.[40] But such negative influence as his notoriety exerted was one that bespoke a fellowship to the broad West. Grand County's heroes identified with the larger community rather than pointing up the community's distinctiveness.

The San Juan, on the other hand, was very much concerned with inner self and developed an extremely well-articulated system of traditions demarking its unique identity. The core of this was what may be called the Hole-in-the-Rock mystique. If looked at rationally, the honor of being involved in this unparalleled endeavor may be somewhat dubious. But San Juaners did not look at the matter rationally. They had been given a charge. In the face of insuperable odds they had carried it out. Given the strong emphasis of the Mormon teachings on duty, they could feel with justification that they had taken a place high on the scale among those who had sacrificed for the success of the kingdom. It is true, strong ambivalences existed about the validity of the purpose underlying their charge. This, however, resulted in those who survived in the country assuming an even more assertive position that the deed was unique and that, as its doers, those who continued to fight San Juan's elements were unique—a chosen community. During the years of colonization, duty continued to be an important element in San Juan's concern with itself. To true believers, the Indian's need for enlightenment provided a duty strongly tinctured with altruism. Thrust into a center of Indian population, the people found it easy to regard this duty as one that lay on the San Juan Mission in a special way. As economics provided the basic flux of Grand County's character, so the mission lay at the base of San Juan's. The village, as contrasted to business, mining, or ranching, was dominant. Cooperativism reduced the centrifugal effects of competing economic interests to a minimum.

Finally, it should be noted that San Juan produced its own heroes. It is true that stock raising and Indian fighting found responsive chords in the community, but even in this realm its heroes, like old Indian Scout Thales Haskell, possessed qualities that marked them clearly as belonging to the San Juan. As ever in the Mormon Church, the San Juan community was unable to ignore the stature lent by wealth. But this notwithstanding, the great heroes are still homegrown, typified by Uncle Ben Perkins, a shotfire from the mines of Wales, who blasted the road down the Hole-in-the-Rock and across the canyons to Bluff. In Moab the figure of Bishop Jens Nielson, feet and legs twisted and crippled by frostbite, his wallet thin from much time spent in the service of the Church, could never have emerged as the single dominant folk-hero. But Nielson, Haskell, and Perkins all lent themselves admirably to the Hole-in-the-Rock mystique. Like the character of the community for which they became symbols, they were people apart.

40. Kelly, *The Outlaw Trail*, pp. 16-19, 36-40, 44-48, and 220.

Chapter IV

Indian Relations on an Emerging Frontier

Few regions have a history of more persistent friction between Indians and whites than does southeastern Utah. Conflict began with the first effort to colonize and extended into the 1920s. On the other hand, discord was neither sensational nor of such magnitude as to attract wide attention. Remote and desolate, the region was something of a redman's refuge—both for groups displaced by whites and for tribal outcasts. As a result, a varied and disaffected though relatively small Indian population frequented the area. Partly because of Indian hostility, white settlers came late and were few in numbers. Small numbers made the whites vulnerable—both in fact and in appearance—predisposing Indians to violence. The sparseness of settlement also invited whites in adjacent areas to push unwanted Indian population into southeastern Utah. Convinced that Indians would respond to Mormon teachings and reluctant to call for army intervention, Latter-day-Saint settlers followed a policy that mixed paternalistic altruism, self help, and frontier bias. Thus, while the Indian relations of the region were not of national significance, they did add up to a distinctive and highly interesting episode in the broad story of Indian affairs. In the regional sense the give and take between white and red men has been of primary importance, contributing to the essential character of the country and influencing its various functions, including the affairs of the La Sal National Forest.

Tribal Makeup

From the time the first Anglo-Americans passed through southeastern Utah, the Utes appear to have dominated the area. Utes were well acquainted with it as early as 1840 when bands from central Utah and from New Mexico traversed the area to visit each other. In 1853 Gunnison met numerous "Utah Indians" as he made his way down the river that bears his name. These he found to be fully aware of the Walker War then in progress between the Mormons and Utes in central Utah. He also learned that Uncompahgre Utes followed migrating deer and elk to the La Sal Mountains and that they considered the La Sals to be an important place of gathering.[1]

In 1855 the Elk Mountain missionaries found several distinct Ute bands in the Moab area. Some they called Elk Mountain Utes— a name indicating that they lived on or near the La Sal Mountains. Another band came from the crossing of the Green River and still others from farther north. Arrapeen, a chieftain from central Utah who paused at the Elk Mountain fort while on a trading trip to the Navajos, was well acquainted with the country and with many of the Indians assembled at the fort. Furthermore, Ute guides showed the Elk Mountain missionaries over well-used Indian trails between the La Sal and Blue mountains and pointed out paths leading to Sleeping Ute Mountain in present Colorado.[2]

Later, after the creation of reservations in Colorado, Uncompahgre Utes and Weeminuches (the western band of the Southern Utes) spent much time in the La Sal Mountains and on Indian Creek. Others passed to and from reservations in the Uinta Basin and southern Colorado or made special hunting trips to the La Sal Mountains.

This and other evidence points to a mobile and dominant population of Utes. For some of these the area was home. Others came for various reasons but seemed to be based elsewhere.

Navajos also came and went in the region. Recent work in dendrochronology suggests that they ranged on the Elk Ridge as early as 1620. According to archaeological evidence they occupied areas north of the San Juan River, including parts of the La Sal National Forest, from 1700 to the beginning of this century. Kigalia, an aging chief whom the Mormons found claiming an Elk Ridge spring to which they gave his name in the 1880s, was born at the same spring in 1801. Driven by punitive expeditions or foraging for their livestock, others penetrated as far as the La Sals, White Canyon, and even to the Henry Mountains.[3]

Navajos welcomed the Americans after the Mexican War but by the 1860s were in a state of open conflict with them. After several years of preliminary skirmishing, Kit Carson and his New Mexico volunteers broke the Indians' will to resist in the harsh winter campaign of 1864. The defeated Navajos then were forced through the

1. Beckwith, p. 57.
2. *See* Diary of Alfred N. Billings, and Diary of Ethan Pettit.
3. J. Lee Correll, "Navajo Frontiers in Utah and Troublous Times in Monument Valley," *Utah Historical Quarterly* 39 (1971): 141-57.

Petroglyphs in Pack Creek. U.S. Forest Service photo.

terrors of the "long walk" and confinement at Fort Sumner, New Mexico.[4] Some, however, evaded Carson and scattered. Some went to Black Mesa north of Oraibi and from there raided the Mormon frontier. Others struck for the remoteness of Navajo Mountain. Such a one was Hoskaninni to whom tradition soon attributed the discovery of a fabulous silver mine called Pishlaki.[5] When the Fort Sumner exile ended in 1868, the tribe returned to a reservation situation, but the Monument Valley-Navajo Mountain refugees remained, claiming their hideaway as traditional grounds.

Thereafter, some quickly became owners of sizable herds of horses and sheep which they ran south of the San Juan as a rule. However, William T. Tew, who was in the country in 1881, saw two Navajo sheep herds, one numbering 6,000 head, north of the river. Kigalia and other Navajos ran sheep as far north as the crest of Elk Ridge. Inveterate traders, the Navajos had long carried on an intercourse with the La Sal Mountain Utes that was as much a matter of thievery as it was trade.[6]

---

4.   Ruth M. Underhill, *The Navajos* (Norman: University of Oklahoma Press, 1956).

5.   Correll, pp. 150-51. *See also* Charles Kelly, "Chief Hoskaninni," *Utah Historical Quarterly* 21 (1953): 219-26.

6.   Journal of William T. Tew, 30 March 1881, original owned by Mrs. Melba T. Hayes, Bloomington, Utah; xerox, Utah State Historical Society. *See also* Diary of Alfred N. Billings, 5 August 1855.

A final tribal group inhabiting the area were the Paiutes. It is not entirely clear who the Paiutes were or where they came from. However, some of them were apparently in the country when the first whites came—at least Jim Mike, a White Mesa Paiute of advanced years (he claims to be over one hundred), tells that he heard the explosions when the Hole-in-the-Rock company dynamited their way through the cleft in 1880.[7] Early whites often failed to distinguish between Ute and Paiute, but by 1900 the latter term was applied to a group of Indians usually found near the Blue Mountains. Although a few Navajo and Ute outcasts were included in this group, neither tribe acknowledged relationship with it.

Fort on the Firing Line

There was a distinctive style in the Indian relationships of the Mormons. In part this was the product of a strong sense of mission on the part of the Mormons. According to the Book of Mormon, Indians were the rightful heirs to America and to the saving principles of Mormon doctrine. Consequently, Mormons at Bluff and elsewhere approached them in paternalistic hope, teaching and waiting against the day when Indians would become converted and would share fully in the gospel. But this alone does not explain the different mood in which Mormons approached their Indian neighbors. Nearly as important was the fact that Mormon Utah was reluctant to invite army intervention. At loggerheads with the United States Government over questions of polygamy and mixing religion with politics, Mormons regarded military posts as potential bases of operation against themselves.

Instead of inviting the military, Mormons developed a "feed rather than fight" policy which was calculated to do three things: pacify the Indians; attach them to the Mormon cause; and, if possible, convert them. Generally keeping the peace, this policy broke down on the occasions of the Walker War of the 1850s and the Black Hawk War of the 1860s. When such hostilities did develop, frontiersmen retracted from vulnerable points, forted up, called minutemen, paid such tribute as the situation demanded, carried on skilled diplomacy through Indian missionaries, and, at times, reacted with hate and vengeance.

In San Juan, the Mormon approach to the Indian was in keeping with this brief outline. The Bluff missionaries regarded it as their responsibility to establish a buffer community to help limit incursions on more centrally located areas of Utah. Actually there was little danger that the handful of Indians that inhabited the region could have broken out of the natural barriers that defended them from white control to carry on raids of any consequence. But given the Mormon antipathy for military intervention and the region's

---

7. Interview with Lynn Lyman, Blanding, Utah, February 1970.

remoteness, local control of the natives was as essential to white colonization as if danger to communities beyond San Juan's bounds had been real. It should be understood that in the broad sense the existence of the Mormon colony on the San Juan did constitute an effective barrier to the Indians. Without it there is good reason to believe the entire region would have been designated an Indian reservation.

There can be no denial that the San Juan colony was both concerned with and deeply involved in Indian relations. Men like Thales Haskell, noted for their skills in dealing with Indians, played important roles in the affairs of the colony. There was no effort to eject the Indians as the whites moved in. Indeed the policy was to draw the Indians in, to become acquainted with them, trade with them, and if possible to teach them something about civilized ways, including Mormonism.

The Mormon right to a share in the country was quickly established, and a workable and lasting modus vivendi developed which permitted mutual occupation with a minimum loss of life. While it doubtlessly fell short of satisfying either party, this arrangement consisted of the following essentials: Indians tolerated Mormons in the country, accepted their paternalistic overtures, took advantage of trade opportunities, and limited their own depredations to a heavy, but tolerable tribute in the form of stolen livestock, and with rare exceptions limited their threats to the community to bluster, which resulted in no loss of life. In return the Mormons tolerated and in form at least welcomed the Indians; minimized their effort to involve outside forces to control the Indians; limited their punitive efforts to sortees to reclaim stolen stock; and until the mid-nineties did not seek their expulsion, and then only as specific situations seemed to require. The unexpressed factor in this situation was the most important. For whites, the arrangement led to increasing control of the country and its resources; for Indians, it led to subjugation and poverty.

Life under these conditions was not friction-free. Indeed, confrontation short of bloodletting was almost constant. To pioneers without benefit of hindsight, theft and rangeland slaughter of stock was a sore trial. If murder of Mormons was actually recognized as unwise policy by the Indians, they had the good sense not to tell the former, and expeditions and negotiations to reclaim stock were always fraught with tension, threat, and acute danger. Tremendous fears developed on both sides. The record is replete with accounts of whites thinking they escaped from destruction at the hand of some Indian whose cruelness led him to make the threat. If the mind of the Indian could be read or his campfire reports of meetings with the whites committed to our record, we would doubtless see fear and frustration in their most profound dimension rather than hostility or insolence at the root of the redman's conduct.

The narrow margin upon which good relations stood is evident throughout the entire tradition of the colony. Repeatedly, violence was avoided only by desperate diplomacy. The Indians often confronted the Mormons on the range or along the roads and even occasionally threatened the safety of Bluff itself. Some Indians were bold enough to take single-handed action over some real or pretended slight. Such was Mancos Jim, a sub-chief of some local fame, about whom Albert Lyman tells the following story. On one occasion when he was carrying goods into the Co-op Store in Bluff, Lyman became irritated with Mancos Jim's dog and gave it a hard kick. Seconds later the old Indian stormed into the store, grabbed Lyman, and in high fury informed him that he had killed the dog. He emphasized his de-

Mancos Jim and Forest Supervisor J. W. Humphrey, about 1914.
U.S. Forest Service photo.

mand for payment by declaring that he was a dangerous man, having killed several of the whites lost in the battle of Pinhook near Moab. A serious upshot was avoided when a sober-eyed grandchild who was tugging at Mancos Jim's shirttail during the entire conversation finally got the old man's attention to inform him that the dog had revived.[8]

That occasional whites sometimes dealt severely with Indians is apparent in another story relating to Mancos Jim. Lemuel H. Redd, one of the Hole-in-the-Rock missionaries who was at the time managing the Bluff Co-op, noted that Mancos Jim was bringing in small amounts of good wool in more or less regular installments. Suspicious, he did some checking and learned that a pile of wool had been seen in a distant corn field. Studying the matter further, he found a hole in the back of the warehouse where wool was being taken from the Co-op, whereupon he got a bear trap and set it inside the hole. The next morning he found Mancos Jim, one arm through the hole, his hand caught in the trap. Redd's disciplinary action was straightforward but harsh. He kicked the old Indian soundly and admonished him to refrain from such conduct in the future.[9]

Mormon policy may have been strict and was certainly paternalistic, but in a more important sense it was successful. For one thing, there was a minimum of bloodshed. Indeed, it appears that only one Mormon of the Bluff colony met his death at the hands of Indians, and that was Amasa M. Barton, killed at a trading post ten miles below Bluff at the Rincon crossing of the San Juan River. Sent there in the spring of 1887 by F. A. Hammond, stake president, and helped in their efforts by a small church appropriation, Barton and his brother Joseph were dispatched as part of a general effort to control grazing for the Mormons in the San Juan area.[10] While no source spells this out in its entirety, it is my opinion, from pieced-together information, that the Bartons were specifically charged with controlling the crossing of the Navajo herds at the Rincon. In any event, Amasa Barton was mortally wounded on June 9, 1887. A few days later about one hundred angry Navajos showed up at Bluff. Since there were only six men in town, it was a tense situation, but bloodshed was averted by the negotiations of aging Bishop Jens Nielson.

Barton's death and the subsequent show of ill will at Bluff are understandable in the context of the Mormon attempt to control the country's grazing. Willing to live and let live if the Mormons did

8. Interview with Albert Lyman, Blanding, Utah, April 1970. This was not the only occasion on which Mancos Jim claimed to have been involved in the bloody melee at Pinhook. In 1886 he told Ed Nolan of Durango about the battle. According to his own account, he was in command of the group that slaughtered nine whites who had been isolated in a gully. He admitted to losses of eighteen men of his own in the encounter; *Idea* (Durango), 26 June 1886.

9. Interview with Lynn Lyman, Blanding, Utah, June 1970.

10. *See* p. 96 and Francis A. Hammond Journal, 22 February 1887.

not overextend themselves, the Navajos felt their rights had been in-fringed upon in this case. The fragile balance in which the modus vivendi hung had been overburdened by the Rincon trading post and its intended control of river crossings. Significantly, the so-called Texas Cattle Company soon made its headquarters in the Rincon area, verifying its strategic location to the control of livestock in the country. However, "made to realize how much they were at the mercy of the Indians," no Mormon attempt was made to revive the post at the Rincon.[11]

On other occasions the modus vivendi held. Contributing to these successes was the fact that Bluff settlers refused to join punitive expeditions against the Indians. A dramatic example took place in 1881 in connection with the hostilities that culminated in the deaths of nine whites at Pinhook east of Moab. Beginning their de-predations by killing two cowboys and stealing a large number of horses and considerable paper money near the Colorado border east of Monticello, the Indians moved south and west, evidently heading for refuge in the rough canyons of Grand Gulch and Navajo Moun-tain. As they passed Bluff, they picked up additional horses belong-ing to that community. Several whites rode out and amidst much angry talk and flourishing of weapons reclaimed their animals. The modus vivendi is most apparent. These same Indians, who numbered about thirty able-bodied men, had just been involved in the killing of two whites and would kill nine more within the month, but they per-mitted "some 8 or 9 of the boys" to take such animals as belonged to Bluff. On the other hand, the Bluffites did not presume to reprimand the Indians for depredations committed against other whites. Al-though they recognized some of the horses and saw that "they had plenty of greenbacks," no hand was lifted against the Indians.[12] The delicate balance of their Indian relationships would not permit it.

Cowboy Wars and Other Indian Troubles, 1855-1890

Elsewhere in southeastern Utah, bloodshed was not avoided. Settlers were sometimes at no great pains to keep the peace. The military was called in frequently. Even the Mormon Indian mission was less successful than in San Juan. Indeed, the record of violence began with the Elk Mountain Mission during the summer of 1855. Specifically charged to establish good relations with the Indians, the Elk Mountain Mission consisted of forty-four men, although the active force was often below that number. At first contact, the Indians were friendly. Entry was made into the Little Grand Valley with little friction, although a few arrows were shot into livestock. This action, however, was passed off by laying it to boyish pranks. The chief men came declaring their goodwill, and numerous Indians submitted

---

11. Perkins, Nielson, and Jones, p. 68.
12. Journal of Platte D. Lyman, p. 39.

to baptism; some became elders in the Church. Generally, missionary efforts seemed to be succeeding. Whites came and went about the fort and carried on explorations without fear. Five of them made a long and what in retrospect must be regarded as a daring journey into northern Arizona. Betraying no sense that trouble was imminent, Alfred Billings, president of the mission, depleted his force

Marker near site of Pinhook Battle.

to eighteen men in September and a day or two before hostilities broke out even permitted two young men to go hunting in the La Sals.

However, a careful reading of the mission journals reveals some evidence of danger. Tension was high between the Utes and Navajos and the missionaries had involved themselves in the controversy. As the summer wore on, theft increased sharply, and Indians redoubled their efforts to trade for guns and ammunition.

But the missionaries showed no alarm until the morning of September 23 when they moved their livestock to a more defensible pasture. Offended, "quite a number" of Indians came to the fort in "a saucy and impudent" frame of mind and protested the change. At last sensing "mischief," the whites loaded their guns, but one permitted himself to be lured away from the fort and was mortally wounded. A general melee ensued during which Alfred Billings was shot in the hand and several Indians were wounded or killed. The two young hunters were intercepted as they returned from the mountain and were killed. After a day or two of siege, Billings ordered his men to abandon the fort, thus breaking up the mission.[13]

There is no record of violence during the next twenty years, but efforts to revive settlement in the 1870s were immediately resisted. Indeed, the next effort to settle in Moab Valley resulted in bloodshed. The account is vague. Two men, George and Silas Green, who came in 1874 or 1875, lost their lives. Reoccupying the old fort, they ran cattle nearby until the winter of 1876-77 when, it is thought, both were killed by Indians.[14]

Even before this incident, Indians had displayed their displeasure with the resurgence of white interest in the country by chasing off a party from the F. V. Hayden Geographical and Geological Survey. During August of 1875 two survey crews under Henry Gannett and James L. Gardner joined forces to explore the La Sal Mountains because of disquieting reports that Indians there were hostile. Noting that the area was bounded by the Navajo, Paiute, and Ute tribes, one of them reflected the attitude of the surveyors:

> The most desperate rascals from each congregate there. . . . and acknowledge no authority but their own chieves—[sic] murderers and robbers everyone. The bands number respectively from 7—20 about as poor and desperate as mountain brigands usually are. . . . Their regular trading is done with the native tribes from whom they obtain arms, ammunition and horses in exchange for proceeds of hunting for game or men.[15]

But the survey had no trouble while it was on the La Sal Mountains. An Indian camp was visible below them on the mountain side, but only one surveyor met Indians; these were peaceable. The camp below was strengthened by several lodges a day or two before

---

13. Diary of Alfred N. Billings, pp. 19-25.
14. Tanner, p. 27.
15. *New York Times,* 9 September 1875.

the explorers planned to leave for the Blue Mountains, but since their departure was imminent they saw no threat in this fact. Leaving the La Sals on August 15, they were attacked late in the afternoon when they were well out into Dry Valley. The attacking party numbered no more than ten, but even this small number caused real concern to Hayden's men, who had only seven rifles and three heavy service pistols. With dark approaching and no cover in reach, Gardner ordered a halt, and saddles and packs were used to erect a makeshift barricade. The attackers did not expose themselves but maintained intermittent fire from cover until about midnight. The next morning the surveyors pushed on, hoping to mount the plateau in the neighborhood of present Peter's Hill. Frustated for a time, they were finally able to force their way up when two of the party succeeded in getting to higher ground than the Indians. Thereafter it was deemed prudent to abandon packs and equipment. Leaving the record of the La Sal Mountain survey, they moved ahead by forced marches to Parrotstown, a village on the Mancos River.[16]

The 1875 report of C. G. Belknap (Ute agent) includes reference to the incident that merits citing here:

> You are aware that the Utes objected to Messrs. Gardner's and Gannett's surveys in the outset, and that the parties of these gentlemen have lately been actually driven in from their work. A few days since Mr. Gardner was here, and, in conversation with Ouray, was assured that the attacking Indians, according to his description of them and of the place of attack, must have been a well-known band of outlaws, formerly Pi-Utes of Utah, now acknowledging no authority, though some disaffected Utes had joined them.

The next year, Belknap gave further information:

> As to the attack upon the surveying party, it was made by a little patriarchal band of outlaws, called by the head-chief, Ouray, Pi-Utes, but admitted by many others to be Weminuche [sic] Utes. Up to within a few months they acknowledged allegiance to no one. During this summer, at the bidding of Ouray, they appeared at our agency. . . . According to their story, which can hardly be credited, all the shooting was done by one man, and he a Pi-Ute from Nevada. . . .[17]

Later, as more settlers came into the Moab country, they recognized the problem constituted by the Indians and exercised some caution. Yet the individualism that characterized their settlement invited Indian hostilities. It was an invitation that was not long ignored. In June of 1880, two young brothers, Joe and Ervin Wilson, were attacked while trailing stock up Pack Creek, over Black Ridge in the

---

16. *Ibid.*, 5, 9, and 25 September 1875. The Monticello office of the Bureau of Land Management has located the site where the surveyors abandoned their equipment. Artifacts are on display at the Monticello office.

17. *Annual Report to the Commissioner of Indian Affairs* (Washington, D.C., 1875), p. 232; and *Annual Report to the Commissioner of Indian Affairs* (Washington, D.C., 1876), pp. 18-19.

direction of Coyote Ranch—now La Sal. The younger boy was badly wounded but escaped when friendly Indians helped him back to Moab. Contemporary accounts indicate that Indians near Moab were divided in their feelings toward the whites and that one group was definitely hostile.[18]

Earlier the same year two prospectors, James Merrick and Ernest Mitchell, were killed in Monument Valley, probably by Paiutes. Both men had been on the San Juan during the summer before when Mormons of the San Juan Exploration Expedition visited the area.[19] Evidently Merrick was a prospector of some experience who had stumbled on what may have been the fabled Pishlaki mine. Mitchell was a young man but one well acquainted with Indians. Apparently a member of the Mitchell family that had taken squatter's rights at the mouth of Montezuma Creek, he was promised a quarter interest in the trip's proceeds for going with Merrick as his interpreter. That Merrick sensed the midwinter expedition into Monument Valley might be risky was suggested by a Mormon explorer named George Hobbs, who wrote that Merrick also offered him a quarter interest in an attempt to strengthen his prospecting force.[20] Years later Hoskaninni-Begay (the son of Hoskaninni) told Charles Kelly that the two men had found his father's mine earlier and had come back for samples of silver. Following their tracks in the snow, he and other Navajos came on a party of Paiutes as they were robbing the bodies. Mitchell lay near one of the Mittens and Merrick near the butte that has since borne his name.[21]

The following year, 1881, was the most tragic in the region's Indian relations. In May, Paiutes struck a lonely ranch near the Utah-Colorado border, killing John Thurman and R. W. (Dick) May, and took a large herd of horses along with a good amount of money in greenbacks.[22] Communications were almost unbelievably bad. Garbled reports of the incident spread slowly at first, then in a rush, with misinformation and half-truth more prevalent than fact. A Navajo called Little Captain is said to have given the first report of the killing to May's brother several days after its happening. Although they saw the offending Indians with stolen horses and money in their possession, Mormons at Bluff admitted to hearing of the incident only after two weeks. Newspapers got the story somewhat earlier, but

---

18. Tanner, pp. 33-35. *See also* Silvey, pp. 10-11, and *Deseret News*, 2 September 1880.

19. Miller, pp. 89-92.

20. Miller, p. 92.

21. Kelly, p. 223.

22. Edgar C. McMechen, ed., "Jordan Bean's Story and the Castle Valley Indian Fight," *Colorado Magazine* 20 (1943): 19. *See also* Journal of Platte D. Lyman, p. 39, and A. M. Rogers, "A True Narrative of an Indian Fight," *Cliff-dwellers' Echo*, National Archives, Region IV Papers (Washington, D.C., April 1912).

accounts in the *Durango Herald* and the Denver press, were unsure of their facts, contradictory, and incendiary in tone.[23]

In the beginning it was thought that the Weeminuches had been involved, but as facts were sorted out it became apparent that Paiutes who had been holding horse races in the area were responsible. Supporting this conclusion is the fact that the hostiles made their way south and west to Butler Wash below Bluff. Later, while haggling cowboys and miners gathered in a motley force in the towns of southwest Colorado, the Indians turned north over the Blue Mountains to Indian Creek where they dallied for several days before picking up a party of Uncompahgre Utes and crossing Dry Valley to the west side of the La Sals.

Meanwhile, the cowboys and miners became increasingly incensed. Army intervention was requested, but no detachment was called out— at least not until the cowboy posse set out for Utah amidst much talk and more confusion. Its leading figures were William Dawson of Rico and Billy May, brother of one of the murdered men. The expedition was poorly handled from start to end, and the Indians displayed a clear superiority in terms of logistics and mobility, if not in leadership.

Finally, with the whites divided, hungry, and dispirited, the Indians were overtaken on the northwest side of the La Sal Mountains at a spot called Pinhook Valley. Upon making contact, Dawson, who was well ahead of May and the bulk of the men, dispatched a small force, which was cut off from the rest of his party and pinned down in a draw. During the course of a bloody day, nine men were killed; seven (Dave Willis, Tom Click, Jimmy Heaton, Harg Tarter, Wiley Tartar, Jack Galloway, and Hiram Melvin) were from Dawson's command. The Wilson brothers, Alfred and Isedore, who, hearing the battle, had come toward the fight and were killed, were from Moab. An additional nine or ten men from Moab also took part.[24]

The Indians, who according to various reports lost from seven to eighteen men, did not tarry but moved out during the next night.[25] The whites began a dejected trip back to Colorado with all vestiges of braggadocio knocked from them. En route they met two rescue parties. One was another citizens' group. Headed by Worden Grigsby, it was of a kindred spirit to the defeated parties and was warmly greeted. Less welcome was the army which had belatedly left Fort Lewis with "four companies of the Ninth Cavalry under Captain Carroll, and a detachment of the Thirteenth Infantry."[26] Jordan

23. Journal of Platte D. Lyman, pp. 39-40. *See also Durango Record,* 12 May 1881.

24. *See* Rogers and McMechen for the casualty listings used here. Perkins, Nielson, and Jones, *Saga of San Juan,* p. 241, add the name of George Taylor to casualties from the Dawson command.

25. For other accounts of the Pinhook Battle see Cortes, Silvey, and Tanner.

26. *Denver Tribune,* 25 June 1881.

Bean, who was wounded during the battleground fiasco, reminisced in later life that they met Carroll and a company of Negro soldiers where Monticello now stands. In a story that hints why the United States Army had not moved out earlier, Bean has Carroll threatening the entire cowboy party with "arrest for attacking and disturbing the Indians." According to Bean, "Bill Dawson drawed his rifle out of the scabbard and told Carroll he just didn't have 'niggers' enough to arrest his men. Every man pulled their guns. Grigsby and his men too, never faltered."[27] Evidently contact with Grigsby had restored some of the group's bravado—or perhaps passing years had restored it to Mr. Bean.

Indian problems continued during the next few years. In 1883 at least one man, Peter Tracey, was killed. Postmaster at a small station not far from the confluence of Montezuma Creek and the San Juan River, he was said to have been murdered by a Navajo named Sore Leg.[28] However, 1882 and 1883 were quiet compared with 1884. Although the Pinhook Battleground killings register 1881 as the most disastrous year in the colonization of southeastern Utah, the problems of 1884 were more general, involving not only the cowboys and Paiutes but Navajos, Southern Utes, and the army as well. In the main, the Mormons again held themselves aloof, only a few being involved and these incidentally. Trouble spots appeared at Monument Valley, at Mitchell's Ranch at the mouth of Montezuma Creek, and on the Blue Mountains, and extended to Soldier's Crossing halfway down White Canyon some sixty miles west of Blanding.

Hostilities began when Samuel Walcott, an aging prospector, and his youthful companion, James McNalley, who had outfitted at Mitchell's, were killed in Monument Valley about the end of March.[29] Emboldened Navajos surrounded Mitchell's in mid-April, maintaining a siege until about April 23, when a Lieutenant Kreps arrived from Fort Lewis with a small force. At Mitchell's he found twenty-three whites, who reported that in repulsing Navajo attacks they had killed one Indian and wounded three, one of whom subsequently died.[30] In the face of Kreps's detachment the Navajos sullenly withdrew, moving back a two-day ride from the river.

A few days after the Mitchell's incident, Navajo Agent Denis M. Riordan's Indian scouts brought Hoskaninni-Begay into the Fort Defiance Agency in Arizona. The young Indian's father and Ganado Mucho, a powerful chief from the neighborhood of Ganado, accompanied him. Antagonistic because no action had been taken against the whites for the Navajos killed and wounded at Mitchell's, Ganado

---

27. McMechen, p. 23.
28. *Southwest* (Durango), 1 September 1883.
29. Correll, pp. 145-61.
30. Ibid., p. 155. *See also* Major Hall, commanding Fort Lewis, to the Adjutant General, Santa Fe, New Mexico, 23 April 1884, Fort Lewis Military Records, National Archives, Record Group 77.

Mucho angrily refused to turn the younger Hoskaninni over to Rior-dan. Although the military was later brought into the Walcott-Mc-Nalley affair, the accused man escaped apprehension during the summer, and a hearing held in November failed to render an indictment against him.[31]

In the meantime a small detachment of infantry was left at Mitchell's, and relations in Utah appeared to be on the mend until an incident early in July precipitated a month of maneuvering and fighting involving both the Utes and Paiutes. Cowboys gathering horses on the south slope of the Blue Mountains shot an Indian during an argument over a horse. This in turn resulted in an immediate and general outbreak of the Indians in the area. Seizing the horses gathered by the cowboys, the Indians attacked a roundup camp, wounded one man, and drove the whites from the range. Mounted troops were moved in at once. But before the cavalry, under a Captain Perrine, got to the scene, hostilities flared again at Mitchell's, where the sergeant in command seized five Utes, who boastingly reported that they had been at the Blue Mountains uprising. With Ignacio, chief of the Southern Utes, protesting that no members of his tribe were absent from the agency, forty or fifty of them, under a subchief called Red Jacket, arrived at Mitchell's in a bellicose frame of mind and demanded that their five tribesmen be surrendered. Thinking that Perrine's command was routed through Mitchell's, the sergeant stalled for time. When he learned that Perrine would not be coming, he yielded to Red Jacket's threats and turned the five prisoners over to him.[32]

Sometime before July 15 Perrine's cavalry arrived at the Blue Mountains, where it was joined by a sizable number of cowboys. Traveling light and depending upon the country for water, they followed the Indians west across Elk Ridge, by the Bear's Ears, and around the south bend of White Canyon in forced marches. The campaign quickly assumed a critical turn because the Indians exhausted water holes along the way. On July 15 Perrine's force, now under straitened circumstances for lack of water, overtook the fleeing Indians at what has since been known as Soldier's Crossing—actually a narrow cleft in an otherwise impassable mesa that forms the west boundary of the White Canyon drainage. Calling a halt because of the crossing's obvious potential for ambush and because of the need to hunt for water, Perrine reluctantly allowed a hotheaded young cowboy called Rowdy Higgins and a government scout named Worthington to check out the canyon trail ascending to the pass.[33] As Perrine had feared, the trail up was easily commanded from the top,

31. Correll, p. 160.

32. *See* dispatches from Major R. H. Hall to the Adjutant General, Santa Fe, New Mexico, Fort Lewis Military Records, 17 July-2 August 1884.

33. Silvey, p. 38. *See also* Hall to Adjutant General, Santa Fe, New Mexico, 20 July 1884, Fort Lewis Military Records.

Graves at Soldiers' Crossing.

and both Higgins and Worthington were shot. The rest of the command fell back unscathed but abandoned seven saddled horses in its haste. Rescue operations impossible, the thirsty whites waited out a terribly hot day while their two comrades died. The strain was made worse for the whites when Mancos Jim, whom many of them knew, jumped into view and (mimicking one of the dying men) "hollered":

> "Oh, my God, boys, come and help me," and before a bullet could reach him, dropped down again. This he kept repeating every few minutes all afternoon, as we supposed mocking Warrington's talk when he was dying. Being directly over him he could hear him much plainer, of course, than we could down below. Sometimes he would substitute, "Oh, my God, boys, a drink of water."[34]

An effort to bring in the bodies after dark was abandoned when the detail assigned found Indians mutilating the bodies and collecting the loot left behind in the disordered retreat. Although a handful of cowboys proposed to ride south along the mesa looking for another pass by which they could get behind the Indians, Perrine wisely ordered the thirsty, choking company to retreat. The offending Indians remained in White Canyon for the remainder of the year, living nicely on cattle belonging to Bluff stockmen.[35]

34. Sam Todd, "A Pioneer Experience" (typescript, Utah State Historical Society, 1925).
35. Perkins, Nielson, and Jones, p. 243.

The years 1885 and 1886 seem to have passed quietly. Even 1887 saw no recurrence of the general disturbances of 1881 and 1884. However, Amasa M. Barton was killed by Navajos at Rincon on the San Juan River in June.[36] As we have seen, broader trouble was averted in this incident. But a seemingly unrelated killing in July resulted in two rather tense months. An employee of the LC Cattle Company, who was on the east slope of the Blue Mountains, was shot. Wild reports were circulated, tempers flared, and detachments were sent out from Fort Lewis. The soldiers camped for the rest of the summer in the mouth of Recapture Wash to protect Bluff, and at Soldier's Spring south of Monticello. Their presence was sufficient to maintain the peace.

A number of changes on the part of the white settlers are apparent in this situation. The Mormons broke with their usual policy and joined in the requests for army intervention. Equally notable was the fact that the cowboys were less volatile and more willing to wait for the military to give protection. Behind each of these shifts may be seen broader changes. Mormon willingness to permit the army to get into the act was not an indication that the long controversy between polygamous Utah and the United States government was ended, but it does suggest that to San Juan settlers, at least, the end of conflict seemed sufficiently near as to make it foolish not to take advantage of such help as the army could offer. With reference to the cowboys, the years between 1884 and 1887 had seen the balance of power shift from small stockmen running cattle from Dolores, Durango, and elsewhere in Colorado to large Utah-based cattle companies carrying with them a certain amount of control and implying some modification of the strong individualism of the early 1880s. Put differently, American civilization was touching both Mormon and cowboy, and each in his own way had changed as a result.

Ute Removal: The "Great Invasion of 1894"

In the years after 1887 the general nature of tensions between Indians and whites in southeast Utah also took a sharp turn. As we have seen, the problem of the 1880s had been one of recurrent violence. During the next eight years, the main concern grew from a proposal to move the Southern Utes from Colorado into Utah's sparsely settled San Juan County.

The removal movement began soon after the Southern Ute Reservation had been established in 1880 for the tribe's three bands, the Muaches, the Capotes, and the Weeminuches.[37] Amounting to about

---

36. Above p. 61. *See also* Francis A. Hammond Journal, 27 November 1887.

37. In 1863 and again in 1868 treaties had established reservations in Colorado and New Mexico for the various Ute bands. In 1873 the San Juan region in Colorado was taken from the reservation, which was later enlarged by executive order in 1875. In 1880 the Southern Utes were located on the Southern

one million acres, the reservation lay 150 miles along Colorado's southern border. It was adjacent to a rich mining country and was part of an important grazing empire that had begun to fill with cattlemen well before 1880. Numerous affluents of the San Juan River flowed through the reservation from north to south, giving it considerable agricultural potential. Furthermore, its location made it important to transportation, and trails and wagon roads to New Mexico as well as the railroad that served southwestern Colorado's mining country crossed it. In short, the Southern Ute Reservation lay in the center of things, and Colorado whites, led by a handful of avid removers at Durango, were determined to have it.[38]

At least three solutions to this dilemma were discussed at various times and by various groups. Some advocated relocation of the Southern Utes on the Uintah Reservation in northeastern Utah, as they had done with the Uncompahgre Utes. Others felt that severalty, (individual ownership of land) held the best promise for the Indians. But during the period under consideration here, neither plan gathered serious support from whites, and Indians appear to have been united in their opposition. The Southern Utes argued that the Uintah Reservation was too distant from their traditional homes. Their attitude toward severalty and a future working one farm was neatly summed up by one subchief when he said: "Trees don't work, God don't work, Indian don't work, white man works."[39]

On the other hand, the third option, removal to Utah's San Juan County, appeared to have much to recommend it. The country was well known to the Utes, and many of them, particularly the Weeminuches made more or less regular sorties into it. In the eyes of the Durango removers, it was a land ideally desolate, not too distant, yet beyond the realm of their own economic interests. No more than 800 whites lived in all of San Juan County, and its two mountains and vast desert valleys and canyon lands seemed well suited to a people determined to follow their ponies and goats from water hole to water hole or hunt and squabble among themselves. As a consequence, pressure mounted to get the Department of Interior to propose a new reservation in Utah and to get Congress to establish it.

But there was much opposition even to this alternative. In the first place the Southern Utes saw little to be gained in removal to

---

Ute Reservation where they were a matter of acute concern to stockmen, miners, and Colorado railroaders. For a complete and balanced treatment of the Southern Ute Reservation question, see Gregory Coyne Thompson, "Southern Ute Lands, 1848-1899; The Creation of a Reservation," in Robert Delaney, ed., *Occasional Papers of the Center of Southwest Studies*, no. 1 (Durango, 1972). *See also* Forbes Parkhill, *The Last of the Indian Wars* (New York: Crowell-Collier Publishing Company, 1962).

38. For information about the Uintah reservation, see Floyd O'Neil, "A History of the Ute Indians of Utah" (Ph.D. diss., University of Utah, 1973).

39. *Durango Herald*, 19 September 1895.

an area which was open to them anyway on an informal basis. It also appears that, while not given to agriculture, the Muaches and Capotes were genuinely satisfied with the land they had. Supported by the Southern Ute agents and much of the time by the Department of Interior, the Durango removal proponents worked to create a desire among the Indians to move. Pursuant to this, Chief Ignacio and several of his fellows were taken to Washington, D.C., in 1886, where they showed some interest in removing to Utah and took part in preliminary discussions.[40]

The proposal gathered steam during the following year. In 1888 a commission consisting of J. Montgomery Smith, Thomas S. Childs, and R. B. Weaver was appointed and in July proceeded to the agency with instructions to negotiate a treaty expediting the removal. On arriving at Ignacio, the Southern Ute agency, the commission found the Indians to be strongly opposed to the move.[41] For several months the commission worked, promoting the removal treaty. After touring the Southern Ute Reservation, stumping among rank and file tribesmen, taking a delegation of chiefs to San Juan County and, more important, taking part in eight long council meetings—each of several days duration—they wore down Indian resistance. At about the middle of November an agreement was reached. According to its terms, an estimated 2,912,000 acres in Utah, an area corresponding with San Juan County, would be exchanged for the smaller tract in Colorado. To entice the Indians it was necessary to offer as boot $50,000 in annuities and $20,000 worth of sheep to the whole tribe and, as a special bribe, $2,000 to the negotiating chiefs. In addition, the Indians were told they could have free access to the La Sal Mountains for hunting purposes. Utah's Paiutes, who, according to the commission, expressed great pleasure at the prospects, were to be incorporated with the Utes.[42]

But Ute removal had other opponents. Most notable among these was the Indian Rights Association. Its attack on Southern Ute removal generally, and, after 1889, on the treaty of removal was two-fold. In the first place it conducted studies of its own, sent its own commissions, talked with Indians, sampled feelings in Colorado, and took an unenthusiastic look at southeastern Utah. Publishing reports that contradicted the Ute Commission's findings and recommendations, the IRA then invaded the halls of Congress, where it lobbied effectively against removal.[43]

---

40. "Report of the Ute Commission of 1888," *Senate Executive Document* 67, 50th Cong., 2d Sess., 1889, p. 20.

41. Ibid., p. 11.

42. Ibid., pp. 2, 14.

43. *See* "Annual Report of the Indian Rights Association" for 1890 and 1892; C. C. Painter, "Protest of the Indian Rights Association Against the Proposed Removal of the Southern Ute Indians" (1890) and "Removal of the Southern Utes" (1890); and F. F. Kane and F. M. Riter, *A Further Report to*

Interestingly, San Juan's big cattlemen divided on the issue. Most of them undoubtedly opposed moving the Utes. At least one worked actively against the treaty. This was the Pittsburgh Land and Cattle Company which ran on the La Sals, but like the IRA was based in Pennsylvania.[44] On the other hand, the Carlisle Company, which from its ranch just north of present-day Monticello ran the largest cattle outfit in the region, looked favorably upon the proposition. With a Mormon village rising in their backyard, the Carlisles let it be known that their home ranch was available as an agency site for the proposed reservation.

Utah was, for many years, the sleeping giant in this situation. Nowhere has evidence been found that the territory pushed back questions of political rapprochement between the Mormon church and the United States government or paused in its quest for statehood to give any thought to the removal question. F. A. Hammond did draw up a statement showing that about sixty Mormon families had improvements and claims valued at $53,852 in the county and that non-Mormon claims, including the Carlisles,' amounted to $33,280. In his letter of transmittal, Hammond called the Ute Commission's attention to the cost of establishing homes in San Juan County, to the lack of prospects elsewhere, and to the inconvenience of moving. But his purpose appears to have been to get a just settlement, not to oppose removal as such.[45]

In 1894 Utah awoke with a start to find that a *fait accompli* had almost—but not quite—taken place while it slumbered. The first evidences that something critical was afoot were noticed by San Juan stockmen during November. An unprecedented number of Utes were camping along the streams and by the springs of the Monticello, Dry Valley, and Indian Creek areas. By the latter part of November it was apparent that the entire tribe—900 men, women, and children—had arrived, complete with ponies and goat herds. The Indians announced that the country was theirs. Washington had acted, and their agent, David F. Day, had told them that the long wait was over; they could occupy their new land and the whites would have to go.

The immediate causes of this invasion are difficult to know. The treaty was still unsigned. There is no doubt that Day directed the Indians to make the move. It is not clear, however, just how he hoped the unannounced removal would be effective. The military command at Fort Lewis must have been apprised and appears to have backed Day, but not to have been involved as an instigator.

the *Indian Rights Association on the Proposed Removal of the Southern Utes* (1892). Copies of these are found in the Indian Rights Association Collection, Pennsylvania Historical Society, Philadelphia.

44.   Correspondence between Robert Smith, J. C. Blood and others of the Pittsburgh Company, and the Indian Rights Association, Indian Rights Association Collection.

45.   "Report of the Ute Commission of 1888," pp. 79-84.

In any event, the arriving Indians triggered great consternation, first in San Juan and Grand counties and, after residents of these counties gave the alarm, in Utah generally. The Indians were armed and wary. In addition to the Southern Utes there were the usual Paiute bands and some "200 to 300 Navajos" in San Juan County. To Willard Butt, San Juan's sheriff, it looked "as if the Utes were making some kind of alliance" with the Navajos "for the purpose of getting the best of the fight they are expecting." Matters were made worse in San Juan by the fact that there were only about 120 white men in the county and these were scattered over its vast length and breadth.[46] Local officials called for aid quickly to save feed that was badly needed and, more important, to avert violence, as it appeared the situation could only go badly for the whites. The aid they requested was of three sorts: first, political intercession by Utah's Governor Caleb W. West to Hoke Smith, secretary of interior, and to Congress; second, arms for men already in the southeast; finally, armed intervention by the U. S. Army if possible, but if it failed to act quickly, then by the Territorial National Guard.

Grand County was also disturbed; many of its residents ran livestock in San Juan and others had mining interests there. Of equal importance were reports that the Indians intended to crowd whites out of the Moab area. In general the tone of official protest from Grand County was more excited than that coming from San Juan. Furthermore, its demands tended a little more toward violent action against the Indians. Two reasons suggest themselves: first, the Indians were not walking the streets of Moab as they were in Monticello, permitting greater luxury of expression there; second, the character of the Moab community was a little more given to activist solutions than was the society of San Juan County.

But even Moab's residents were less belligerent than the cowboys of the La Sal and Indian Creek areas. Characterized as "long haired Armenians" by Day, these gathered in Dry Valley in a meeting reminiscent of those that had led to the cowboy wars of 1881 and 1884.[47] Fearing that Utah's public officials would either fail to act or would act with insufficient decisiveness, the cowboys planned to "start a fight in order to get quick action and federal troops in and a federal investigation."[48] Publicizing their plan through a letter-writing campaign, the stockmen set a deadline of December 15 for the initiation of hostilities and waited to see if Governor West could get the Indians expelled without their drastic measures. Day immediately sent a telegram to the governor which cast more than a few aspersions at his management of affairs and implored him "to stay the

46. Butt to Governor Caleb W. West, 23 November 1894, Caleb W. West Papers, Utah State Archives.
47. David F. Day to Caleb W. West, 5 December 1894, West Papers. *See also* Silvey, p. 48.
48. Ibid.

avenging hand" of the cowboys. Angered, the governor forwarded to Secretary of Interior Hoke Smith the entire text of Day's "impudent and blackguard telegram."[49]

The press quickly took up the controversy between Day and West which, coupled with the frantic appeals coming in from the southeast, led West to move to protect Utah interests. Since broad sections of the public were unsympathetic to the cattlemen, West based his case for action on the needs of squatters and homesteaders and made preparations to send in the National Guard. Arms and ammunition were collected. Five cases of rifles and 7,000 rounds of ammunition were distributed in Grand and San Juan counties. The man directly responsible, E. W. Tatlock, inspector general of the Utah National Guard, headed south on December 6. A meeting was set at Monticello to which were invited the governor, Colonel Tatlock, Agent Day, Colonel H. W. Lawton (inspector general for the Colorado Department), and various local and Indian leaders. By December 8 the federal wheels finally creaked into motion, enabling Hoke Smith to wire the governor that the War Department "will doubtless prevent any outbreak. Agent Day has been instructed to return the Indians to their reservation."[50]

During a nightlong meeting on December 12, the news was given to the Indians. To them the frustration must have been almost beyond our ability to comprehend. Told that the country was theirs, they had been met by a hostile people. Encouraged on the one hand to stay, they were ordered back on the other. With women and children and their entire holdings, they had made one hard winter trip—now they were asked to make another. As Tatlock reported at the meeting, the Indians were "defiant and said they would occupy and retain the land, regardless of orders." However, they were given no chance to negotiate but were told flatly that "they could go back peaceably, or troops would force them back."[51]

Protesting, they left. Day and Lawton saw the first bands out of Utah. Others tarried, causing some concern among the residents of the southeast. But as they were able, they made their way back to Colorado, and before 1895 was many months old the great invasion of San Juan County had ended. With it died the chance that the county would become an Indian reservation.

Although what Forbes Parkhill called "the last of the Indian wars" continued to mar relations until the death of the Paiute chieftain Posey in 1923, a more or less permanent social equilibrium had been achieved by 1895.[52] The white population remained small and rela-

---

49.   Telegram to Caleb W. West, 5 December 1894 and telegram to Hoke Smith, 5 December 1894, West Papers.
50.   Hoke Smith to Caleb W. West, 8 December 1894, West Papers.
51.   Tatlock report to West, 18 December 1894.
52.   Parkhill's *The Last of the Indian Wars* is the best secondary source for the Indian-white troubles extending into the twentieth century.

tively untouched by mainstream influences. Mormons, particularly in San Juan County, continued to regard themselves as special emissaries to the Indians although the immediacy of obligation lessened with time. Serious thought of moving the Southern Utes to Utah was abandoned and the prospect of continued Ute occupation of the reservation in southwestern Colorado was accepted. Even before 1895 the Navajo Reservation had been drawn to include Utah south of the San Juan River and its confluence with the Colorado River. A few years later the Aneth extension added a substantial area north of the San Juan along the Colorado border, bringing the Navajos even nearer to white communities. A permissive carryover from the era of the mission Mormons, coupled with limited white population, enabled several small bands of Paiutes and Utes to remain in the region. During the winter these Indians annexed themselves to Bluff and later to Blanding and in the summer roamed the Blue Mountains. All in all, it made for a distinctive society—one in which the tradition of earlier conflict, natural conditions, and federal policy brought Indians and whites into a close and lasting—if not altogether satisfying—relationship.

Chapter V

The Livestock Frontier

The livestock frontier of the La Sal Forest area was both spectacular and important. Few range regions can boast a more varied or more exciting past. Its story includes cowboys, cattle barons, outlaws, Mormon cooperatives, Indians, sheep, and always the threefold threat of nature—drought, canyonlands, and remoteness. The story began late but once started moved quickly and with a lusty vigor quite in keeping with the best traditions of the stockman's frontier. Actually three frontiers converged in the area during the 1880s. Stockmen, Mormons, and Indians each acquired new interest in the country at about the same time. The interplay among them left its peculiar imprint upon the area. Elsewhere in this study Mormon colonization and Indian relations have been treated. In the pages that follow, the development of the livestock industry in the vicinity of the La Sal and Blue mountains will be summarized.

The course of the livestock frontier's development up to the advent of the National Forest in 1906 falls into five rather clearly delineated subdivisions: that of the cowboy; the cattle empire; the Mormon; the sheepman; and the period of adjustment and developing balance. These phases developed irregularly and with much overlapping, but in a general way they followed in sequence.

Of Tom Ray, Spud Hudson, Racehorse Johnson, and Other Cowboys

Small stockmen, or what I have chosen to call cowboys, were the first to arrive. Beginning in the mid-1870s they came, washing ahead of the main tide of colonization. They were a breed apart, not refugees from the law in the sense that some riders for the big companies would be at a later period, but nevertheless an aggressive, independent, and adventurous set. Many of them might be termed drifters, having moved from place to place about the West. Character-istic was Tom Ray, who in 1877 became the first settler at what is now Old La Sal. Ray and his family had pioneered in Ten-nessee, moved to California in the early 1870s, back to Mount Pleasant in Utah, and finally to La Sal.[1] Another rolling stone was Preston Nutter. Born in Virginia in 1850, he worked as a cabin boy on the Mississippi River, joined a wagon train for the West when he was thirteen and, coming by way of Nevada, San Francisco, Idaho, the mines of Colorado's San Juan District, San Diego, and after an interval of freighting in western Colorado, arrived with a growing herd of cattle in the Thompson-Cisco country north of the La Sal Mountains in 1883. Although he followed the cattle business for the rest of his life, he ranged widely in Arizona, Utah, and Colorado be-fore finally stabilizing in the Nine-Mile area of eastern Utah in 1902.[2]

The small stockmen came from everywhere. Many, like Nutter or like "Spud" (his real name was Joshua B.) Hudson, who moved two thousand cattle onto the Blue Mountains in 1879, came from Colo-rado—Nutter from Montrose, and Hudson from the "Picket Wire" near Trinidad. Some, like the O'Donnel brothers, merely followed herds from the Dolores Valley or from elsewhere along Colorado's southwest border to Utah's San Juan. Al Nunn, who is said to have crossed the Colorado line near Paiute Spring with 1,200 head of cattle, and Charley ("Race Horse") Johnson must also be included in this class. Many of the Colorado cowboys maintained headquarters in Colorado, limiting their Utah operations to summer grazing. Others broke with Colorado and in time became part of the Utah scene.

Many of the cowboys came from Utah settlements. The real pioneers in this movement from the west appear to have been the Green brothers, George and Silas, whose arrival in Moab Valley about 1875 and subsequent deaths have been noted. Memory of their point of origin is vague, but in 1877 others migrating from the Utah settle-ments were guided across the Wasatch Plateau to the Green River by one of the Green brothers, suggesting that Green's own herd of cattle had been driven east over the same trail.[3] By the late 1870s a clearer pattern began to emerge, with the McCartys, the Taylors, the Wilsons, J. H. Shafer, and others bringing cattle from un-designated points west of the Wasatch range to run on the virgin ranges near Moab, and Green Robinson, John E. Brown, Dudley

1. Silvey, p. 6. Portions of this chapter have appeared in my essay "San Juan in Controversy: American Livestock Frontier vs. Mormon Cattle Pool," in Thomas G. Alexander, ed., *Essays on the American West 1972-1973*, Charles Redd Monographs in Western History, no. 3 (Provo, Utah: Brigham Young University Press, 1974): 45-68.

2. Virginia N. Price and John T. Darby, "Preston Nutter: Utah Cattleman, 1886-1936," *Utah Historical Quarterly* 32 (1964): 236.

3. Tanner, p. 27.

Reece, and a Mr. Peters joining Spud Hudson and other Colorado cowboys near the Blue Mountains.[4]

The economics of this process are interesting and important. Utah herds had stocked Great Basin ranges to capacity and beyond before 1879. An acute drouth during that year and in 1880 complicated the problems of overstocking. As a result, large numbers of cattle were sold or herded to new ranges. The Bennion family, who customarily ran cattle in Skull and Rush valleys of west-central Utah, moved 2,000 head into Castle Valley at about this time.[5] Others, like Lester Taylor and his family, pushed on across the Green and Colorado rivers to make southeastern Utah their home. The economics of this situation also attracted buyers from Colorado. With the Colorado market bringing $25-$30 per head on a straight-run basis, cattle which sold for about $10 each in the Utah settlements obviously offered good profits. In 1881 Preston Nutter transferred $6,100 to a Manti bank to cover the cost of cattle he purchased in Sanpete County for trailing to Montrose. If the reports of the going price are accurate, we deduce that Nutter purchased about 600 head

Branding scene in southeastern Utah, about 1915.

4. Perkins, Nielson, and Jones, p. 90. *See also* Silvey, pp. 6-7.
5. The Bennions summered near Fish Lake and wintered on Ferron Creek. Glynn Bennion, "The Story of a Pioneer-day Cattle Venture" (typescript, present writer's possession).

of stock. In 1879 and 1880, Spud Hudson purchased cattle in the Utah settlements, turning a handsome profit on the differential between Utah and Colorado prices.[6] Others, including Dudley Reece and Green Robinson, also bought cattle in Utah to fatten near the Blues and sell at a good profit in Colorado.

It is difficult to determine exactly what routes were followed by the first herds trailed from central and western Utah. Later, the Scorups, J. A. and James, came from the Salina area by way of Grass and Rabbit valleys, crossing the Colorado at or near Hite's Crossing, and worked through White Canyon to get into the country back of the Blue Mountains.[7] Spud Hudson and the others who brought herds in at the end of the 1870s could have done what the Scorups did, but evidence indicates they did not. In 1884 Platte D. Lyman blundered more than explored to Hite's Crossing, which was called Dandy Crossing by Bluff settlers. Two years earlier, A. K. Thurber had "looked out" a trail from Rabbit Valley in Wayne County to the west side of the river, but there is no evidence of large herds being taken that way as early as the mid-1880s.[8] In 1886 Lyman and a dozen other small owners drifted "a little over 1000 head of cattle" through Rabbit Valley to the Colorado River and into the San Juan. It appears, however, that most of these cattle came east by way of Hall's Crossing not via the Hite's Crossing-White Canyon route. As early as 1880, a leg-weary herd of Texas cattle which, in a far-ranging quest for grass had dwindled from 1,500 to 800 head, were attached to the Hole-in-the-Rock expedition and taken through to McElmo Creek in western Colorado by Tom Box. According to one account, cattle and horses totaling 1,800 head accompanied the Bluff pioneers.[9] Other herds doubtless came in by the same route, but I have found no clear mention of them in the early record.

What all this adds up to is the strong likelihood that not only the Rays, the Taylors, and other cowboys who ran on the La Sals, but also Hudson, Peters, and other Blue Mountain graziers arrived by way of the Old Spanish Trail, crossing the Green River at the ford of the Spanish Trail, and the Colorado, at Moab. Taken together, references concerning herds coming to eastern Utah over this well-marked trail indicate that tens of thousands of cattle were trailed out from the settlements before an equilibrium in numbers staunched the flow by 1885.[10]

6.   Silvey, p. 7.

7.   Stena Scorup, *J. A. Scorup, A Utah Cattleman* (n.p., 1944), p. 28. See also Neal Lambert, "Al Scorup: Cattleman of the Canyons," *Utah Historical Quarterly* 32 (1964): 301-20.

8.   Journal of Platte D. Lyman, pp. 64, 73.

9.   "Reminiscences of George W. Decker," in Miller, pp. 201-2.

10.   It is interesting to recall that the Spanish as well as the Indians had driven herds of horses and mules numbering into the thousands from California to New Mexico during the 1830s. As far as I have been able to ascertain, the first herds of cattle and sheep to be driven over the route by Anglo-Americans

I have referred to this period of development as the time of the small cattlemen or the cowboys. In the main, the picture conveyed by this nomenclature is accurate. As Don Walker has noted in his excellent article on the Carlisle Cattle Company, the cattlemen of the earliest period were "usually both owner and manager."[11] For most of them beginnings were humble. Some of the earliest ran dairy herds. Tom Ray reportedly brought sixty head of Milking Shorthorns to Old La Sal in 1877. Ray, who was the first stockman to settle on the south slopes of the La Sals, followed a pattern that was characteristic of Utah livestock development when he pushed out ahead of other cattle herds with his dairy cows. Tom May, one of the first settlers in Paradox Valley, also ran a dairy, hauling butter salted down in whiskey barrels to Durango markets.[12] Many of the earliest Mormon forays into the cattle business had involved summer dairying operations in which no more than 150 cows were milked.[13]

Beef cattle operations were also small. A Frenchman and a Negro, who occupied the old Elk Mountain Fort at Moab in 1877, are reported to have had small herds of cattle, perhaps about forty head each. While specific evidence is lacking, such settlers as the Silveys, who moved again and again in quest of ranges not overrun by the big outfits, and who spent much of their time riding for the big outfits, probably had relatively small herds.

And there were also the true cowboys, men with few or no cows, who drifted from one job to another for their board and a few dollars. Many of these came and went from Durango and other Colorado towns. Often unemployed and broke, they holed up at remote camps, waiting out off-seasons, and were easy prey for get-rich schemes, including stock rustling. Indicative of their life-style is Jordan Bean's report that fifteen cowboys spent the winter of 1880-81 at Burnt Cabin Springs near the Utah border, drifting out about May 1 to find jobs as the spring roundups began.[14]

On the other hand, this early period was not entirely dominated by small stockmen and cowboys. If we can accept as valid the breezy tallies of old-timers upon whom the count depends, there

were the sheep belonging to a Mr. McClanahan and his partner, Mr. Crockett, and "the fine herd of cattle" of the Burwell brothers which were driven to the California markets in the wake of the Gunnison exploration in 1853. The Gunnison diary does not record how many sheep and cattle were in these herds but does indicate that they came through in good shape. *See* Beckwith, pp. 6, 75.

11. Don D. Walker, "The Carlisles: Cattle Barons of the Upper Basin," *Utah Historical Quarterly* 32 (1964): 270.

12. Silvey, p. 2.

13. "Diary of Albert F. Potter's Wasatch Survey, July 1 to November 22, 1902," Region IV Papers, Record Group 95, National Archives, Washington, D.C. *See also* Andrew Karl Larson, "I Was Called to Dixie," *The Virgin River Basin: Unique Experiences in Mormon Pioneering* (Salt Lake City: Deseret News Press, 1961), pp. 236-48, 588.

14. McMechen, p. 19.

were a dozen or more stockmen each with more than 1,000 head of cattle. Spud Hudson, who first claimed what was later Carlisle Ranch, brought in 2,000 head in 1879. The following year he "made a number of trips to the settlements, returning each trip with larger herds of cattle."[15] The Taylors had 3,000. Between them, Philander Maxwell and Billie McCarty boasted 2,000 head, while a Mr. Peters, whose first name has escaped generations of historians, ran 2,000 cattle from his headquarters at the spring that now bears his name. Even horse herds were counted in heroic figures. Hundreds of head are said to have been trailed in behind the Bluff settlers during the winter of 1880. The following summer, Joshua Alderson and John Thurmond brought in 1,500 horses from Nevada and Oregon.[16]

Later, wild horses ran in great numbers, as evidenced by the fact that the Scorup brothers slaughtered as many as 700 head in a single hunt in their effort to free grazing lands for cattle.[17] Spared the demands of Forest permits, and virtually beyond the count of County Assessor L. H. Redd, who began to ride the country in 1881 in an attempt to build the tax rolls, it was a time when enthusiastic if not entirely accurate counts were tolerated.[18] But even discounting exaggerations on the part of the old-timers, it is evident that some aggressive and fortunate men quickly built herds of substantial numbers.

Of Ranch Kings and Cattle Barons

But the day when the small stockman was dominant was over almost before it began. The kind of profits that enabled Spud Hudson to turn successive herds of cattle into gain during 1879 and 1880 did not go unnoticed. Furthermore, big companies financed from the money marts of America and Great Britain were hard on the heels of the cowboy ranchers in their quest for investment opportunity. In the years after 1883, the prime ranges around what later became the La Sal National Forest were taken over by big operations, and the smaller ranchers were forced into successively more remote corners. The movement of the small outfits to less attractive spots may be traced by a couple of examples. Green Robinson and John E. Brown, who ran on the Blues until 1883, sold their cattle and claims to the Carlisles. Buying more stock in the Utah settlements, Robinson set up operations at Coyote, taking John E. Brown in with him. Almost immediately, the Pittsburgh Cattle Company (PCC) bought out Robinson at his new headquarters. Little more is seen of him, but John E. Brown then moved to Indian Creek where he located a ranch in 1887.[19] The Silvey family is another case in point. Selling their La Sal interests to the PCC in 1887, they moved first to the east end

---

15. Silvey, p. 7.
16. Rogers.
17. Lambert, p. 307.
18. Perkins, Nielson, and Jones, p. 179.
19. Silvey, p. 36.

of Lisbon Valley, running cattle in a remote canyon fourteen miles above Paradox Valley and four miles from the Dolores River before moving in 1889 to Hatch Point. Finding good grazing but an inadequate supply of water, the Silveys pulled back to Hatch Ranch in Dry Valley the following year, and by 1895 were at Rattlesnake Flats southwest of La Sal.[20]

While it oversimplifies the situation, it may be said that southeastern Utah was divided into six great cattle provinces during the years after 1883. Tucked in and around these great outfits were smaller operators, some of whom ran respectable ranches, and a few of whom succeeded to claims upon the great provinces as the years and changing fortune made opportunity.

What I have called the great provinces developed along a simple geographic pattern. Beginning in the north near the Denver and Rio Grande Railway tracks, they extended south to the San Juan River where they turned west and north again to take in the region behind the Blue Mountains. On the extreme north beyond the Colorado River was an area dominated first by Preston Nutter; the south slopes of the La Sal Mountains were held by the Pittsburgh Cattle Company; Dry Valley and the north and east drainages of the Blue Mountains made up the domain of the Carlisle Company; South Montezuma Creek was the preserve of the L C (Lacy Cattle Company); the Bluff Mormons operated south and west of the Blue Mountains; and, somewhat later as pressure for grass forced cattle into increasingly forbidding country, the Scorup brothers came to control first White and Dark Canyons and finally Indian Creek.[21] The genesis of each of these subdivisions will be traced briefly in the paragraphs that follow.

After dabbling in the grazing business during the early 1880s, Preston Nutter moved into the triangle formed by Thompson's Springs, Cisco, and Hill Creek in 1886-87. Unlike several of the other cattle giants, Nutter was not backed by corporate financing during these years; but by astute trading, skilled management of livestock, and more than a little luck, he worked toward a goal of 15,000 to 20,000 head of cattle.[22] In 1888 he entered a partnership with Ed Sands and Tom Wheeler, forming the Grand Cattle Company. The following year Nutter bought out his partners and, obtaining contracts to supply beef for the army and Indian agencies at Fort Duchesne, pushed his operations farther into the Book Cliffs area. But as much

20. Ibid. *See also* Silvey, "When San Juan County Was Given to the Southern Ute Indians" (typescript, Utah State Historical Society).

21. Among the larger operators not mentioned were Lester and Albert A. Taylor. Entering the country with 3,000 head, they were among Moab's most important stockmen. In 1900 they added to already extensive holdings by leasing 21,707 acres from the State Land Board. *See Emery County Progress* (Castle Dale, Utah), 24 November 1900.

22. Price and Darby, p. 236.

the rugged individualist as Preston Nutter was, even he fell prey to corporate blandishments, and in 1893 joined New York business-men in forming the Strawberry Cattle Company. To avoid a con-flict of interest, he sold his Grand County operation to the Webster City Cattle Company, which subsequently ran stock in the country north of the Colorado River, as did the Turner family.[23]

A few years before Nutter moved on to the vast ranges north of the Colorado River, the Pittsburgh Cattle Company took over the south La Sals and north end of Dry Valley. Organized in 1884 by a group of Pennsylvania financiers, the PCC sent Charles H. Ogden and James Blood to the La Sal area, where they bought the cattle and ranches of Green Robinson, the Maxwells, and the Ray and Mc-Carty families. After consummating this transaction in 1885, they held most of the claims and improvements at La Sal and Coyote. Green Robinson's Cross H brand was taken over by the company, and Og-den, Blood, and Frank S. Smith became responsible for its local opera-tion. In 1887 J. M. Cunningham was brought in as manager, and Thomas B. Carpenter as ranch foreman. They proved to be a par-ticularly effective team and together ran the operation for many years. There is evidence that the PCC ran cattle in both Colorado and Utah and that it handled 15,000 to 20,000 head, although tax rolls for San Juan County suggest a figure not more than one quarter of that number.[24]

In 1895, Cunningham and Carpenter, joined by Fred N. Prewer, organized the La Sal Cattle Company to buy the PCC stock and ranches. During this same year, ranch headquarters were changed from La Sal to Coyote. Because the post office was moved from La Sal to Coyote without changing its name, the latter came in time to be known as La Sal, and the older town was called Old La Sal, Pine Lodge, or merely "the other ranch." A ditch cut high on the east slope of the mountain drew water from La Sal Creek to the flats below Coyote, permitting the development of several hundred acres of farmland. In 1896 Fred Prewer oversaw the planting of an orch-ard and a grove of cottonwoods and the construction of a large ranch house. The house sat a half-turn out of line with the world, but dominated the ranch then as it does now.[25] Below the ranch house was a dirt-roofed bunkhouse. And, demonstrating that sur-vival demanded adaptation even by the big cattle outfits, "Chihuahua," a row of cabins used by Mexican sheepherders, lay east across the main ditch from the bunkhouse.[26]

In 1898 Prewer left the company. Thereafter it was known as Cunningham and Carpenter. Capable in their management, these

23.   Ibid., p. 242. *See also* Walker D. Wyman and John D. Hart, "The Legend of Charlie Glass," *Colorado Magazine* 46 (1969): 40-54.

24.   Minutes of San Juan County Court, 1880-1900, 27 July 1892, p. 127.

25.   Perkins, Nielson, and Jones, p. 181.

26.   John Riis, *Ranger Trails* (Richmond: The Dietz Press, 1937), p. 6.

two men diversified to sheep, acquired ranges in the Book Cliffs and on the east slope of the Rockies east of Denver, and otherwise showed every evidence of steady growth. After being a dominant force in the north end of San Juan County for more than fifteen years, they began to sell out in September of 1914. The first sale involved Book Cliffs interests, amounting to "nearly 10,000 acres and several thousand head of cattle and sheep" which were sold to the Taylor brothers of Moab and Grand Junction for a reported $100,-000.[27] Justifying their action by reporting that the Book Cliffs operation had been too distant from their La Sal headquarters to permit efficient operation, they disclosed their real intent when they sold out their remaining interests in November for $230,000 to "a local association made up of Lemuel H. Redd, J. A. Scorup, Kumen Jones, Hans Bayles, Nielson Brothers, J. F. Barton, J. P. Larson, and F. B. Hammond, Sr."[28]

The largest, and in many ways the most exciting of the corporate outfits, was the Kansas and New Mexico Land and Cattle Company or, as it was known in southeastern Utah, the Carlisle Company, or simply the Carlisles. Two English brothers, Harold and Edmund S. Carlisle—purportedly of noble lineage—funded the operation with British capital at $720,000, a good share of which was their own. They paid $210,000, or an average of $30 per head, for 7,000 cattle running on the Blue Mountains and belonging to Spud Hudson, Green Robinson, Dudley Reece, and Peters. The newcomers took over the Blue Mountain and Dry Valley ranges of these same men. They adapted the "three bars" on the left hip brand that Peters had used, by separating the bars and placing one on the left hip, one on the side, and one on the shoulder to become the "Hip-Side and Shoulder" company of Judge Fred Keller's famous Blue Mountain ballad.[29] In addition to its Utah holdings, the Carlisle Company had sizable herds in New Mexico and 400 head in Kansas.[30]

The Carlisles' Blue Mountain operation began big and grew quickly. A few statistics indicate its magnitude. As early as 1884 the brothers were reported to have 11,000 head ready for market. In 1885 their cowboys branded 5,300 calves and in one grand roundup bunched 10,000 head from the sandy flats and dry gulches of Dry Valley alone. In the early 1890s drought and the incursions of sheep brought drastic reductions in cattle numbers, and the Ute in-

27. *Grand Valley Times*, 4 September 1914.
28. Ibid., 27 November 1914. *See also* Perkins, Nielson, and Jones, p. 182; and "Historical Information, La Sal National Forest," p. 55.
29. One verse of Judge Keller's song runs:
    For the brand L. C. I'll ride and "sleeper calves" on the side.
    I'll own the "Hip-Side and Shoulder" when I grow older
    "Zapitaro" don't tan my hide.
See Perkins, Nielson, and Jones, p. 95.
30. Walker, p. 271. *See also Durango Daily Herald*, 31 May 1883; and Silvey, *Northern San Juan County*, p. 35.

Cattle losses at a Blue Mountains bog.

vasion of Dry Valley in the winter of 1894-95 is said to have resulted in the loss of 50 percent of the stock wintering in that locality. Yet when the Carlisles bowed to low returns and bad times and sold their cattle in 1896 they still gathered 30,000 head of stock. It seems likely that during peak years their herds numbered substantially more than this figure.[31]

31. Franklin D. Day, "The Cattle Industry of San Juan County" (Master's thesis, Brigham Young University, 1958), p. 37.

As Don Walker notes: "At the level of man to cow in the new cattle empire, it was still old-time know-how, mostly Texan, that handled things."[32] The first Carlisle foreman, John Mosely, apparently came with the Carlisles from Kansas. More important in the tradition of the country was foreman Mack Goode, a one-time Texas cowboy, whose crew was made up mainly of Texans. Frank Silvey, who rode with Goode during the mid-eighties, recalled that the regular Carlisle crew was comprised of about a dozen men during the Goode period. Much better known throughout the southeast than Goode, and perhaps more than even the Carlisles themselves, was William E. or Latigo Gordon, son of Mrs. Harold Carlisle by an earlier marriage, and longtime foreman of the operation. Gordon, who came near to being the complete product of his times and environment, was a colorful and effective figure. He rode and brawled with the rowdiest of his cowboys, dealt shrewdly as local manager when the Carlisles came to spend less time in Utah, made the transition from cattle to sheep, married a Mormon girl, and stayed on in the country after the Carlisles sold out.

When they first came to southeastern Utah, the Carlisles established their headquarters at Paiute Spring. Their Paiute Spring buildings were still standing in 1888 when the Southern Ute Commission surveyed San Juan County, but the company had long since moved into Spud Hudson's old Double Cabins Spring headquarters six miles north of present Monticello. There they built a substantial home ranch, consisting of barns, corrals, bunk cabins, and developed hundreds of acres of irrigated fields.[33] In about 1887 they built a large frame house which came to be known as the "White House," and fenced huge areas of the public domain, including several sections just north of Monticello.[34] This enclosure cut off the road between the south and north ends of the county, and started a running controversy between the Carlisles and the traveling community. Fences were cut, gates were let down, and stock were driven out on the one hand, and threats were made and bully tactics used on the other, including several shooting incidents. In 1891 the trouble was eased when the San Juan County Court (the territorial equivalent of the county commission) directed Harold Carlisle to open the county road. Carlisle complained, so the court relented, and established a new right-of-way around the east fence of the Carlisle claim which the company agreed to accept.[35]

From its headquarters ranch, the Carlisle Company dominated a wide range, including the Vega Creek and other north and east drainages of the Blues, and extending east into Colorado and north deep into Dry Valley. F. A. Hammond, who, as the guiding spirit of

---

32. Walker, p. 274.
33. "Report of the Ute Commission of 1888," p. 17.
34. Francis A. Hammond Journal, 4 March 1887 and 22 March 1888.
35. Minutes of San Juan County Court, 1880-1900, 30 December 1891.

a Mormon drive to force the cattlemen out of the country had occasion to look carefully at the various operations, reported that the Carlisles claimed all "these mountain streams" and had "some 80 to 60 miles" for stock range.[36]

Actually, the Kansas and New Mexico Land and Cattle Company does not appear to have owned one acre of ground. The fact that both Edmund and Harold Carlisle were English nationals complicated their plans to secure land title. Nevertheless, they applied the standard "rubber forty" operating technique of the time, and Edmund S. Carlisle and confidants among their employees entered claims to about fourteen key spots, enabling them to control the water sources and consequently the country served by this water. Records in the Salt Lake City Land Office were confusing and in some ways misleading, but T. S. Childs, who studied the matter for the Southern Ute Commission, found that:

> All these fourteen entries . . . are made . . . directly or indirectly in behalf of the Carlisle Cattle Company, an English company, none of whose members are American citizens, but one of whom, Edmund C. Carlisle, has declared his intention of becoming such. There are grave questions in regard to these entries. . . . It is claimed by those who are familiar with the territory that these desert land entries will not hold, on the ground that the land is not in a proper sense desert land.[37]

Several of the Carlisle claims which had been filed in 1885 were shortly judged invalid because claimants had failed to meet the time requirements of the law for reclaiming the land from its desert condition. It was later decided that Mrs. Esther E. Carlisle rather than Edmund had filed on the single entry actually under the Carlisle name and that the status of other claims was questionable because they were on unsurveyed ground. At least 4,920 acres were entered, none of which appears to have been proved up.[38]

Problems with land claims notwithstanding, the Carlisles were an influence to be reckoned with. When F. A. Hammond computed the values of private holdings at the request of the Ute Commissioners, Carlisle holdings amounted to nearly one-third of the San Juan County total.[39] As one of the commissioners put it, the Carlisles were in a position to "command money and use it. . . ."[40] However, the company appears to have been remarkably easygoing in matters politic, and, some rather fundamental differences notwithstanding,

---

36.   Francis A. Hammond Journal, 17 March 1887.

37.   Childs to William F. Vilas, Secretary of the Interior, 15 November 1888, in "Report of the Ute Commission of 1888," p. 73. "Rubber Forty" was a term applied to the practice of acquiring deeds to small plots adjacent to streams and springs and using control of water to monopolize vast regions of unwatered grassland.

38.   Ibid., p. 72.

39.   Childs to Vilas, 9 October 1888, in "Report of the Ute Commission of 1888," p. 84.

40.   Childs to Vilas, 15 November 1888, p. 71.

manifested more than a little patience with their Mormon neighbors. Indeed, the brothers Carlisle appear to have been "cricket" in most of their Utah dealings and left a tradition that is in most respects superior to that of the general cattleman's frontier.

According to historical information collected in about 1940 by Leland Heywood, then supervisor of the La Sal National Forest, the Carlisles operated a sheep outfit for a few years after selling their cattle. In 1911 they sold their sheep and range rights to a company consisting of Henry Dalton, John E. Adams, Hyrum Perkins, and L. H. Redd for $90,000. Some Carlisle lands were later entered under the Homestead Act, passing into possession of various private parties.[41]

The L C, or Lacy Company, adjoined the Carlisle ranch on the south with its Utah headquarters at the junction of Recapture and Johnson creeks. Its line cabins were near present-day Verdure. The area of its customary range was the southeastern slope of the Blue Mountains, including the South Montezuma, Devil Canyon, and Bulldog Canyon drainages, and extending south and east along Montezuma Creek onto McCracken Mesa. For a time in the late 1880s the L C tried to push its western bounds south along Recapture Creek. Mormons from Bluff also were moving toward Recapture grazing grounds, and as a result a confrontation ensued.

I. W. Lacy, the founder of the L C, came into the country early—the *Saga of San Juan* states that the company reached the Blue Mountains in about 1880. Corroborating this judgment is the reminiscence of Jordan Bean, an early Colorado cowboy, who recalled that Lacy had run his stock in Montezuma Valley in 1879.[42]

The Lacy Company was usually acknowledged to have been one of the largest outfits in the San Juan but was considered to be smaller than the Carlisle ranch. One report from the mid-1890s pegged its numbers at 10,000 head.[43] On the other hand, Al Scorup reported that when the L C Company went out of business in about 1896, the firm sold a number of cattle locally and still drove some 22,000 head to Dolores. It will be recalled that the Carlisles drove 30,000 to Albuquerque at the same time.[44]

More than most of San Juan's cattle companies, the L C had a history of violence. Its original owner, I. W. Lacy, was killed at Fort Lewis in a brawl. Thereafter, the operation was handled by his

41. "Historical Information, La Sal National Forest," p. 52. *See also* Amasa Jay Redd, ed., *Lemuel Hardison Redd, Jr., 1856-1923, Pioneer-Leader-Builder* (Salt Lake City, 1967), p. 50.

42. Perkins, Nielson, and Jones, p. 190. *See also* McMechan, p. 17.

43. Silvey, *Northern San Juan County*, p. 47.

44. Franklin Day, p. 37, quotes Scorup on these figures. Reports in the "Historical Information, La Sal National Forest" raise question as to both the date and ownership involved in this sale. Indeed it suggests the 22,000 head were sold in 1892-93 and may have been made up of Bluff Pool cattle as well as L C stock.

widow's brothers, the Brumleys, under whom the bloodletting continued. In 1884 and again in 1887 altercations with the Indians led to
the killing of L C employees. In 1886 an L C foreman, Bill Ball, was
ambushed and mortally wounded by two drifting riders who had
taken advantage of temporary refuge offered by Ball to steal several
head of L C horses. A few years later a nephew of I. W. Lacy,
George Brooks, who succeeded Ball as foreman, was killed by Indians
at the Big Bend of the Dolores River. Thereafter the L C brand and
livestock were traded to a Dr. South of Trinidad, Colorado, and Bob
Hott took over its Utah management. When ownership passed from
Lacy family hands, the chain of bad luck was evidently broken, as no
more killings were recorded.[45]

The L C apparently did not establish legal claim to any of its
land. Its improvements were not extensive as evidenced in a report
prepared for the Ute Commissioners listing its holdings at $2,600.
This sum nevertheless ranked it as the third largest concern in the
county after the Carlisles and the Bluff Pool.[46]

By 1885 big cattle companies were in control of most of southeastern Utah. The only area not fully claimed was the region south
and west of the Blue Mountains, tenuously held by Bluff City Mormons. Efforts to make the Mormon farming village pattern function
had failed, and, as we have seen, Bluff settlers had come near to
giving up the effort. With the problems inherent in the San Juan
River's unsuitability for farm villages still unsolved, Mormon settlement was confronted by tremendous pressures from the encroaching
livestock frontier during the middle 1880s. That the Mormons did not
withdraw entirely was due in large measure to a shift in emphasis
from the farm village to cooperative livestock production and to the
person of Francis A. Hammond, who, as new president of the San
Juan Stake, was instrumental in putting together a policy implement-
ing this shift. The Mormons took the offensive after 1885, mounting a
program that led to a confrontation which was in many ways like the
characteristic competition of squatter and cattle baron. In other ways
it was the meeting of the two livestock frontiers—Mormon co-op herd
on the one hand, and the big cow outfit of the general frontier on the
other.

In the short run the Mormon offensive enabled Bluff settlers to
exclude interlopers from the region south and west of the Blue Mountains and to strengthen San Juan Mormons by the establishment of
Monticello and Verdure and later Blanding. Its long-term effects
were two-fold. First, the Mormon co-op herd system was modified
as it impinged upon the more general livestock frontier. Second, this
adaptation led to ultimate Mormon dominance of southeastern Utah's
livestock industry; the great names in the twentieth century have been

---

45. Perkins, Nielson, and Jones, pp. 70-71, 90. *See also* Walker, p. 283.
46. "Report of the Ute Commission of 1888," p. 84. It should be noted
that Hammond did not figure the Pittsburgh Company holdings in his report.

Redd Ranches and Scorup-Somerville rather than Carlisles, or Cunningham and Carpenter.

With failure of the Mormon effort to colonize southeastern Utah a very real possibility, Francis A. Hammond was called to preside over the San Juan Stake in 1885. The announcement of his appointment preceded him; in an action of questionable legality but of major significance to Mormon control of San Juan, he was elected Electman of the San Juan County Court in the August election of 1885, thus giving him an important political position several months before he left his home in Huntsville.[47] With his large family and 500 head of cattle in tow, Hammond made his way almost the full length of the territory during the fall of that year. Fortunately, he kept an extensive diary of not only the trip but of his doings during the critical years of Bluff's confrontation with the livestock frontier. Apparent even before he arrived at Bluff was his determination to encourage involvement in the cattle industry. He talked about it as he traveled, observed ranges, and expressed concern when non-Mormons indicated interest in the country.

Once in Bluff, Hammond discovered that the Saints had waited almost too long to initiate the shift to livestock. By his reckoning there were 100,000 head of cattle in San Juan County—inevitably they were crowding into Bluff's ranges.[48] On December 17, 1885, Hammond learned that "10,000 sheep were making for Recapture"— a pasture he hoped to utilize for his own cattle. The Navajos, too, were moving across the river onto Bluff herd grounds but were easily dealt with by a few men delegated to push them back.

Far more threatening was the expansive conduct of Bluff's nearest neighbors on the northeast, the L C Company. George Brooks first visited Hammond, announcing his intent to drive a large herd to Elk Ridge, and then turned 600 head "loose on our Range [Hammond's]," in the more immediate vicinity of Bluff.[49] Adding insult to injury, Colorado cowboys, led by a man named Fayette Wilson, asked Mormons to guide them in search of range on Elk Ridge, and, when they were dissatisfied with that area, to the country around Lake Pahgarit.[50]

On January 16, 1886, Hammond initiated the first step of his offensive by organizing a cooperative herd—the so-called Bluff Pool. On the nineteenth co-op members established "a guard on our eastern border along the White Mesa for 100 days." Two men maintained a constant vigil against invasion, with pool members providing ten days' herding for every fifty head of stock.[51] Taking advantage of

47. Francis A. Hammond Journal, 8 December 1885.

48. Ibid., 17 December 1885.

49. Ibid., 27 January, and February 7, 11, and 23, 1886.

50. For several years Mormons had been running a few cattle in the vicinity of Lake Pahgarit along the Hole-in-the-Rock road. Journal of Platte D. Lyman, p. 70.

51. Francis A. Hammond Journal, 16 and 19 January 1886.

connections in the north, the Bluff Pool also petitioned the Territorial Legislature for a tax on all stock passing into Utah from Colorado.[52] Finally, letters were written inviting Mormon stockmen to "come immediately and help us stock up the range."[53] In response to these invitations, Platte D. Lyman and about a dozen other western Utah stockmen drove cattle to ranges east of the Colorado River late that year.[54]

The growing emphasis upon cattle and the fact that outside herds were pushing to break Bluff's hegemony of the area forced Mormons to expand onto the last virgin summer ranges in southeastern Utah during 1886. They had recognized the potential of "the summit of the Elk Mountains" as early as 1883, but because their own needs had not been pressing had allowed it to remain essentially in the hands of the Indians, who hunted and ran their ponies and goats there.[55] In this case as in so many others, Mormon friendship with the Paiutes paid off. In the years before 1886, the Paiutes had dominated the Elks—in essence holding it for the Mormons. In a treaty arrived at sometime before March 1, 1886, Mormons were given exclusive right to Paiute claims there. By the end of the year Hammond could report that Bluff Pool cattle numbering 2,000 head had pastured safely on the Elks—"the first stock ever ranged there."[56]

But this breakthrough did not go unprotested. Indeed, Fayette Wilson's Durango cowboys, who toured the Elks looking for grasslands in February, returned to Colorado in a huff where they reported that they

> had talked with the Mormon leaders at Bluff and [were] informed that they were not welcome to locate there. The Mormons had made a treaty with the Pi-Utes and one of the provisions was that no white men should locate stock in that region.

In an ominous afterthought they noted that Mancos Jim and other Indians were in Bluff being "fed by the Mormons."[57] Hammond, in reply to Edmund Carlisle's accusation that the Mormons and Indians were "banding together to keep the cattlemen out from the Elks," replied that "nearly all the report [Fayette Wilson's] was false."[58] He also wrote to the *Idea*, the Durango newspaper in which the report of the Mormon-Indian collusion had appeared, and in a neat bit of double-talk denied that "range hunters were informed a treaty existed" but "pleaded guilty" to

> . . . making a treaty with Indians who claim Elk Mountains as their hunting ground—with the understanding that we were to put our stock

52. Ibid., 27 January 1886.
53. Ibid., 11 February 1886.
54. *Journal of Platte D. Lyman*, p. 97.
55. Ibid., p. 64.
56. *Deseret News*, 29 December 1886.
57. *Idea*, 6 March 1886.
58. Francis A. Hammond Journal, 17 March 1886.

there without being molested. We have paid them in part and expect to pay them more, knowing that it is cheaper to pay them a little for their undisputed claim than to attempt to drive them out and thus place ourselves at their mercy.[59]

Recognizing that a confrontation over grazing rights was imminent, the Carlisles moved to improve their claims even before Hammond arrived, making entry in the names of themselves and employees during 1885.[60] By the end of 1886 they also had fenced the home ranch and other key properties.[61] While the Lacy Company did not bother to make legal entries, George Brooks kept the pressure on; by February of 1887 L C cattle accounted for a large portion of the "4000 owned by outsiders now on range near Bluff. Brooks, who was demanding grazing for an additional thousand cattle, met with Hammond in a futile attempt to work out a range division that would satisfy both parties.[62]

Moreover, by the winter of 1886-87 threats were coming from many directions. At the end of December, 6,000 sheep were loosed almost literally in the backyards of Bluff settlers. Later in the year, a Mr. Gahleger located 2,000 head of Texas "stock in the Comb Wash in the heart of our Winter Range. . . ."[63] In the words of Albert Lyman, who recalled the advent of the Texans, they came:

> [a] great bawling herd, a mile long . . . straggling down the river through Bluff—yellow cattle, white, black, brindle; all of them starving and hollow from the long trail; all of them coyote-like in form, little better in size. And horns! such a river of horns as you might see in a nightmare—horns reaching out and up, out and up again in fantastic corkscrews.[64]

Gahleger, who was not above trafficking in the tension created by the arrival of his Texas steers, offered half-interest to the Bluff settlers. Ignoring their poor quality, he asked $18,000, a price far beyond Bluff's ability to pay, and indicated half-interest had already been sold to Mr. Reid, county treasurer for La Plata County.[65] Within a few days of this contact, Hammond learned that another Texas herd numbering 1,000 head was approaching the Elk Ridge range by way of Indian Creek. Gahleger's Texas outfit established

---

59. *Idea,* 19 April 1886. Among the Mormon claims to grazing rights on the Elks was J. F. Adams's story that he bought the range from Chief Kigalia, who "was located at the spring now known as Kigalia when the Bluff people took their cattle to the mountain in 1890. The Indians were very much concerned and told the whites to move on. Mr. Adams unpacked, cooked dinner and invited the Indians to eat. Adams then traded Kigalia a pony and a piece of beef for the land on the South Elk Mountain." *See* "Historical Information, La Sal National Forest," p. 51.
60. "Report of the Ute Commission of 1888," p. 72.
61. Francis A. Hammond Journal, 4 March 1887.
62. Ibid., 27 February 1886.
63. Ibid., 27 October 1887.
64. Lyman, "The Fort on the Firing Line," 52:820.
65. Francis A. Hammond Journal, 29 October 1887.

headquarters at the Rincon, and, ignoring Mormon claims to prior rights, wintered in Comb Wash and Grand Gulch and summered on the Elks from which the company took its ELK brand and name.

For Bluff, which had concluded it could not survive as a farming community, the spring of 1887 was a time of challenge. Hammond and his co-religionists met this challenge with a vigorous self-interest that justified the name "Bluff Tigers" by which they began to be known.[66] While the local literature accords him little credit—or for that matter, blame—F. A. Hammond appears to have been the catalyst that pushed the Mormons into the livestock business. He was also the force behind a drive in 1887-88 which kept the Mormon toe-hold upon the country and in the long run had more than a little to do with the fact that the great names in San Juan livestock are Mormon and Utah in background and not gentile and Colorado.

The 1887 campaign saw the Mormons shift from the defensive to the offensive. Springs and crossings were claimed, and Indians were maneuvered to Mormon advantage. Ranches were taken up, improvements built, and a number of new villages were planned and settlement initiated.

The first step in this campaign had been launched in January of 1886 when the Bluff Pool was organized. Unity in the Pool as well as in the Church itself was essential. In an effort to achieve this, a few individuals were either replaced or brought into line. Joseph Barton and the Hyde brothers were sharply reprimanded when they refused to cease their vengeful conduct toward the Navajos after Amasa Barton's murder. With Hammond's backing, Jens Nielson, bishop of Bluff, "began to prune up the ward," and several Church members were dropped or otherwise reproved.[67] Of even more significance to the success of the campaign, Hammond faced down an effort on the part of L. H. Redd—perhaps the most willful and self-directed member of the Pool and certainly one of its most successful men—to break the Pool's joint marketing agreement.[68]

Working to bring discipline to the Pool, Hammond laid out his strategy early in 1887. Amasa and Joseph Barton were called to the Rincon, a major Colorado River crossing for Navajos with sheep.[69] John Allen and Thales Haskell were directed to locate Indian farms in the heads of Allen and Cottonwood Canyons, and the Paiutes were encouraged to take up residence there, thus hindering access of outside cattle herds to Elk Ridge through these routes.[70]

Of great significance were calls to settle three new towns. Joshua Stevens was designated to head a settlement at the head of Indian

66. Riis, p. 51.
67. Francis A. Hammond Journal, 18 and 19 July 1887.
68. Ibid., 10 March 1887.
69. Ibid., 28 February 1887.
70. Ibid., 28 February and 15 March 1887.

Creek. Frederick I. Jones was called to lead a group to Monticello and Verdure, or North and South Montezuma as the respective camps were known during the first year. The Church was approached and evidently made an appropriation to aid the San Juan Stake in these undertakings.[71] Much of this effort came to naught. Barton was killed, forcing abandonment of the Rincon. Before the year's end, Gahleger's Texas cattle moved into the vacuum left by this failure. Joshua Stevens failed to hold the Indian Creek-North Cottonwood access to Elk Ridge as planned but established a ranch at Mormon Pasture, giving a point of Mormon control high on the mountain.[72] The Paiutes moved into Allen and Cottonwood canyons, establishing camps that became more or less permanent, but it is difficult to assess the effect this had upon grazing development.

In moving to Monticello and Verdure, Mormons threw the gauntlet directly in the face of the Lacy and Carlisle corporations. Other less critical points were let slip while every effort was made to crowd into the very front yards of the greatest cow outfits in the country. The L C and the Carlisles had claimed and used all the land the Mormons took up, and the Carlisles had filed on all the waters flowing in the various branches of Montezuma Creek. Ignoring such rights as these claims gave, F. I. Jones and his co-workers laid out a town, fields, and ditches at Monticello and established two dairies, a sawmill, and small farms along Verdure Creek. The sites for these developments were chosen in March of 1887, and the claims occupied and worked by the Mormons during that entire season. Perkins, Nielsen, and Jones in their *Saga of San Juan,* are of the opinion that the pioneers withdrew after establishing the claims in March of 1887, but this is clearly in error as the Hammond diary makes repeated reference to the activities of F. I. Jones at Monticello and N. A. Decker at Verdure during the entire summer.[73]

The Mormons recognized they were moving onto land previously claimed and expected trouble. In this they were not disappointed as frictions developed immediately and persisted for many years. On the whole, however, the Mormon invasion and conquest was accomplished with little real trouble. This was due in part to the conduct of the Carlisle brothers, who were restrained and even friendly in their opposition. They conferred frequently with Hammond and clearly preferred lawyers to guns. Much top-level negotiating took place around Durango, as both Hammond and the Carlisles spent most of their time in Colorado during the summers of 1887 and 1888.

71. Ibid., 28 February 1887.

72. Stevens, his brother Alma, and Brigham Young, Jr., organized a cattle company in October and wintered for several years between Elk Ridge and the Colorado and used Mormon Pasture as summer headquarters. *See* D. L. Goudelock File, U-Adjustment, Manti-La Sal National Forest Records, Record Group 95, Denver Records Center.

73. Francis A. Hammond Journal, summer, 1887.

A lawyer named Prewit represented the Carlisles; a Mr. Rupell—whose advice was "keep possession"—represented the Mormons.[74] Carlisle restraint may have been related to the fact that they had been thoroughly chastened in a New Mexico controversy the year before when three herders who invaded the Carlisle range were killed. New Mexico's governor became involved, revealing a very negative attitude toward the Carlisles personally and cattlemen generally. Perhaps the "'hurrah outfit,' reckless, and . . . irresponsible" brand he had given them stayed any recklessness in Utah.[75]

Critical confrontation with Carlisle and L C cowboys was averted during the summer of 1887 when the Navajos and Paiutes both turned to hostile action, killing Barton at the Rincon and an L C rider not far from Verdure. The tense times which followed served the Mormons well. With cattlemen and Mormons alike requesting protection, two detachments of troops came from Fort Lewis. One was stationed at the mouth of Recapture Wash on the San Juan River; the other was at Soldier Spring one-and-one-half miles south of Monticello. Because fear of the Indians was high, and federal troops were camped only a stone's throw away, the Mormons proceeded with their expansion unmolested during 1887. Without the Indian hostilities, an entirely different chapter might have been written in the history of southeastern Utah.[76]

Not surprisingly, water rights quickly became the issue upon which success or failure turned. The Carlisles had filed on all the water in Montezuma Creek—or, put more accurately, its agents had. As it proved, the two ranchhands who filed on North Montezuma Creek were no longer employed by the Carlisles and were willing to deal with Hammond. Hammond appears to have acquired their claims and thus established what in the long run proved to be a valid right to about half the Montezuma runoff.[77] In the water controversy, Mormon control of the county court, which also sat as a "Water Commission," proved useful to the settlers of Monticello and Verdure. Composed entirely of Mormons, the "Water Commission," which awarded title and adjudicated disputes, naturally did not offer much hope for a settlement favorable to the Carlisles. Nevertheless, Edmund S. Carlisle requested a hearing in November of 1887 but failed to show up as scheduled. The following summer the "Water Commission" awarded certificates to F. I. Jones and others and to N. A. Decker and others for all the waters of the North and South Forks of North Montezuma Creek. The Carlisles then appealed to the Territorial Water Commission and got an injunction forbidding Monticello's use of North Fork Water. After much litigation, a settlement

---

74. Ibid., 17 May 1887 and 23 April 1888.
75. Walker, pp. 279-81.
76. Francis A. Hammond Journal, July and August 1887.
77. Ibid., 9 August 1887 and 26 April 1888.

was reached which can only be regarded as a defeat for the Carlisles, as it gave the interlopers half the water of Montezuma Creek.

Controversy was not limited to the courts. Heavily armed ditch riders patrolled the ditches. Cows were run off or killed. Bells were taken from milk cows, and, when padlocks were put on the bells, cows heads were cut off, enabling cowboys to take both padlocks and bells. According to Henry Honaker, who rode for the Carlisles as a young man:

> The foreman [once] took me to a swale and pointed to a pile of bones bleaching in the sun. "See what happens to Mormon cattle when they come on our range," he said with an oath, "there was 300 head in that bunch."[78]

Old-timers think the foreman exaggerated, but the incident does indicate the attitude that prevailed. While the real challenge to the Mormon invasion came in the form of water litigation, cowboys continued for years to harass settlers at Monticello. A number of killings grew from it which are, of course, lamentable in the highest degree, but the cowboy harassment had its humorous side, and is responsible for some of Utah's richest frontier traditions.[79]

In 1886 or shortly thereafter, the Bluff Pool had turned to buying out invaders. Two New Mexico sheepmen brought "their huge herd of sheep" to Bluff in the winter of 1884-85.[80] Protests were lodged, but nothing was done until the winter of 1886-87 when the Bluff Pool borrowed money from a Durango bank, and, paying more than the value of the sheep, purchased the herd, and thus removed this outside threat.[81] The Texas cattle were also bought out. Run locally by a Mr. Crosby, their nuisance value led the Bluff stockmen to purchase the entire herd, probably in 1888. Thereafter, L. H. Redd, H. J. Nielson and others managed the so-called ELK Cattle Company for the Pool.[82]

By these methods the Bluff Pool held its rights to the south side of the Blue and Elk Mountains and spread into surrounding areas as years passed. The settlers of Bluff and other San Juan villages had in a symbolic way come through a second Hole-in-the-Rock. In following the farm village pattern, they had gone at things wrong just as surely as they had taken the wrong trail to San Juan in 1879-80.

78. Perkins, Nielson, and Jones, p. 106.
79. *See* Walker; Perkins, Nielson, and Jones; and Albert R. Lyman, *Indians and Outlaws: Settling of the San Juan Frontier* (Salt Lake City: Bookcraft, 1962).
80. Perkins, Nielson, and Jones, p. 77.
81. *Deseret News*, 8 December 1886. *See also* Redd, pp. 39, 42.
82. Minutes of San Juan County Court, 1880-1900, 26 July 1894, and 25 October 1897, pp. 169, 249-50. The Texas cattle were of poor quality and many of them reverted to total wildness in the canyon breaks of southeastern Utah. Texas renegades, as they were known, were later run down and roped one by one and literally dragged to market by the Scorup brothers and other hard-riding cowboys. *See* Karl Young, "Wild Cows of the San Juan," *Utah Historical Quarterly* 32 (1964): 252-67.

But they made the shift to cattle and later sheep, met the competition on the ranges, and survived. Their survival spelled doom for Texans, the L C Company, the Carlisles, and, in 1914, for the successors of the Old Pittsburgh Company. The Pool itself was abandoned in 1897 as declining competition permitted the luxury of individualism, but the stand taken by F. A. Hammond and the Bluff Pool in the years after 1886 rather than drought or even changing times was the major cause of the great cow outfits' recessional in southeastern Utah.

A Large Space of Stone—The Scorup Holdings[83]

The last of the provinces to be claimed by a great cattle operation was the rugged and arid canyon land that lay west and north of the Elk Mountains. Including White Canyon, Dark Canyon, and Beef Basin, it was so forbidding that even Platte D. Lyman, who had accommodated himself to much of the world's worst real estate, judged it a "rough and worthless country."[84] It became the first base of the Scorup brothers, J. A. and James. Coming into the area first in 1891, J. A., or Al, Scorup found a few skulking cowboys who were running remnants of the Texas cattle there. After hanging on through fantastically adverse times, the Scorups emerged as major factors in southeastern Utah's cattle scene by 1910. A decade later, and after Jim's death, Al Scorup incorporated with Moab's Somerville brothers to buy out the Indian Creek Cattle Company and, as Scorup-Somerville, became Utah's largest cattle outfit.[85] However, most of the Scorup saga belongs to the era of the Forest and will be developed in later sections of this study.

Sheep-cursed

Like cattle, sheep played an important role in the settlement of Utah's southeast and in adjacent areas of the other Four Corners states. However, the sheep story has not been as well told as that of cattle and cannot be here. The formal record of the sheep industry is scanty, and sheep have not provided the stuff of frontier romance; consequently I have found relatively little information about sheep. What is available indicates that they played a significant role in the early development of the La Sal Forest region. The pages that follow will undertake to trace this role in general terms but will provide little detail because it is lacking in the record.

It is difficult to know when sheep first entered the country. Herds could well have been driven over the Old Spanish Trail during the pre-American days, but if such is the case I have found no evidence of it. On the other hand, sheep products—primarily blankets—

---

83. "Report of the Ute Commission of 1883," p. 43.
84. Journal of Platte D. Lyman, p. 64.
85. *See* Scorup; Lambert; and David Lavender, *One Man's West* (Garden City, N.Y.: Doubleday, 1956).

Abandoned sheep pen near Monticello.

were a major trade item during the heyday of Old Spanish Trail commerce. In 1853 two sheepmen, McClanahan and Crocket, attached themselves to the Gunnison exploration and trailed a "large flock of sheep" from the Missouri River to California, passing by way of the Book Cliffs and the Green River crossing.[86] There is no evidence that sheep were included in the stock brought to the area by the Elk Mountain Mission in 1855 or by the earliest settlers of the La Sal and Blue Mountains.

Very probably the first sheep in the region of the La Sal Forest belonged to Indians. William T. Tew, who passed through the San Juan Valley in 1881, observed several herds of sheep and goats—one estimated at 6,000 head—belonging to Navajos.[87] Monument Valley Navajos as well as the renegade Paiute bands of the Navajo Mountain area also had flocks of sheep and goats by 1880 which were moved around pretty much at will. The Navajo subchief, Kigalia, is said to have pastured a herd of 300 sheep on Elk Mountain at a very early time.[88] In 1883, a Durango newspaper reported that 5,000 head of sheep were purchased by the Southern Ute Agency at the price of

---

86. Beckwith, pp. 6, 75. For a general treatment of the sheep industry, including useful summaries of the business in Utah, see Edward Norris Wentworth, *America's Sheep Trails* (Ames, Iowa: Iowa State College Press, 1948).

87. Journal of William T. Tew, 30 March 1881.

88. Kumen Jones as quoted in Perkins, Nielson, and Jones, p. 279.

$2.40 each and distributed among the Utes. The latter had no interest in sheep and quickly disposed of them for as little as fifty cents apiece, selling to Mexicans and other sheepmen.[89] Indian agents and others took advantage of this situation to acquire large herds and evidently ran them on the Indian reservation of southern Colorado during much of the 1880s.[90]

At least as early as the winter of 1884-85, New Mexico sheep (the Daniel-McAllister herd) were trailed to winter pasture near Bluff, and the next winter 10,000 head grazed along Recapture Wash. From this time sheepmen from Colorado and New Mexico grazed large numbers in Utah during the winter months. In 1888, T. S. Childs of the Ute Commission reported to the secretary of interior that "sheepmen will soon begin as usual to drive thousands of sheep over into San Juan County for the winter. One man here will soon start 14,000."[91]

Determined to hold the Bluff area for its own stock, the Bluff Pool bought the Daniel-McAllister herd. Thereafter the Pool ran increasing numbers of sheep. Other southeastern Utah stockmen probably began to purchase sheep at about the same time, and by the early 1890s a shift from cattle to sheep was in full swing.

This change sprang, of course, from economic reasons. The easy money had been creamed from the country during the 1880s by the first cattlemen. The aggressive Mormon effort to control grazing resulted in additional pressures as did falling prices caused by glutted markets and the Panic of 1893. Sheep with two products—wool and mutton—and somewhat stronger prices, seemed to offer a promising option. When those who made the change first appeared to prosper, others followed suit; by the mid-90s all but the most die-hard sheep haters were running some sheep.

The big cattle ranchers first tried to meet the threat by organization.[92] But by 1897 even they had succumbed, and sheep were dominant. With proud names of the cattle frontier like Carlisle, Gordon, and Taylors leading the way, sheep became big business. Finally, in 1900 even the Cunningham-Carpenter Company fell in with the trend, shipping their cattle to ranges east of Denver and planning to devote their Utah range to sheep, "claiming they are compelled to do this in self protection."[93] Shearing sheds dotted the country, wool wagons were a familiar sight, and herds numbering in the tens of thousands grazed in Dry Valley and other lowland areas in the winter and on the mountains in the summer. In 1897, a Mr. Ortiz from just across the border in Colorado shipped 253,768 pounds of wool in 46 cars to a Boston commission house. He is said to have "pocketed not less than

89. *Durango Herald*, 22 May 1883.
90. "Report of the Ute Commission of 1888," p. 16.
91. Ibid., p. 75.
92. *Durango Herald*, 16 April 1897.
93. *Grand Valley Times*, 17 May 1901.

$40,000" from this transaction.[94] Three Moab owners shipped $30,000 worth of mutton in 1899. L. H. Redd was reported to have 30,000 sheep by the turn of the century, and by 1906 Goslin Brothers of Cisco shipped "over a quarter of a million pounds" of wool, supposedly the "largest individual wool clip ever made in Utah."[95]

The Denver and Rio Grande Railroad recognized the economic value of all this, and catered to sheepmen. In addition to providing loading corrals and warehouses for wool at Thompson, Cisco, and elsewhere along its line, the railroad ran ads in local papers, calling the attention of sheepmen to grazing lands adjacent to the railroad at various points, and offering accommodations to sheepmen.[96] With this surge, which was reenacted all over the state, Utah quickly became one of the great wool-producing states, and by 1901 the National Association of Wool Manufacturers reported that it stood fourth in wool production after Montana, Wyoming, and Idaho.[97]

The change to sheep in southeastern Utah was accompanied by some friction but was on the whole carried off without violence. Sheepmen were met with understandable hostility as they entered ranges long grazed by cattle. But the sharpness of the confrontation was eased because many of the sheep that came into the country were imported by local cattle ranchers making the transition to sheep. Utah sheepmen often met trouble when they drove herds onto Colorado ranges. In 1893, 25,000 head of sheep are said to have been trailed into Mesa and Garfield counties in Colorado, mostly from southeastern Utah. Cattlemen met this onslaught with poison, and what a Durango newspaper called a "life and death struggle" ensued. At least 300 head of sheep were killed.[98] A few years later, Alex Reed, who wintered in Grand County, lost 2,500 head of sheep to a "band of masked men at a point about 20 miles northwest of Gunnison, Colorado."[99] In 1904 a group of Fourth of July revelers wrapped bunting "used in the celebration" at Moab around themselves and rode up Spanish Valley, bent on devilment and looking for a sheep herd. They first struck the Carlisle and Gordon herd, dispersing it but evidently doing no serious damage. They then crossed the valley to the Daniel Hyde herd, shooting at herders and killing and maiming "a number of sheep."[100] Unexplained poisonings and fires at sheep ranches often begot rumors of foul play and arson, but evidence substantiating the rumors was lacking, and continues to be lacking. On the whole, incidents of violence were rare. The transition to sheep was accomplished with a minimum of bloodshed.

---

94. *Durango Herald*, 6 October 1897.
95. *Grand Valley Times*, 27 April 1906.
96. Ibid., 31 July 1896.
97. *Emery County Progress*, 14 December 1901.
98. *Daily Southwest* (Durango), 13 June 1893.
99. *Grand Valley Times*, 7 June 1901.
100. Ibid., 21 July 1904.

Economic troubles were much more important. Wool and mutton, like beef before them, quickly glutted the market, and by 1895 wool often piled up at Thompson or Cisco with no buyers, or, if sold, went at prices that fell far below the break-even point. In 1896 there was a disastrous dip in wool prices. This was reflected at Moab where the *Grand Valley Times* repeated the sheepman's lament:

> There are no buyers at any price, but it is reported some have received offers of four cents per pound. This condition is laid to the war, but war makes prices higher and especially is wool affected by it.[101]

The slack conditions of 1896 were often repeated, though rarely did prices collapse to four cents a pound. More often, wool buyers were to be found, but the market was clearly in their hands and prices running from ten to fifteen cents a pound rather than twenty to twenty-five cents were the norm. Mutton prices, too, were often low. With sales down, the tendency was to build herds, and overgrazing quickly became a serious problem. But such matters belong to the development of the National Forest and shall be considered in that context.

Frontier Recessional

In the years after the turn of the century, the economy of southeastern Utah began to stabilize. Put in another way, it passed from its frontier and experimental stages and worked out a balance of livestock, small agriculture, and mining that was to be characteristic of it during the entire first half of the twentieth century. The emerging balance was reflected in a reversal of the movement to sheep, and by 1904 big ranchers were diversifying, running both sheep and cattle. The cattle empire had been swept away. Now the day of sheep monopoly was also passing. The Bluff Pool—another of the devices with which the country's pioneers had experimented as they sought a workable equilibrium—was also disbanded in the late 1890s. Its individual owners now operated privately or formed partnerships and corporations. The Pool had been instrumental in breaking up the cattle empire, but now the cooperative patterns on which it rested were being remolded radically in the direction of individualistic capitalism.

Other evidence of change was to be seen in developing governmental regulation during the years around the turn of the century. San Juan County had been organized in 1880 and Grand County ten years later, but government in those first decades was of little importance. It was true the county court held forth in both counties. Roads were by far the matter of greatest governmental concern, followed by water regulation, land and mining claims, and education—usually in that order. Livestock rustling and violent crimes were

101. Ibid., 29 April 1896.

common and never effectively coped with until after the turn of the century. Justice of the peace courts existed in the southeastern counties during the territorial period but more important crimes were taken to United States district courts in Provo and elsewhere or not dealt with at all. Law enforcement officers were lonely and underpaid figures. Education was almost a complete travesty—at least as a function of county government. The San Juan County Court appointed school superintendents from a very early time. Often performing other official functions as well, school superintendents were given appropriations counted by dollars rather than by hundreds or even tens of dollars. A characteristic entry in the minutes of the San Juan County Court notes that twenty-five dollars was appropriated to Kumen Jones, Superintendent of District Schools "to pay for books."[102] In 1883 Jones resigned his posts as supervisor of the Bluff Road District and as superintendent of schools. The clerk of the court laconically recorded that "Ten ($10.00) was appropriated to Kumen Jones for services as Superintendent of District Schools for the years 1881-2."[103] The record is silent as to what Jones received for his efforts on the Bluff road.

Statehood in 1896 was hailed with joy in southeastern Utah, but it brought responsibilities to San Juan and Grand counties that over-burdened their underdeveloped sources of revenue. In the main, new expenses were connected with the system of state courts that was established at this time. Criminal cases previously taken north at territorial expense were now handled locally by the Seventh District Court at county expense. San Juan County was particularly hard hit. The county commission was taken over by a gentile insurgency in 1896 that saw some 200 voters (this was by far the heaviest vote cast in the county before 1900) elect Thomas B. Carpenter and David L. Goudelock as commissioners. Revenues from property tax had never been great, but the county court, which had always been controlled by Mormons, had placed heavy taxes on saloons (there were no more than two or three of them) and had successfully collected the liquor tax. Carpenter and Goudelock pushed through drastic reductions in liquor taxes and adopted a very easy policy with regard to assessing property tax at the same time mounting costs of law enforcement made new demands upon the county's puny treasury. The result was financial disaster. For several years San Juan County wrestled with this problem before finally bringing its revenues into line with its expenditures. During this time of adjustment there were repeated moves to annex San Juan to Grand County. These proposals do not appear to have had the support of a majority of the citizenry in either county but were nevertheless of considerable importance.

Also indicative of the move away from frontier conditions was the growing effort to regulate the livestock industry. From very early

---

102. Minutes of San Juan County Court, 1880-1900, 7 June 1880, p. 9.
103. Ibid., 4 June 1883, p. 18.

times brand and estray ordinances had existed at the county and state level.[104] During the 1890s San Juan and Grand County Courts passed fence laws, licensing laws which included transient herd fees, and ordinances to control rustling. Furthermore, livestock came to be counted more realistically for tax purposes, as growing demands for roads and education, and the mounting cost of county government demanded greater revenues.[105] State laws governing livestock also became far more stringent and were more effectively applied. To obtain a fair adjustment of taxes and license fees in a situation where herds normally moved through many counties in the course of a year, a major license law was enacted by the state legislature in 1900.[106] The State Board of Sheep Commissioners also applied laws regulating the health of sheep, and by 1905 dipping was required to control the scab, and inspectors were appointed to enforce compliance. Federal inspectors, too, had become commonplace by 1905.

Obviously times had changed. The frontier of the late 1870s had been supplanted. Cattle had been crowded from the range. Sheep were in turn yielding to diversified livestock culture. The Mormon-gentile confrontation had become more a matter of rhetoric than reality. Government was setting in motion what has proved to be an ever-expanding wheel of regulation. By 1905 the frontier had passed. The next turn of government's regulating wheel brought the Forest Service to southeastern Utah and the modern period began. The pages of the next section of this study will be devoted to an analysis of the La Sal Forest and its impact upon southeastern Utah.

---

104. Levi S. Peterson, "The Development of Utah Livestock Law, 1848-1896," *Utah Historical Quarterly* 32 (1964): 198-216.

105. Minutes of San Juan County Court, 1880-1900, pp. 132, 277-78, 305; and Minutes of San Juan County Court, 1900-1920, pp. 4, 5, 33.

106. *Grand Valley Times*, 16 February 1900.

Part Two

Developing Hinterland: A National Forest's Impact to 1950

Chapter VI

Establishment of Forests in Southeastern Utah

The turn of the century was a time of beginning for the Forest Service in Utah. The pioneering period was past, and Utah had become a state. The first easy resources had been skimmed off. Stream pollution and floods pointed to misuse of these resources and raised fear of impending crisis. Law and order had in large measure supplanted the experimentation and individualism of the raw frontier. Changing times also were apparent in the establishment of forest reserves, which began in 1897, and extended through most of the twentieth century's first decade. First the Uintah Reserve, next the Fishlake Reserve, then, in a rush, reserves totalling some four million acres of forest were proclaimed along the Wasatch Range from Cache Valley to Escalante. Finally, almost unnoticed, the La Sal and Monticello reserves came into existence.

By the end of the nineteenth century the concept of "conservation through wise use" had been formulated by a dedicated group of Americans, and a strong movement was advancing it into the public and the official consciousness of the nation.[1] Foremost spokesman of this movement was Gifford Pinchot, head of the forestry movement, who attracted the support of President Theodore Roosevelt. Applied first to the preservation of forests, the movement had extended to other natural resources by the time Utah's reserves were created.

In 1875 meetings were held that led to the establishment of the American Forestry Association. Together with other scientific and conservation-minded groups, the association studied the problems of forestry, sought to popularize the protection of forests and big game animals, and called for the creation of reserves and a national park system.

---

1. Henry Clepper, ed., *Origins of American Conservation* (New York: Ronald Press, 1966), p. 5.

To begin with, government officials were indifferent, but by 1877 men such as Carl Schurz, secretary of the interior, were beginning to give conservation official support. In March of 1891 Congress authorized the President to designate certain areas in the public domain as forest reserves. The first reserve was created the same year, and during the next half-dozen years thirty-three million acres in thirty forest reserves were set aside by executive order. In 1897 Congress provided for the survey and organization of the forest reserves and for their administration under the General Land Office of the Department of the Interior. As early as 1876 Congress had authorized the appointment of a forestry agent in the Department of Agriculture. In 1881 this office was made the Division of Forestry. By 1900 the Division of Forestry had grown to employ 123 persons and was headed by Gifford Pinchot. The following year, it was advanced in rank to the Bureau of Forestry, and President Roosevelt recommended that the forest reserves be transferred from the Department of the Interior to the Department of Agriculture. This change was effected in 1905, and the bureau simultaneously became the Forest Service.[2]

Conservation in Utah at the Turn of the Century

Conservation started early in Utah and continued during the first decades of the twentieth century. Utilization of water, timber, land, and grazing ground for the good of the community characterized the earliest settlement. During the 1890s, Utah played a leading role in the National Irrigation Congress movement. In 1892 the Territorial Legislature made it illegal to pollute streams. Concern for recreation led to the early establishment of a fish and game commission. During the last months of Grover Cleveland's administration, support from Utah encouraged him to include the Uintah Reserve in the 21,379,400 acres he withdrew from entry for forest purposes.[3] By 1899 Governor Heber M. Wells and many others recognized the relationship between water supply and "the increasing spoliation of our timber." In the governor's annual message of that year, he declared that the federal government was the only "source to which the citizens of the state may look for protection of the timber growing upon the public domain."[4] With reference to this, he noted that the Uintah Reserve had been withdrawn from public entry and was subject to all the rules and regulations of the Department of Interior through a special agent whose headquarters were at Coalville.[5] In 1898 the Second State Legislature requested a grant

2. Ibid., pp. 5-15, 38-46; *see also* Gifford Pinchot, *Breaking New Ground* (New York: Harcourt, Brace, and Co., 1947); and Arthur H. Carhart, *The National Forests* (New York: Alfred Knopf, 1959).
3. Heber M. Wells, *Annual Message*, 10 January 1899, pp. 31-32.
4. Ibid., p. 31.
5. Ibid., p. 30.

of certain lands near Fishlake in Sevier and Wayne counties. Supported by Representative William H. King, this request led to the establishment of the Fishlake Reserve in 1899.[6] The Mormon Church, which had wholeheartedly backed the Irrigation Congress movement, voted at its April conference in 1902 to support federal withdrawal of public lands for protection of watersheds, and by the end of the year various communities, including Salt Lake City, Manti, and Monticello, had petitioned the federal government to withdraw their watersheds from grazing use.

But for all its support of conservation, Utah was not conservationist in the way national leaders of the movement were. At the head of the national movement stood what Thomas Alexander has called "advanced-progressive conservationists," who favored governmental development and suspected the motives of state and business interests. By contrast, most Utah leaders were what Alexander termed "business-minded conservationists." They favored some federal action but believed that private and state interests "ought to be included in conservation considerations."[7] This stance was apparent in the attitudes of each of Utah's first three governors. Wells, who, as we have seen, favored positive action by the federal government, reacted with fear when "something over 4,000,000 acres of land," extending in an almost unbroken line from the northern boundary . . . "to within a few miles of the southern limits of Utah" were withdrawn after 1902. He saw no way in which the withdrawal of vast tracts could prove beneficial "in a public and general sense."[8] Similarly, his successors, John C. Cutler and William Spry, favored close connection between state and federal interests in conservation but had sharp misgivings about the loss of local control and opportunity because of the magnitude of Utah's National Forests.[9]

Most Utah congressional leaders of the era also may be called "business-minded conservationists." In 1897, when Cleveland had exercised his executive prerogatives in a last-minute action to create reserves in Utah, Senator Frank Cannon joined Senator Clarence D. Clark of Wyoming and other western senators in protesting this action. But by comparison to his western colleagues in the Senate, Cannon's protest was low-key and responsible. He pledged full support to an amendment which would drastically limit the withdrawal but went on record as favoring forestry reservations.[10] During the years around the turn of the century, Representative William H. King

6. Ibid.

7. Thomas Alexander, "Senator Reed Smoot and Public Land Policy, 1905-1920," *Arizona and the West* 13 (1971): 247.

8. Wells, 15 January 1901, p. 11, and 13 January 1903, pp. 20-21.

9. Elmo R. Richardson, *The Politics of Conservation: Crusades and Controversies, 1897-1913* (Berkeley: University of California Press, 1962), pp. 45, 94, 100; and John C. Cutler, *Annual Message*, 15 January 1907, pp. 44-45. See *also* the Governors' Papers of Wells, Cutler, and Spry at Utah State Archives.

10. *Salt Lake Tribune*, 27 February 1897.

also supported the forest reserve concept. In 1898 he pushed for the creation of the Fishlake Reserve but insisted upon limitations including restoration of the reserve to the public domain at the pleasure of Utah's people; an option for an outright grant to the state; and the employment of Utahns to administer the reserve.[11]

Senator Reed Smoot also falls in the category of responsible supporter. He was always sensitive to local petitions protesting excessive forest regulation and proposed withdrawals but supported President Theodore Roosevelt and subsequent conservation leaders. He was twice chairman of the Senate Public Lands Committee and supported the national parks movement. Refusing to be stampeded, he left Utah open to further reserve development when anti-reservation senators amended the Agricultural Appropriations Act of 1907 to prohibit the creation of forest reserves in several neighboring states.[12] Obviously, the door to development of the forest reserve system in Utah was open. Public opinion was not hostile. Important leaders favored it, though not without limitations. The Mormon Church had given its blessing to the concept, and numerous official and private groups had petitioned for the withdrawal of various areas for the purpose of watershed and flood protection.

Albert Potter's Wasatch Survey, 1902

Given this frame of reference, it is not surprising that vast mountain areas in Utah were organized into forest reserves during the new century's first decade. A major step in this process was the Wasatch survey of Albert F. Potter, chief grazing officer of the Division of Forestry (later the Forest Service). Conducted during the summer and fall of 1902, Potter's Utah tour took 145 days and covered more than 3,000 miles.[13]

Canvassing the state's mountains from Logan to Escalante, Potter had an extraordinary opportunity to observe conditions and attitudes. Much was common to the entire region. Aside from the physical similarity of the mountains, there was sameness in the drouth of the year as there was in the burden of livestock that grazed the country. But there was also diversity. Striking differences existed in the intensity of forest utilization. In 1902 the far south, particularly the Thousand Lakes and Boulder Mountains area, was still a wilderness, except for the heavy grazing use. To the north, society had swarmed

---

11.   William H. King to Heber M. Wells, 1 July 1898, as quoted in Wells, *Annual Message*, 10 January 1899, pp. 32-33.

12.   Alexander, "Senator Reed Smoot," pp. 249, 251, 256.

13.   For a more complete treatment, see Charles S. Peterson, "Albert F. Potter's Wasatch Survey, 1902: A Beginning for Public Management of Natural Resources in Utah," *Utah Historical Quarterly* 39 (1971). For the primary source on the Wasatch Survey see Diary of Albert F. Potter's Wasatch Survey, 1 July to 22 November 1902. This diary was located several years ago by Arnold R. Standing, a Forest Service career man who devoted much of his time to the history of the Forest Service and Utah.

over the Wasatch Range. This was especially apparent in Cache Valley, where settlers had encroached far up the mountains in a wide variety of ways. The forested areas had been heavily lumbered for years. Power plants had long since invaded mountain streams, and a surprising number of mining operations scratched for subsistence.[14] Humanity's imprint likewise had been laid on the Cache highlands in the form of farms and gardens, fenced areas, and private and public roads, as well as the inevitable livestock operations.[15] In sum, Potter's survey of the Cache Valley area revealed a heavily worked but not overly productive forest whose users were beginning to recognize the need for regulation.

Potter made careful observations of the livestock industry. Throughout the entire region of his survey, cattle operations were of sharply limited size. Settlers and Mormon villagers, who characteristically owned small, irrigated farms, generally ran from ten to 150 head of cattle as part of their operations. These cattle were grazed on the mountains during the summer and were grazed or were fed on lowland bottoms and fields in the winter. For such operations, mountains with their grazing resources, as well as water for irrigation, were essential.[16] A few cattle operations of more than modest size came to Potter's attention. At Heber, for example, owners pooled their stock and leased range on the Uintah Reservation at a cost of $12,000. This sum enabled the Heber pool to utilize approximately 77,000 acres, which constituted one of the largest ranges held by any single interest.[17] More characteristic of big cow outfits generally was the Ireland Land and Cattle Company. Headquartered in Gilson Canyon near Salina, it sprawled through several locations and ran thousands of animals. Potter noted that it had been unusually aggressive in extending its grazing lands. Public domain amounting to 40,000 acres had been illegally enclosed by its fences. Exploiting lax state land laws, the Ireland Company had also claimed most of the water holes in its vicinity and, using the "rubber forty" technique, stretched control of the water to dominate the entire area. Elsewhere, Potter found evidence of the past existence of numerous mountain dairy operations. Milking up to 150 cows during summer months, these dairies had taken advantage of virgin pastures in the 1870s and 1880s to raise a calf crop and at the same time make cheese and butter. By 1902, however, mountain dairying had passed, because the lush grazing on which they depended had been preempted by sheep. These sheep, in Potter's words, now "grubbed away at the grass roots."[18]

---

14. The Logan Electric Company's first power plant dated back to 1880, only one year after Thomas Edison perfected the incandescent lamp. See Joel E. Ricks and Everett L. Cooley, eds., *The History of a Valley: Cache Valley, Utah-Idaho* (Logan: Cache Valley Centennial Commission, 1956), p. 227.

15. Diary of Albert F. Potter's Wasatch Survey, p. 7.

16. Ibid., p. 36.

17. Ibid., p. 13.

18. Ibid., p. 46.

Albert Potter in 1918 with elk calf in his arms. U.S. Forest Service photo.

By the time of Potter's visit, sheep formed the basis for Utah's biggest grazing industry. He saw sheep everywhere, but mountains adjacent to Cache and Sanpete valleys were areas of concentration. Potter estimated sheep on the Cache Mountains at 150,000 head. In boasting moods, Sanpete residents claimed that a million head ran their forests, a fact—if indeed it were a fact—which gave them claim to being the nation's largest sheep county. In a lament, one Salina cattleman informed Potter that no fewer than 150,000 sheep had scoured the Salina watershed during the summer of 1901.[19] Sheep raising was not tied to farm property but was a matter of running the animals summer and winter in the public domain and of unbridled competition for feed. Many sheepmen with whom Potter came in contact ran sheep on Utah's West Desert in the winter, summered them in the Wasatch Range or trailed them to Idaho, Wyoming, or Colorado. Conversely, out-of-state herds invaded the Utah East Desert and crisscrossed what came to be known as the Manti National Forest, tramping its plateau tops to a veritable dust bed.

People and their attitudes were of primary interest to Potter, and he took every opportunity to sample local feelings on a wide variety of subjects. Sentiment against sheep and those who ran them was widespread. Typical was the opinion of one villager who said that "when a man gets sheep he loses his conscience and gets a good supply of gall instead. . . ." The vocabulary of the era reflected this antipathy. The country was "sheep-cursed," the water "sheep-flavored," or the sheep themselves a "pestilence."[20] Antisheep sentiment was especially strong with cattlemen. With their customary range rights under a continuing challenge from sheep, some cattlemen were downright hostile, evincing an attitude that in 1897 had seen masked cowboys intimidate herders and slaughter 800 bucks near Vernal.[21] Yet, to Potter, relations between Utah sheepmen and cattlemen seemed remarkably amicable. Among the latter he found feeling that cattle should be protected, but he also saw a willingness to "give the devil his due" that boded well for "give and take" when forest regulations were established. In some places, sheepmen, too, were submissive, agreeing to cooperate with regulatory efforts.

With reference to forest conservation, Potter found interest and in most cases, clear-cut though differing attitudes. Division on this question varied geographically. Beaver County, having experienced neither shortage of timber nor difficulty with its watersheds, was generally opposed to forest conservation. The town of Levan was not

19. *Ibid. See also Manti Messenger,* 17 July 1897; and W. H. Lever, *History of Sanpete and Emery Counties, Utah* (Salt Lake City: Tribune Job Printing Company, 1898), p. 39.

20. *Manti Messenger,* 27 February 1896. *See also* Charlie R. Steen, ed., "The Natural Bridges of White Canyon: A Diary of H. L. A. Culmer, 1865," *Utah Historical Quarterly* 40 (1972): pp. 61, 65.

21. *Manti Messenger,* 31 July 1897.

"interested in the forest reserve," which apparently meant that it was in opposition.[22] At Manti and Logan, sizable groups favored the establishment of reserves and petitioned accordingly. Everywhere the pros and cons divided according to economic interest in sheep. Cattlemen, farmers, and townspeople generally favored reserves; sheepmen and people involved in associated activities were opposed.

A deep-seated commitment to private ownership also was expressed. Time after time Potter was told that the problem of resource management would best be solved by opening public lands to entry or purchase. Some thought the appetite for private land was insatiable, and one sheepman of rugged optimism opined that every acre in the vast Wasatch Plateau would be quickly purchased if offered for sale.[23]

Mines, sawmills, fires, floods, and various other matters also came under Potter's scrutiny, but the materials discussed above provide an adequate basis from which to consider his tour in the broad sense. In 1902 Utah was well into its social and economic development. Hundreds of agricultural villages and towns had been established, most of them in the area of the Wasatch Survey or near it. For fifty-five years, stewardship of the state's natural resources had been largely in private hands. Mormon cooperation and frugality had led to careful development of primary water resources. Mining came late but by 1902 played the major economic role. Western railroading extended two important lines into Utah and sent numerous local spurs through its valleys. After slow beginnings, livestock had boomed to become a major industry following 1885. Each of these and other forces affected Utah's forest regions.

Potter assessed the impact of this human use, finding that it had seriously impaired the productivity of the state's natural resources, and that floods, erosion, and water pollution were becoming threats to human life and to property. Many Utahns were cognizant of the problem, and to Potter it seemed that the on-balance opinion favored the protection and management of forest resources. Confirmed in its forest reserve policy, the Forest Service moved during the next five years to place the mountains of central and western Utah in national forests.

Resource Problems in Southeastern Utah

Potter's peregrinations did not carry him onto the La Sal and Blue mountains, but had they done so he would have found conditions similar in most respects to those observed elsewhere in the state. Overgrazing had become a real problem. Mining and lumbering had not yet made serious inroads on mountain resources but were being carried on with an unregulated disregard for the future. Floods and erosion were changing the landscape, and they had ren-

22. Diary of Albert F. Potter's Wasatch Survey, p. 25.
23. Ibid., p. 29.

dered limited water supplies more precarious. Furthermore, the public was beginning to recognize the need for governmental help in developing the country's natural resources and controlling those already in use.

As seen in an earlier section of this study, white settlers first used the La Sal and Blue mountains as cattle ranges. Later, hard times had led to stocking with sheep, and the continuing struggle to survive in a marginal country resulted in overgrazing by the mid-1890s. Overworked ranges in turn caused intensified competition.[24] With drought added to overstocking, crisis sometimes became disaster in the years around the turn of the century. There was often simply not enough feed to carry all the stock. We have learned earlier of the strained balance between stock numbers and feed in Dry Valley in the winter of 1894-95. At that time, the unexpected addition of the goat and pony herds of the migrating Utes (even though it was only for a few weeks) is said to have led to the death of up to 50 percent of the cattle running between La Sal and Monticello.[25] As competition intensified, more stock was taken onto the mountain earlier, and of necessity it came down earlier in quest of feed. Typical was the experience of C. E. Krofford of neighboring Emery County, who reported in 1900 that he moved his horse herd from Joe's Valley during the first days of September because there was no feed.[26] As early as 1893, it was necessary to drive sheep herds numbering 25,000 from the La Sal Mountain area to Mesa and Garfield counties in Colorado, where, according to some reports, they were turned into pastures and alfalfa patches of farmers, who responded by poisoning and killing upwards of 300 sheep.[27]

Not only did the mounting numbers of livestock result in competition between sheepmen and cattlemen and involve them in conflict with squatters, but miners also reacted to the onslaught of hungry herds. In 1900 La Sal Mountain miners met at Mill Creek and passed resolutions protesting "against the encroachment upon mineral lands by those seeking to use land for grazing." The assembled miners also protested the policy of the State Land Board which often selected prime mineral lands under Utah's grants from the United States Government.[28] Robert R. V. Reynolds, Bureau of Forestry inspector whose report led to the creation of the La Sal Forest Reserve, indicated that by 1904 the miners group numbered 250 men.

Short feed, overstocking, and competition inevitably leveled grass stands, giving opportunity for hardier undesirable species to supplant nutritious plants. By 1900 people in southeastern Utah were begin-

---

24. Glynn Bennion, "Some Things I Have Read, Heard and Seen Relating to Range Use in Utah" (typescript, present writer's possession), p. 8.
25. See pp. 74-76. *See also* Silvey, *Northern San Juan County*, p. 53.
26. *Emery County Progress*, 8 September 1900.
27. *Daily Southwest*, 13 June 1893.
28. *Grand Valley Times*, 7 September 1900.

ning to worry about weeds. In 1901 their concerns were sharpened
by reports of sheep lost to poisoning. In Rabbit Valley west of the
Colorado River, for example, three sheepmen lost 1900 head when
drouth forced their herds to eat weeds usually passed over.[29] With
such problems in mind, representatives of southeastern Utah stockmen joined their colleagues throughout the state to pass a resolution
which noted that the "effects of unknown vegetable poison" were causing the loss of thousands of livestock on Utah ranges and called for
the appointment of researchers to ascertain wherein the problem
lay.[30] Of more serious concern generally than poisonous weeds were
trash plants. In the years immediately after the turn of the century,
several new varieties established themselves. On the La Sal and Blue
mountains, the earliest and hardiest of these were Russian thistle and
Indian tobacco. Larkspur and sneezeweed also came early but likely
not before the La Sal Forest had been established.[31]

Local lumbering had developed by 1900. The first lumber on both
the La Sal and Blue mountains had been whipsawed at a rate of no
more than 300 feet per day. Obviously, there was little threat of irresponsible use in this. But as the mining frontier moved west
from Colorado's San Juan district, the matter of lumbering assumed a different complexion; timbers were required for supporting tunnels, and lumber was needed for building mining camps.
As early as 1881, for example, a Durango newspaper asserted that the
average weekly sales of the San Juan Lumber Company amounted
to 50,000 feet of lumber and that other companies sold enough to
make weekly sales total 75,000 or 80,000 feet.[32] Some idea of the
mushroom growth of mining towns may be obtained from William
T. Tew's 1881 report: ". . . We came to the beautiful city of Durango.
There was not over 13 or 15 houses here last fall, now there is a large
city of about 250 or 300 houses. Business houses of various kinds."[33]
By the end of the century, people at Durango were deeply concerned
because of dwindling timber supplies. Lamenting that thousands of
young trees had been cut in getting access to saw timber and that
vast areas had been fired in the process of burning tops and limbs,
the *Durango Herald* called for a policy of preservation for southern
Colorado's forests.[34]

Furthermore, timbered areas adjacent to the La Sal Mountains
had been exploited to provide charcoal to carry on the smelting process. That this had become a problem was apparent as early as 1887
when Secretary of the Interior L. Q. C. Lamar requested that Attorney General A. H. Garland investigate charges against Alvin C.

29. *Emery County Progress,* 16 February 1901.
30. Ibid., 19 January 1901.
31. *Grand Valley Times,* 4 September 1903.
32. *Durango Herald,* 1 September 1881.
33. Journal of William T. Tew, March 1881.
34. *Durango Herald,* 6 February 1899.

Tree cutting for mine timbers had denuded many Utah forests by 1902.

Dake of Dake, Colorado, who had illegally cut and removed 39,000 cords of pine and spruce wood from government lands to supply the Grant Smelting Company with charcoal. The secretary further requested that criminal proceedings be brought against Dake, and that a civil suit for $150,331 be instituted against him and the smelting company jointly if investigations upheld the charges.[35]

Early timbering operations on the La Sal and Blue mountains were limited and primitive. The first mill had been set up northwest of Paradox Valley in 1881. At least four other mills were operated on the La Sals prior to 1900. On the Blues, the first sawmill was placed in operation in 1887 at Bulldog Canyon.[36] To begin with, operators apparently cut with no formal restrictions, supplying local mines and the towns of the region. However, on February 15, 1900, the Department of Interior issued orders limiting the purposes for which

35.   Ibid., 27 June 1887.
36.   "Historical Information, La Sal National Forest," pp. 108-11.

timber could be cut and controlling cutting and removal.[37] There-after, a minimum of regulation was observed.

Forest fires were not particularly severe in the La Sal Forest tim-berlands. Indians are said to have fired certain areas at times, either to flush out game, or to seek revenge for being driven out by whites. While some people speculated that fires accounted for deforested areas, such fires do not appear to have been extensive, or by general standards, destructive. However, the dry summer of 1900 resulted in one major fire on the north slope of the Blue Mountains. Begin-ning late in July, it continued burning into the first weeks of August, and, according to Moab accounts, blazed so fiercely that its "light could be seen plainly on the Mesa above Moab, 60 miles from the fire."[38] Reports then and later indicate that this was an unusual burn.

It was recognized from the first that water was the key to the development of the entire country. The paramount role played by the La Sal and Blue mountains as the chief source of manageable water was apparent in the nature of the area's economy as it was in the location of its towns and ranches. By the mid-1890s overgrazing, and, to a much smaller degree, timbering, had upset the balance of the La Sal and Blue mountains' water flow, making runoff more erratic and reducing its manageability. Creeks and water courses that had been overgrown and limited in size in the 1870s opened up, be-coming broad water courses as unretarded spring runoff and rain-storms flushed off the mountains.[39] The region's potential for flood-ing runoff is apparent in the account of the first storm observed at the present site of Moab by the Elk Mountain missionaries in 1855. What Oliver Huntington called an "awful rain" fell within a few days of their arrival. His account is one that anyone who has ob-served a thunder shower in the canyonlands can appreciate, but it also provides dramatic evidence of the area's tendency to flood and to erode. Sitting out the rain under his wagon cover, Huntington wrote:

> I looked out of the wagon and saw a wonderful sight. More than 20 creeks running, leaping and pouring off the mountain precipices all around from one to 300 feet high. The mountains all arround [sic] us are barren soft and red sand rocks carved and molded into every shape and now all the molded water courses are streaming with the creeks and rivers rilling tumbling and pouring down the mountain sides. This is a great blessing and God God [sic] sends to us and our crops. The whole valley which is ten miles long N. W. and S. E. by 2 miles wide is all sand except about 2 miles square near the river which is good meadow land made by the Spring Creek we are on, settling on the valley.[40]

37. *Grand Valley Times*, 2 March 1900.
38. Ibid., 3 August 1900.
39. A. N. Ray, who came into the country in 1877 with his father, later reported that a man could "jump across Mill Creek." Similar reports exist for other streams; La Sal National Forest Historical Document (1936), p. 4.
40. Oliver Huntington Diary, 13 June 1855, typescript, Utah State Histori-cal Society, p. 98.

Later floods along the San Juan River played a significant role in the long decline of Bluff City. It is worth repeating that the spring of 1884 brought floods of unprecedented magnitude which washed away sizable amounts of farmland and dumped trash and rocks into the lower part of Bluff itself. Overgrazing probably had not become a major problem by 1884, but the potential of water flow to frustrate man's efforts was apparent.

The next references to serious flooding appear in the mid-1890s. High water between Thompson and Moab interfered with mail service during September and October of 1896. At Moab, Mill Creek and Pack Creek widened to become major watercourses and washed away bridges, irrigation works, and a few outbuildings.[41] While the direct threat of floods to property and human life was clearly recognized, the full meaning of the threat had not yet made itself felt, and many regarded the floods more as spectacles than as adverse elements of a deteriorating ecology. Typical was a *Grand Valley Times* item reporting that one particular flood was "a glorious sight, being about four hundred yards across."[42] After a brief respite during the last years of the 1890s, heavy rains resulted in flooding throughout southeastern Utah in 1901. These brought comparisons with the high waters of 1897, and reports of diverse calamities, including the drowning of more than 500 head of sheep belonging to the Nielson Brothers on the Blue Mountains and loss of irrigation works in Grand and Emery counties.[43] After another lull in 1902 and 1903, several bad years followed. Floods now came with explosive energy, and, on occasion, with little or no warning. A flood which illustrates both points occurred early in August, 1904, and was reported as follows:

> Utah is the only state where they can have a flood without a rain. Tuesday there was not a cloud visible in the sky at Moab but the mountains were obscured as with a blanket. . . . In the middle of the afternoon there was a sudden noise of rushing waters. Instinctively the inhabitants turned toward Mill Creek. A large volume of water, well loaded with sediment and drift-wood, filling the banks to overflowing came down the stream, washing out dams and carrying away fences. Two sons of Alma Molyneaux's, Superintendent of Schools, and Cecil Taylor were bathing at the time of the flood. The Molyneaux boys lost their clothes and the Taylor boy just escaped with his life.[44]

The following year also was marked by unusual floods. One particularly heavy storm resulted in the following writeup in the local press:

> Mill Creek has been booming . . . making heavy cuts into the banks on both sides taking our corrals, fences, and hay stacks, the swinging bridge at the old Darrow place going out. At Lee Kirks place the corrals, stacks and chicken yards, including all his hay crop, was carried away. . . .

41. *Grand Valley Times*, 25 September 1896.
42. Ibid., 24 September 1897.
43. Ibid., 2 August 1901. *See also Emery County Progress*, 27 August 1901.
44. *Grand Valley Times*, 5 August 1904.

> Nearly one-half the residence lot of James Moore was cut away and a big
> cut made into the Stewart and Goudelock places. All places along the
> creek received more or less damage. The water came over the banks
> above Robertsons place flooding his cellar and yard and down the street
> and into the yard of Mrs. Larry Burr's, flooding the place up over the
> foundation of the house and it took on the part of the men who came
> to the rescue some active work to prevent serious damage.[45]

While floods periodically assumed crisis proportions in the minds
of southeastern Utah's citizenry, people were generally more sensitive to the problem of polluted streams. Every town in the entire
region depended upon springs and streams for domestic water.
Townspeople often dipped directly from streams or from the ditches
that ran by their homes for drinking and cooking water. In this
respect southeastern Utah was not unique. Indeed, the problem was
regarded as of sufficient moment to require action by the Territorial
Legislature in 1892 when a law was passed prohibiting sheep from
watersheds within seven miles of a city.[46] In 1900, continuing problems with contaminated domestic water led residents of Monticello to
request a ruling from A. C. Bishop, state attorney general, as to the
meaning of the 1892 law. The attorney general's ruling, as reported
by the *Emery County Progress*, held that herding

> sheep within the seven-mile limit of a city, town or village where the
> filth may drain into the water supplying the inhabitants of such a city,
> town or village is a misdemeanor. If the sheep camp, however, is not
> within the drainage area it is not a misdemeanor to herd them within
> the seven-mile limit. In measuring from the town to determine the
> seven-mile limit the attorney holds the course of the stream should be
> followed and not a direct line. A community of three families where
> there is a post office and a school maintained constitute a village
> within the measure of the statute, the attorney general thinks.[47]

Under the Bishop ruling, some progress was made during the
next years toward controlling grazing in community watersheds. In
March, 1901, Robert Hill of Lawrence, Emery County, was charged
with befouling the waters of Huntington Creek. In the course of
Hill's trial it was demonstrated that his sheep camp was some five
miles from Huntington in a direct course but seven and three-eighths
miles "by the water course." The defendant was thus discharged.[48]
Later the same year, another Emery County stockman found no such
loophole. On this occasion, a young sheepherder whose pack mules
had fallen from a ledge to their death on the banks of Huntington
Creek was charged with befouling the stream. The defendant pleaded
guilty and in keeping with the attorney general's ruling that such
an offense was a misdemeanor, was fined $21. A similar case took

---

45.   Ibid., 29 September 1905.
46.   *Compiled Laws of Utah*, 1892, p. 70. *See also Revised Statutes of the
State of Utah*, 1898, p. 910.
47.   *Emery County Progress*, 22 September 1900.
48.   Ibid., 9 and 16 March 1901.

place in Grand County the following year. F. B. Hammond and John Tangren of Moab, who had for years maintained a sheep corral on Pack Creek, were charged under the 1892 law, found guilty, and fined twenty dollars each. There is no evidence that they moved their sheep.[49]

As administered in Utah, the law of 1892 was obviously inadequate to protect domestic water sources from contamination by livestock. Continuing concern over the matter, as well as consternation at the mounting costs of floods, led first to petitions to the federal government, then to the Wasatch Survey made by Albert F. Potter, and in the years after 1902 to an increasing number of forest reserves in the state. While they probably were not the first petitions, a number of requests for aid in protecting watersheds were dispatched from the Emery County towns in 1901 immediately following the "Mule Case" cited previously. In 1902 Monticello turned to the Department of Interior for help. For a time thereafter it appeared that the Blue Mountains or parts of them would be withdrawn from public entry and a reserve created. But no evidence has been found that such action was taken at that early period.[50]

Forest Reserves: Surveys and Proclamations

In September of 1904, Robert R. V. Reynolds of the Bureau of Forestry inspected the La Sal Mountains pursuant to their establishment as a reserve. Late the following summer, R. B. Wilson, forest assistant, carried out a similar survey on the Blue Mountains. The reports that issued from these two surveys became the organic documents of the La Sal and the Monticello forest reserves which later were merged to make the La Sal National Forest. Both reports suggest that onsite inspections were made to verify planning already well developed rather than to initiate consideration. Of the two reports, that of Reynolds is more comprehensive and shows greater care and skill in production.[51]

About two weeks appear to have been involved in making each reconnaissance. Reynolds made the La Sal Post Office his base of operations, and Wilson worked out of Monticello. Both men assessed the natural and the human conditions in the neighborhood. In most cases this was a matter of practical observation and hearsay, as few

---

49. Ibid., 10 August 1901. *See also Grand Valley Times,* 25 April and 2 May 1902.

50. On 19 July 1902, the *Emery County Progress* carried the following item: "Notice has been given that 100,000 acres more land located in San Juan County, is to be withdrawn from entry. This is the seventh forest reserve contemplated for Utah. The others are the Wasatch, Uintah, Aquarius, Gunnison, Fish Lake and Logan." I have found several references indicating that Monticello had requested a reserve in 1902. *See* Robert R. V. Reynolds, "The Proposed La Sal Forest Reserve, Utah and Colorado," Region IV Papers, National Archives.

51. Ibid. *See also* R. B. Wilson, "Report on the Monticello Forest Reserve, October 1905," Region IV Papers, National Archives.

or no records dealing with weather, land use, agricultural production, grazing, or timber were to be found. Each inspector observed the deteriorating grazing and watershed conditions, and reported these without undue emphasis. Neither found any popular demand for the creation of reserves except among miners, who seemed to favor anything other than the status quo. Townspeople and cattlemen were unenthusiastic, but the inspectors thought they could be depended upon to support the movement. Sheepmen were all opposed. Running some 90,000 head of sheep on the Blues and 30,000 on the La Sals, they were overstocked and knew it but feared the consequences of regulated grazing. Both reports concluded with recommendations to proceed with the establishment of reserves.

A brief surge of public interest accompanied Reynolds' visit, but if much local thought was given the matter of the forest reserve during the next fifteen months, little word of it has survived. Indeed, the record is silent until December, 1905, when a laconic report in the *Grand Valley Times* indicated that the wheels of bureaucracy had been turning. Announcing that the "Forest Reserve will be made," the *Times* hopefully continued:

> This will be of great benefit in the long run, though it may immediately affect a few adversely. The water supply depends on maintaining the forests. The matter of cutting timber will then come entirely under inspection of a government officer as well as the amount of stock that may be ranged thereon.[52]

On January 25, 1906, President Theodore Roosevelt signed the proclamation designating 158,000 acres covering most of the La Sal Mountains as a forest reserve. In February of the following year, Roosevelt completed the process when he created the Monticello Forest Reserve.[53]

The pattern of onsite inspection used by Albert F. Potter in 1902 had been followed by Reynolds and Wilson. What shortly became the La Sal National Forest had been established with apparent support of a majority of interested parties in Utah, including the residents of Grand and San Juan counties. There remained the task of defining the role of the Forest Service and of clearing up the many problems of administration connected with the multiple use concept which was already emerging as a basic principle of natural resource management.

---

52. *Grand Valley Times,* 1 December 1905.
53. Ibid., 2 February 1906.

Chapter VII

Administration on the La Sal Forest: The Formative Years

Like other forests, the La Sal National Forest was distinctive in no small part because of the people who worked it. This was especially true of the early period. To personnel, add the fact that the Forest came into being late in the period of forest formation; that it was remote and part of an arid canyonland; that its users were among America's last frontiersmen; and, finally, add the reality of grazing's predominance. Bear in mind, however, that the La Sal Forest was a unit in a large whole, and you have an outline of the situation in which early La Sal administrators worked. Some failed—more succeeded. In sum, their efforts met the most pressing needs of resource management and, in the broader sense, helped form southeastern Utah. Administratively, the first step in this process was to define the physical form of the Forest.

Acting upon the Reynolds report, President Roosevelt created the La Sal Forest Reserve on January 25, 1906. With 128,960 acres in Utah and 29,502 in Colorado, the new reserve totalled 158,462 acres. A little more than twelve months later, the president proclaimed 214,270 acres covering most of the Blue Mountains and Elk Ridge to be the Monticello Reserve. Within two months of this action, an executive order was issued changing the title of all forest reserves, including La Sal and Monticello, to national forests. In December, 1907, 101,398 acres from the public domain were added to the Monticello National Forest by presidential proclamation, and in July, 1908, an executive order combined the two national forests. Demonstrating a complete lack of understanding of the Spanish influence upon the area, officers of the Forest Service changed the name of the forest from La Sal—used at least since the time of Father Escalante—to the LaSalle National Forest. The announcement of this change was accompanied by an offhand statement that, since the name La Sal seemed to have no significance, but was much akin to the name of the great French explorer, the Forest's name should be changed to honor LaSalle. Recovering from this miscue, the Forest Service changed the name back to La Sal on March 16, 1909. The basic administrative unit of the Forest had now been created.[1]

Remaining were the more complex tasks of working out the policies, practices, and relationships of a national forest. Basic to these problems were matters of understanding what constituted wise management of the peculiar natural resources that existed in the mountains of southeastern Utah. Equally important, and in some ways more challenging, was the process of winning support of people living adjacent to the mountains, and establishing an effective working relationship with them. A third major task—one always fraught with problems for planners and administrators alike—lay in the development of effective internal managerial systems. These were important and challenging tasks, but by 1906 the Forest Service was well on its way toward developing administrative patterns and structures to direct the process.

The entire effort of the Forest Service rested upon good people, and a national organization characterized by efficiency and esprit de corps existed. As a foundation, there was an excellent Washington, D.C. staff, at the core of which were men trained and educated in the long struggle to establish the conservation movement. Good people had been drawn in from the field, too, thus the service gained the specialized understanding of local conditions. This policy resulted in such men as Arizona's Will Barnes and Albert F. Potter, and Utah's W. C. Clos making lasting contributions to the emerging character of the service. Indicative of the roles such men played is Paul H. Robert's thumbnail biography of Clos,

> who . . . had a large part in developing grazing procedure. He probably was born in Switzerland and certainly received technical training there in Animal Husbandry and Botany. For years he had been the principal employee of John B. Seeley [actually John H. Seely] of Mount Pleasant, Utah, who at the turn of the Century was one of the country's outstanding breeders of purebred Rambouillet sheep. Potter had met Clos while making forest boundary examinations in Utah. He was so impressed with his qualifications he prevailed upon Seeley to agree to Clos's joining the Forest Service. Clos was an encyclopedia on range management. His European antecedents and experience gave him an appreciation for conservation of natural resources and governmental exercise of means to that end. His long association with Seeley imbued him with the viewpoint of the livestock operator.[2]

1. Proclamation and Boundary Folder, Manti-La Sal National Forest Historical Files; and Manti-La Sal Historical Atlas, Region IV, Ogden, Utah.

2. Pinchot, *Breaking New Ground;* and Paul H. Roberts, *Hoof Prints on Forest Ranges: The Early Years of National Forest Range Administration* (San Antonio: Naylor Co., 1963), p. 42.

Mountain mining camp at Clear Creek visited by Albert Potter.

Also contributing to an effective Washington office was the early development of an intern program under which outstanding field men worked in the national office for short stints. A double-barreled policy, this enabled Pinchot and his cohorts to imbue field men with proper professionalism, and at the same time bring the problems of field administration into strong focus in the Washington office. At least two La Sal Forest supervisors participated in this program— Henry A. Bergh and Orrin C. Snow. The latter, who was the first supervisor on the La Sal, was assigned to Washington for a three-month period beginning July 1, 1908 "to take over the work of Acting Chief of the Office of Organization."[3]

Close check of local development appears to have been maintained from the first. Indeed, the whole administration of the Forest Service moved on the process of the inspection. Forests were founded as a result of field examinations. By 1906 inspection districts were in existence, the result being that the names of such inspectors as Robert R. V. Reynolds, W. W. Clark, and R. B. Wilson are seen often in conjunction with the La Sal and Monticello national forests. To begin with, forest contact with the Washington office moved through these roving inspectors. Yet it would be a mistake to think of the inspection district as approximating the regional office. The relationship between the forest and the national level was far more di-

3. *Grand Valley Times*, 6 June 1908.

rect than it has been in the years since the regional office or its early counterpart, the district office, came into existence.

On December 1, 1908, Gifford Pinchot established six forest districts, coinciding in their boundaries with the existing inspection districts, but with headquarters located in each. According to Pinchot's instructions, which were sent to all forest supervisors including John Riis, acting supervisor on the La Sal, "all business now transacted with the Washington Office will be transacted with the district office." A new *Use Book* was announced, and teams trained in Washington were directed to leave for the district offices on December 1. This development was "the culmination of a plan toward which the service has been working steadily." Pinchot expected that it would increase the usefulness of the various forests, reduce delay, bring line and staff officers into more immediate touch, and relieve the Washington office of the heavy burden "of routine it now carries, and enable each one of us to spend more time in field work on the Forests."[4]

Forest contact with the national office was not entirely supplanted by this arrangement, but a new administrative level had been interjected. From the beginning of 1909, the history of the La Sal National Forest was in no small part the history of its relation with the district—later the regional—office in Ogden.

Policy statements, use manuals, and other directives were from the first a way of life. To some forest officers they literally became "the rangers bible."[5] Among these officers was A. W. Jensen, supervisor of the Manti Forest. A lawyer by training—and one is tempted to say by birth—Jensen's legalistic bent found full expression in his application of the *Use Book* and other directives. The letterpress books in which appears the correspondence of Jensen's first three years as supervisor come near being "the complete lexicon of the *Use Book* in practice." While no forest administrator escaped the *Use Book* entirely, early La Sal Forest supervisors by comparison to Jensen appear to have been unfettered by the letter of the law—a fact which led to a much looser administration on the La Sal than upon the Manti and, not surprisingly, to certain difficulties.

The fundamental administrative unity of the La Sal and the Blue Mountains-Elk Ridge forest areas was recognized from the first. Although R. B. Wilson called for the creation of a separate reserve in his 1906 report, he pointed out that the Monticello Reserve did not merit the establishment of a supervisor's office and urged that it be attached to the La Sal Forest for administrative purposes. There is no evidence that he anticipated that this relationship would be temporary, and the fact that the logical step of combining the two units was taken during the summer of 1908—less than a year and a half after the Monticello Forest was created—hints that some such

---

4.   Letter of 5 November 1908, Proclamation and Boundary Folder.
5.   Riis, p. 31.

merger may have been anticipated at the outset. If such be the case, the initial failure to bring the Blue Mountains directly and fully under the mantle of the La Sal Forest may well have been a concession to political sensitivities in San Juan County. Residents of the county had emphatically rejected overtures to become an adjunct of Grand County during the days of financial crisis that accompanied Utah's transition to statehood in 1896-97. However, if San Juan County felt misgivings at the formal attachment of the Monticello Forest to the La Sal, little word of it has survived. After 1908, what had been two distinct forests became one, and was subdivided internally into the north and south divisions with headquarters in Moab. The whole was organized into five ranger districts, two on the La Sals and three on the former Monticello Forest. The ranger districts were themselves broken into grazing allotments. In time, administrative arrangements also were adapted to timber tracts, to watersheds, and to wildlife units.

Gentile and Government Men

In the spring of 1906, Orrin C. Snow, who had grown up in a livestock family in Wayne County, Utah, became the first officer of the La Sal National Forest. On the advice of W. W. Clark, an inspector who had studied the situation, Snow's first headquarters were established at Castleton, where they remained until October of the same year when Snow moved into Moab, taking a humble office over the Williams Drug Company store.[6] Snow was at first designated "Forest Ranger in Charge" but was soon referred to as acting supervisor; before his first year was past he signed his correspondence as supervisor. In the parlance of his forest associates, Snow was "a smart man"—one who could have been regional forester had he chosen to press for professional advancement rather than for private gain. After some college training he had joined other members of his family in an ill-fated agricultural venture in Canada, where a promising beginning was wiped out by unseasonable frosts. With nothing to show for $40,000 invested, Snow returned to the United States. But he was not easily put down and soon found his way into the La Sal Forest position. In December of 1908, he was transferred as supervisor to the Sevier National Forest in Panguitch, where he served until August 3, 1915. During much of his time at Panguitch, Snow engaged in the livestock business on the side and on leaving the service went into the business fulltime. Forming a partnership with a Panguitch banker, he used his intimate knowledge of range and livestock to good advantage, and, before World War I was over, his holdings were said to be worth $200,000.[7]

---

6. *Grand Valley Times,* 11 May and 10 October 1906.
7. For most of the biographical material on O. C. Snow, I am indebted to former La Sal Forest Supervisor J. W. Humphrey of Provo, interview 26 March 1971.

Moab Main Street showing building which housed Forest offices (at left.) U.S. Forest Service photo.

But if Snow was diverted by business opportunity, there is no evidence that he neglected his duties on the La Sal Forest. His staff was small, consisting at first of himself only, then an additional ranger, and finally a full increment of four men, although there is evidence that three of these were seasonal rather than full-time employees. Snow was affable and got along well with people in the locality. Together with the surveys upon which the major additions to the Monticello Forest were based, much of Snow's time must have been spent in establishing a workable relationship with forest users.[8]

John Riis, whose appointment as an acting forest ranger became effective in February, 1907, became Snow's first assistant and stayed on, assuming the latter's duties as supervisor in December, 1908. Unlike Snow, Riis was not begotten of the grazing regions of the West but was by birth an easterner. He had, however, connections with the forest movement quite as intimate and much more dramatic. He was the son of Jacob Riis, one of America's great nineteenth century social historians, and the personal friend and confidant of both Gifford Pinchot and Theodore Roosevelt. Leaving the parental nest, young Riis tried his hand in the West, working in Nebraska and Colorado before ending up on the Cunningham and Carpenter ranch

8. *Grand Valley Times*, 21 December 1906.

at La Sal in the years immediately prior to the establishment of the La Sal Forest. In this connection it is interesting to note that in striking out for himself and later in writing his *Ranger Trails*, John Riis followed Theodore Roosevelt's example, as the president had sojourned in the ranch country of the Dakotas and had committed his experience to history in his autobiography.[9] Tiring of the social relations of cowboying as well as the rigors of its life, Riis told Cunningham of his plans to draw his pay and quit, whereupon the latter urged him to enter the Forest Service. Assigned to Monticello, John Riis found life in the small Mormon community to be at once quaint, irritating, and challenging. As Riis put it, he and the town's inhabitants "were all in a hard place." His very arrival pointed up basic problems which set Riis apart and continued to influence forest relations for many decades. His own appraisal is instructive:

> Almost before I was comfortably warm after the ride in the wind and snow I saw through the window white-haired old Bishop Jones heading a delegation of leading citizens to make a formal call on me. They were frankly suspicious of all "government men." The day when United States marshals rode through the country to arrest all Mormons found living in polygamy was still green in their memory. Since that time the visits of federal officers had been few and far between. . . . They did not know the new forest laws and I did not know the country. They had settled it and felt it was theirs. I was here to tell them they must pay hard cash for the use of the range and their herds must be limited to the capacity of the range. . . . Though respectful and courteous, the Mormons made me feel keenly that I was an alien in the land and my presence was on sufferance only. As far as social functions and the little intimacies of the village hospitality were concerned I was completely ignored. . . .

A gentile and a government man, Riis "was under double suspicion in the eyes of these clannish mountain folk." . . .[10] But he survived the difficulties of this combination and went on to smooth some of the roughest edges of hostility toward the new system.

One illustrative episode in this soothing process involved a rancher named Parley Butt and four of his sons. Unfortunately for the dignity of the Forest Service, Riis had undressed on this occasion and was lying on his bed, clad only in underclothes. The Butts put in a sudden and hostile appearance at Riis's cabin on Monticello's outskirts. Fingering their Winchesters, these "fine specimens of the 'Bluff City Tigers'" threatened insurrection against the government, but, fortunately for Riis, they had a sense of humor and were cajoled into a more reasonable frame of mind. They left the ranger's shack over an hour later following a discussion of overstocking, erosion, and other range problems. Riis, at least, felt the prospects of forest regulation had been improved.[11]

9. Theodore Roosevelt, *An Autobiography* (New York: Charles Scribner's Sons, 1913).

10. Riis, p. 32.

11. Ibid., pp. 51-52.

Serving next as acting supervisor and later supervisor, Riis was in effective charge of the Forest from July 1, 1908, until January, 1910. In this role he appears to have been reasonably competent, although he never really understood the frontier people of the area. To him they were old-fashioned, colorful, and even admirable, but Riis never escaped an undercurrent of supercilious scorn and distrust for them. In the long run, this limited the accomplishment of his administration. He left the Moab office under pressure following a bitter controversy with the Stockgrowers' Association over counting cattle onto the Forest.[12]

Southward You Ride to the End of the Sandrock Trail

Because John Riis has left one of the best contemporary accounts of southeastern Utah during the first decade of this century, it will be useful to pause for a look at society there. The country was remote, raw, and unfettered. It was only yesterday that it had been penetrated by the Spud Hudsons and Billie McCartys of the first livestock frontier. On the other hand, it would be only tomorrow that iron bridges, improved roads, experimental farms, and the forest service would carry the future into the area.

John Riis was one of the first men from the outside to see "Monticell" as many in San Juan's old cow country called the village. In his *Ranger Trails*, Riis left an unusually vivid portrait of the village and of life in it. In the narrative biography of her husband, *Uncle Will*, Juanita Brooks has given additional detail to the Monticello of this era. Riis and another contemporary writer, Burl Armstrong of the *Intermountain Republican*, did the same for Moab. Because they reflect the circumstances in two major towns dealt with by early La Sal Forest administrators, a few passages from each will be worth including at this point. Of Monticello, Riis wrote:

> From Coyote on the slopes of the La Sals, the Blue Mountains are visible twenty miles or more to the southwest. They held a strange fascination for me. Often my eyes turned towards their mysterious bulk and I wondered just what sort of country slept there in its isolation. I was soon to know.

> Late one February afternoon I rode down the wide lane between the barb-wire fences that marked the main street of Monticello, seat of San Juan County. Monticello was in truth merely a wide place in the road. Some thirty Mormon families made their homes there, tending their little farms, grazing their cattle and sheep on the Blue Mountains in the summer and out on the great dry desert on the east in the winter. . . .[13]

> Always the wind blows at Monticello; round and round the mountain like a rollicking dog chasing its tail. Playing an endless tune on the single telephone wire strung along the main street and slapping the loose tin roofs with a noisy gusto. "Does the wind always blow this way?"

---

12. *Grand Valley Times*, 28 January 1910.
13. Riis, pp. 31-33.

I asked a lanky rider who stopped long enough to exchange the cour-
tesies of the road. "No, Stranger," he drawled; "sometimes, p'raps once
or twice a year, she turns around and blows the other way. Adios."
Not even the rind of a grin creased his leather face as he rode off.

Eventually some writer traveling through the West will find Monticello.
He will stop to rest, then stay to write. It lies at the end of the Sandrock trail a hundred dusty miles below the glittering tracks of the
Denver and Rio Grande. Southward you ride, crossing the Grand River
where sleepy Moab nestles deep between the red cliffs, still south over
the sun scorched miles of Dry Valley, then up the long pull between
the pinions and the cedars till you climb out on the plateau and to
Monticello.

Monticello clings to the sky; a little cluster of weather-beaten houses
perched on the mountain side seven thousand feet and more above sea
level. Eastward into Colorado, even to the skyline rolls the great desert,
the winter range of uncounted stock. Purple green in sage it sleeps, a
great inland empire, the dust of distant sheep herds swirling lazily in the
sun. To the west the blunt peaks of the Blue Mountains hover close
over the little Town; a protecting rampart of green-brown slopes of
bunch grass and pine. The old Mormon settlers, trekking south from
Salt Lake at Brigham Young's command to go forth and settle the new
land, stopped here to rest.[14] Too long they lingered looking eastward,
dreaming perhaps of the homeland by the far Mississippi, and the camp
became a town.[15]

In February of 1909, exactly two years after John Riis's arrival
in Monticello, Will Brooks from Utah's Dixie made his way over the
same Sandrock Trail. Expecting to take advantage of a dry farm
bonanza, the gospel of which had been preached to him at the agricultural college in Logan, young Brooks hooked a ride with a freight
outfit at Thompson and inched his way to Monticello through a
furious late winter storm. Arriving with the storm, Brooks found four
inches of new snow at Monticello. His wife has lately recounted
his experience:

Before morning it [the snow] was two feet deep, and it never slacked
until it had covered all the fences. We made paths and tunnels to the
barns, and sat out a full six weeks of repeated storms. We just settled
down in the homes, but had parties almost every night. During that
time I met all the people of Monticello, the best class of people that I
ever associated with in all my life.[16]

Brooks and Dan Perkins, a Monticello boy with whom he was
partner, borrowed $1,000 and with it made down payment on 3,000
acres of state land and took up homesteads. Later, he and his partner
were appointed to take over the State Experiment Farm which already had been started there, getting a little pay and some school
credit for their efforts. Brooks also survived a long bout with typhoid:

14. Actually Brigham Young had passed away some ten years before
Monticello was settled in 1887.

15. Riis, pp. 41-42.

16. Brooks was a Mormon and closest friend and business partner to a son
of Monticello. While old settlers doubtless did not accept him entirely as one of
their own, there was obviously much difference in his reception and that of Riis.

In the fall of 1910 a typhoid epidemic hit Monticello. Many people were sick, and seventeen died in this little village. I got it along with others; Dan's wife Maggie went down at the same time and died, also her brother, Ike Jones. He lived with his parents, but Maggie and I were in the same house with only a wall between us. She died on November 19, 1910, and I knew the instant she passed; nobody needed to tell me that Maggie was gone. I knew it. I myself was so low at that time that the family wondered if I would survive, but the turning point came, and within a few days I was on the way to recovery, with a huge appetite and a happy assurance that I was going to make it.[17]

When John Riis became supervisor, he transferred to Moab and came to know it as well as he did Monticello. Fortunately, he also sketched his impressions of Moab:

Moab nestles between red sandstone cliffs at the foot of the long valley where the brown waters of the Grand River emerge for a bit from a rocky gorge only to disappear again into an even narrower gorge that in the end becomes the Grand Canyon. In the early days of the West the little Mormon settlement with the biblical name was just another stopping-off place on the Sandrock Trail used by the train robbers and other fugitives from the scant laws of the West. The country was almost inaccessible and it was a bold sheriff who would follow the Sandrock Trail in search of his man. So Moab became the rendezvous for gunmen and rustlers. To this day there are old timers who refer to it as "Robber's Roost," who can remember when the flash of pistol fire split the velvet darkness of its cottonwood-shaded streets as cowmen and outlaws celebrated after an all-day session at the bar.

Referring to the Twenty-fourth of July Pioneer Day festivities as "Gentler echoes of that wilder day," Riis conveys a rowdy impression as he tells of horse races, heavy drinking, and wild shooting in the streets. Jail in Moab was a busy place. Riis tells of a man held on a murder charge waiting for trial in that jail during the midsummer. "After two weeks of cooking in his cell, he wrote to the governor offering to plead guilty if they would just send him to the penitentiary. Anything but the Moab jail." Relating the jail to the twenty-fourth of July celebration, Riis continues:

Someone proposed a boxing match and the husky village butcher who boasted a ring career as part of his past and told many tales of his fistic prowess before he settled in the Grand Valley challenged all comers. But the Mormon boys were slow to take him up. Wrestling and horse racing were more in their line. They knew little about boxing and the butcher was a husky lad. So the butcher strutted in his glory until someone thought of a lone hobo sitting in the town calaboose. He had been brought in from the railroad thirty-five miles away for some trespass or other. The Moab jail with its single cell stood out in the open where the heat of the sun intensified by the red cliffs often sent the mercury up to 105 or more. . . . The hobo in the calaboose was offered his choice of freedom if he stepped in the ring with the butcher and staged a finish fight, or sitting in his cell till the court met. He gave

---

17. Juanita Brooks, *Uncle Will Tells His Story* (Salt Lake City: Taggart and Co., 1970), pp. 11-16, 128.

22-Birdseye View of Moab
ur Co.

Bird's-eye view of Moab in early days; exact date unknown.
U.S. Forest Service photo.

one look at the jail and followed the committee down to the hotel where a ring was quickly roped off in the street.

The fight that followed was an epic. The butcher, twenty pounds the heavier, smiled confidently as the hobo crawled through the ropes. He would play with the man a while before putting him out. But the hobo looked back up the street towards the jail squatting in the midday heat. Then he leapt from his corner and tore into the butcher like a tornado, staggering him under a hurricane of blows. For four rounds he rushed the butcher off his feet and when the village champion was a broken idol with his face turned up to the sun the hobo leaped from the ring, grabbed his shirt and coat, and hurried down the road to the ferry, fearful lest the crowd change its mind and send him back to jail. He disappeared around a bend in the road with the cheers of the crowd following him.[18]

Burl Armstrong, a reporter who accompanied a 1907 party from the University of Utah which called itself the "San Juan Explorers," left a colorful account of the party's approach to Moab and his own impressions of the village. While Armstrong was undoubtedly "afflicted with an undisciplined imagination," his vices, in the words of the *Grand Valley Times,* leaned "towards the side of virtue" and contribute to our understanding of the Moab in which Orrin C. Snow, John Riis, and other early La Sal Forest officers worked. Armstrong wrote:

We were half way down the canyon when its beauties were stolen from us by a sand typhoon of uncommon force. The driver, as skilled and

18. Riis, pp. 84-87.

reckless as he was, was forced to stop many times, while the horses, gladly standing still, turned their heads away from the ondriving sand. The wind came up the canyon like it was traveling through a funnel, gathering strength at every turn and hurling a cloud of sand before it. We started on again and ran smack into an immense herd of sheep. Herders were moving 20,000 sheep up the canyon in two flocks.[19] The sheep stood with their heads to the ground, waiting for the sand to blow over. The horses pranced with fright among the sheep and narrowly missed turning the stage over a steep cliff.

When the cloud had passed we found ourselves in the center of a bleating mass of wool. The sand dunes were transformed into a solid mass of gray-white. Shepherd dogs barked, and here and there a herder drove his pony into the flock to urge them on. The sheep swarmed over the trail, upon the cliffs, and were finally lost to sight in another billow of sand.

Grand Valley is a beautiful sight even to eyes filled with sand. The rich green verdure is a relief from the rocks and rills of a canyon where vegetation consists of sagebrush, greasewood, and scrub pines. The Grand River shimmers in the sun like a band of shining silver, and wends its way out of the valley through two solid walls of rock. The last section of the flock of sheep met us at the ferry. The ferryman charges a half cent a head for the sheep, and he makes money. Moab nestles comfortably in the center of the valley. Bounding the pretty garden spot are seemingly insurmountable walls of stone. Off in the distance the La Sal mountains mantled with snow, show up through the haze and give a touch of grandeur to the scene. Moab has 800 people, thrifty, well to do, and eternally busy. They are building an empire down here in a remarkably fertile valley.[20]

Some of Armstrong's commentary was obviously done in fun. Much of it is subject to challenge. Another observer, H. L. A. Culmer, who made a 1905 expedition to the Natural Bridges of San Juan County for the Salt Lake City Commercial Club, was as awed by the trail and as enchanted by Moab as Armstrong, but he came away more impressed with the unhurried and easy of life. Bolstering his own observations by citing Dr. J. W. Williams, Moab's physician, Culmer wrote: "The people get Moab fever after the first year. It is so easy to make a bare living and so hard to get rich here. The symptom of Moab fever is chronic laziness."[21]

The Road to Public Acceptance of Resource Management

Whatever the view of contemporaries, southeastern Utah was just emerging from its frontier period when the La Sal Forest Reserve was established in 1906. In the twenty-five years just past, the West of Spud Hudson and "Race Horse" Johnson had passed progressively from unclaimed cow pasture, to cattle empire, to Mormon

---

19. While Armstrong's descriptions of the wind may not be an exaggeration, his count of the sheep was almost surely overdone.
20. *Grand Valley Times,* 28 June 1907.
21. Charlie R. Steen, "The Natural Bridges of White Canyon: A Diary of H. L. A. Culmer, 1865," *Utah Historical Quarterly* 40 (1972): 65.

country, to a no-man's-land of the cattle-sheep competition, to part of a state, and by 1906 was well on its way to integration into the broad fabric of the United States, with resources previously as free as the air now fair game for government control and administration. The inspections, reports, proclamations, boundaries, and headquarters required by resource management reflected the wavering line of advancing civilization as mid-twentieth century Americans have come to know it.

As important as were inspections and proclamations to this process, personnel was even more important. When he took his lonely post at Castleton that spring day of 1906, Orrin C. Snow was the first figure of a force that enjoyed a modest increment during the formative years of the La Sal Forest. Then, with precedent, growing wealth, and depression lending impetus, that force flooded to full tide as resource managing agencies proliferated in recent decades.

In southeastern Utah this transformation was accompanied by a marked shift in public opinion as to where the best interests of both the commonweal and personal prospects lay. During the formative years at least, the genesis of public opinion from a frontier individualism tinctured with Mormon cooperativism was closely related to Orrin Snow and other foresters who gave resource management not only its public face, but much of its internal character and integrity as well. Gathering to the La Sal National Forest from far and near, Forest officers represented a cross-section of American attitudes. They were themselves barely a first generation of organization men in whom strong ambivalences existed. What may be termed a spirit of professionalism struggled to dominate a spirit of frontier individualism. To state this proposition in another way, the road to public acceptance of resource management was closely related to the success of foresters in playing down individualism in their own responses and assuming a patient integrity which recognizably served the public interest. As a case study pointing up this development, the La Sal National Forest provides some notable opportunities. Its early foresters had flaws in what for want of a more descriptive term may be called professionalism. Orrin Snow, for example, was in a very real way the embodiment of free enterprise—biding its time and not biding it with any great patience. John Riis was an errant son of the Ivy League, something of a playboy, who, for all his grasp of conservation and truly superb powers of observation, was sharply limited in his ability to comprehend and manage his constituents.

Other early La Sal foresters were a cross section of the west. Probably predominating were farmers and cowboys such as Lawrence Adams and Ed Taylor, unable to make a living in Utah's hamlets. Haberdashers from Scranton, and defunct dentists from Iowa, as in the cases of Rangers Fred W. Strong and J. W. Palmer, also were numbered in their ranks. Adding variety and color was Ranger Rudolph E. Mellenthin, a German immigrant in whom the ambivalences of romanticism and Prussian militarism festered to create a sometime drugstore cowboy—silk scarf, high boots, big gun, showy horses, and all—a sometime artist who struck off murals and survey worksheets with great sensitivity, and a sometime autocrat called "the Kaiser" by irritated Forest users. Also to be found were discouraged men such as capable and likable Ranger Sterling Colton of Vernal. His wife dead, Colton appeared to lose hope, and in 1914 went to an early death.

But more useful to an understanding of the internal dilemma confronting a resource management agency as it establishes an image commensurate with its need for integrity and concern for the public interest is a consideration of two other early forest supervisors, Henry A. Bergh and J. W. Humphrey.

Every Other Man a Forest Ranger

On January 1, 1910, Henry A. Bergh assumed his duties as supervisor. Bergh was an enigmatic person and in many ways the most interesting and complex individual connected with the early history of the La Sals. He was energetic and imaginative. He recognized problem areas and worked with enthusiasm and ingenuity to bring about their solutions. During his incumbency, much progress was made toward establishing more practical boundaries, particularly on the Woodenshoe and Dark Canyon allotments of the Elk Ridge district. The range of his vision included upgraded ranger stations for each of the five districts, and much progress was made in this direction. He directed the improvement of drift fences, pastures, ditches, roads, stock trails, and telegraph lines. Under his direction a major timber reconnaissance was conducted during the summer of 1911. Together with the timber survey crew, his forest staff grew to an all-time high of seventeen, ten full-time employees and seven surveyors, which led wags in Monticello to crack that every other man one met in those parts was a forest ranger.[22]

Bergh was a master of at least the superficial arts of public relations, though to his ultimate regret he let more basic elements of his own public image languish. The pages of the *Grand Valley Times* never ran more Forest material than during his days. His inspections, trips, plans, and accomplishments were kept before the public eye. In addition, he drove his small staff to put out the "Cliff Dwellers' Echo," a mimeographed house organ of the La Sal Forest. Announced as a monthly publication in mid-1911, it ran several issues that year, and in 1912 it appeared as a quarterly. Demanding contributions from each of his rangers, for some of whom writing ap-

22. *Grand Valley Times*, 21 July 1911.

pears to have been sheer agony, Bergh presented a surprisingly diverse and well-done periodical. In no small part this was due to the untiring efforts of Howard W. Balsley, clerk, upon whom fell much of the editorial and writing work, as well as the typing and production. But Bergh himself was clearly the one who made the publication. In each issue he wrote long feature articles. Sometimes dealing with prehistory, sometimes with the theory of conservation, but more often with the functions of the Forest, these articles provide a good, though not unbiased, look into the Bergh administration. Bergh also made a real contribution to the history of Indian relations when he invited A. M. Rogers, a participant in the Pinhook Battle, to publish an account of that engagement.[23]

Beyond all this, Henry Bergh comes through in the pages of the "Echo" as a local promoter in the grand tradition of western editors. In each issue he promoted the Forest, transportation, towns in the locality, and a wide variety of enterprises. In his enthusiastic reporting, railroads were just over the hill, and river highways held promise of total metamorphosis for Moab. Clearly among his attributes were the abilities to dream and to convey his dreams to others by way of the written word.

But Bergh was an enigma. In spite of his achievements, he was a failure, indeed, he was a resounding failure. In failure, as in so many other situations, Bergh added his own peculiar flourishes. Close examination indicates that from the outset of his La Sal administration there were checks and fissures in the mosaic of general success he portrayed. Indeed, it appears that Bergh came to Moab under something of a cloud. A story well-known among his contemporaries suggests that many of them saw inconsistencies in his character. These became particularly apparent at the time of a conference at which District Forester E. A. Sherman was making a strong case for forest officers to enforce game laws. Bergh, who was known to ignore game laws both from personal and policy standpoints in the Idaho forest of which he was supervisor, made an obvious and public show of applauding Sherman's position. When Bergh was transferred almost immediately from the more prestigious Idaho unit to the La Sal Forest, it was regarded by some as a demotion meted out in part as a result of his duplicity with reference to game laws.[24]

Once in Moab, Bergh continued to ignore game laws—a policy that probably did not reduce his popularity with either his subordinates or forest users. However, since the official position of the Forest Service was widely known, Bergh's policy could not have enhanced the dignity of the service's position. Matters had de-

23. *Cliffdwellers' Echo*, 1911 and 1912.
24. Interview with J. W. Humphrey, Provo, Utah, 27 March 1971.

teriorated so far that in 1914, when J. W. Humphrey undertook to enforce the game laws, he was met with derision as well as resistance by forest officers and local residents alike.[25]

While it is nowhere cited as one of Bergh's problems, it is apparent to the modern researcher that his aggressive forward movement allowed no opportunity for consolidation. He was simply too expansion-oriented to conclude one project before moving to another. Mistaking momentum for progress, he left many loose ends behind him. Furthermore, the disparity between the image he sought to create and the reality of the Forest's situation was not always subtle, and in some cases the discrepancy was glaringly obvious. One example will suffice to illustrate the point. In his public releases, Bergh talked as if grazing permits were closely and effectively controlled. Characteristic of his buoyant claims was the following from a general grazing report made in 1912:

> I might say that the grazing business on this Forest has undergone a complete revolution. The allotments, the character of the stock, the manner of running the different classes of stock, all have been so radically changed in the past three years that it almost frightens me to look back and note what has been done, and yet there has been no serious conflicts or complaints. . . .[26]

This impression of progress may not have been misleading with relation to control of sheep entering the Forest, as they could be counted by herds. In the case of cattle, however, any allegation that control of numbers had been achieved was untrue—a fact that was known by rangers, users, and the public alike. Although Bergh claimed that effective control had been achieved through counting cattle as they entered the forest in the spring, Forest manpower was insufficient to control points of entry, and the lack of driveways and drift fences, as well as the general topographical relationship of the Forest boundary to the public lands, all precluded control. These factors, together with the reluctance of users to yield to public management, made it clear that Bergh's talk of permits, counting, and control of numbers was without much meaning and suggested that Forest regulations belonged to a paper system.

Furthermore, Bergh was a prime example of the personality split between a nascent professionalism and lingering free enterprise. A professional forester in many of his responses, he was, nevertheless, as freewheeling in his quest for individual gain as Orrin C. Snow, yet he apparently lacked the latter's fundamental integrity. During the period he was supervisor, Bergh came to have a variety of personal enterprises, including a poultry business in Moab, a 400 acre dry farm, and a profitable traffic in Navajo blankets. There is evidence that

25. Ibid.
26. *Cliffdwellers' Echo*, December 1912.

Bergh sometimes mixed Forest Service interests in these personal pursuits. Among the charges later laid against him was the use of public lumber and grain in his poultry business. It also appears that some Forest improvement contracts were compensated through three-cornered deals in which Bergh swapped horses and other goods as part of the arrangement.[27]

Worse, Bergh became involved in a Forest Service wire contract in which he falsely represented a purchase of smooth wire as barbed wire, and was accused of pocketing the difference. He also made trades involving government property, including horse collars and tarps. Howard W. Balsley, forest clerk under Riis, Bergh, Humphrey, and Locke, took testimony in the Bergh case, and recalled that "not much was involved, but he played his favorites among the users, and I always thought he got paid for it."[28] While the Forest Service obviously suffered both internally and in its public relations because of all this, Bergh might personally have survived, had he not capped the entire matter by a morals episode involving a teenage girl who did housework for the Bergh family. When the affair approached the explosion point, Bergh "picked up very suddenly and left for parts unknown" one October evening in 1913. A thorough investigation was made by Homer E. Fenn, A. C. McCain, and Quincy Croft from the district office. Although McCain, district chief of operation at the time, reported that Bergh had "violated eleven of the fourteen criminal statutes," a federal grand jury at Salt Lake City failed to indict him. The jury held that while the points charged had been proved, they were in themselves of small importance so the case was dropped.[29]

Homer E. Fenn, assistant district forester, subsequently reported on one of Bergh's activities. While it involved only a small function, it comes near summarizing the Bergh style. Beginning with a strong touch of irony, Fenn wrote of the Bulldog ranger station near Blanding:

> This station is one of Bergh's star performances. It has six fairly large rooms, is lathed and plastered and has commodious closets, pantry, etc. It cost the Government approximately $1400. Funds in excess of $650 were secured, so I was told, by collecting money direct from the sale of timber to local sawmill operators [one of Bergh's rangers reported the same device had been used to finance Bergh's chicken coops] and by the diversion of funds allotted for drift fences and other improvement projects. The father of the girl with whom Bergh has been charged with improper relations, was employed as a common laborer on this

27. Henry A. Bergh to Iowa Smith, 15 July 1913, Castleton, Utah, U-Adjustment Folder, Denver Records Center.
28. Interview with Howard W. Balsley, Moab, Utah, 23 August 1968.
29. Ibid. *See also* interview with J. W. Humphrey, Provo, Utah, 26 March 1971; and Statement of J. W. Humphrey, "Historical Information, La Sal National Forest," pp. 21-25; and *Grand Valley Times*, 28 November 1913.

project at $5.00 per day [this figure was far out of line with prevailing rates] during the entire course of construction. He was also employed in the same capacity and at the same rate of pay at other projects, including the Cottonwood Ranger Station.[30]

At the time of the Bergh affair, the La Sal Forest had been part of the scene in southeastern Utah for almost eight years. While its accomplishments were substantial, it had neither been effective in winning the respect of its public nor in dealing effectively with problems inherent in the control of grazing. Cuts in the number of stock had been made, and adjustments between cattlemen and sheepmen had been effected, but the real authority of the Forest in controlling numbers, regulating use of allotments, and the length of the season had not been established.

Cowpunchers of Superior Type and a Forest's Image

The personnel situation was recognized as the Forest's most pressing problem. As Homer Fenn put it, the La Sal had been "neglected in two respects from a personnel standpoint." In the first place was the "unfortunate selection of supervisors," and second was the "lack of proper personnel inspection by members of the district office." Morale and discipline had become almost nonexistent. J. W. Humphrey, who replaced Bergh, learned early that loyalty was sadly wanting in certain rangers, for at least one challenged his judgment and action publicly.[31] With the exception of Lewis T. Quigley, whom Fenn judged to be the only really promising ranger on the Forest, the entire force "had the idea . . . that if any manual labor was to be done on their districts, guards or laborers should be appointed for the purpose." According to Fenn:

> The prevailing idea seems to be to carry a riata [lariat] instead of an ax, and assay the role of a cowpuncher of superior type, rather than that of an officer of the government who is expected to do such work as may be necessary to facilitate the use and administration of his district.[32]

Public opinion rated the rangers in about the same way. It was acknowledged that Quigley was diligent. Others were sometimes regarded as lazy, particularly J. W. Palmer, the onetime dentist who suffered from a variety of ailments, real and imagined, and never hesitated to take refuge behind them. Mellenthin's foppish efforts to affect a cowboy style won him only ridicule, and his German background and his autocratic mode of dealing with Forest users led him to be hated as well. It was no secret that hardworking ranchers thought that most of the rangers loafed in the winter. Occasional

30. Homer E. Fenn, Inspection Report, 10 July 1915, Personnel Folder, Manti-La Sal National Forest Historical Files.
31. Ibid.
32. Ibid.

J. W. Humphrey, Ranger Robert Strong and wife at the latter's residence in Moab. U.S. Forest Service photo.

circumstances encouraged this opinion. One story supporting it involves Thomas B. Carpenter of La Sal, who heard Mellenthin and Balsley singing in the forest office over the old Cooper-Martin Store in Moab and dryly commented to bystanders: "That's what the government pays them for."[33] Some foresters were held to be guilty of more grievous offenses. It was generally thought that William H. Keershaw had exceeded more than an ethical code when he "tipped off a relative to the fact that there were some technical violations of the land laws in securing title to the townsite of Grayson, or Blanding." Carl Stockbridge, who was brought in when it became expedient to transfer Keershaw, was "a gun-toting cowboy from Texas," who was feared because of his surly temperament and his reputation as a killer.[34]

The La Sal Forest not only was neglected by the district office, and unfortunate in its first three supervisors, but also it was regarded as one of the most undesirable assignments, if not *the* most undesirable assignment in the entire district. It will be recalled that it was widely held that Bergh had been demoted when sent to the La Sal

---

33. Interview with J. W. Humphrey, 15 April 1971.
34. Statement of J. W. Humphrey, "Historical Information, La Sal National Forest," p. 22.

from an Idaho forest. Orrin Snow also felt he had been moved up in his transfer to the Sevier Forest. While this may have been due partially to administrative decisions placing status and pay on the La Sal below other forests, it was also the product of the extreme remoteness and the higher expense of living on the La Sal. To the latter proposition, Ranger Sterling L. Colton could attest. Unable to rent a house for his family in Grayson, he located them in Bluff, where the "rent and cost of living is exorbitant." Sugar, he reported, sold at $10.50 and flour at $6.00 per hundred.[35] Rangers often found life in their districts to be lonely and hard. Because of overgrazing, most found it necessary to buy grain and carry it on inspection trips to feed their horses, thus excluding the purchase of other necessities with the modest sum allotted for expenses while on extended Forest tours. A story persists that after buying horse feed for the first trip, many new rangers left the Forest in disgust.[36]

The attrition rate was particularly high during the time John Riis was supervisor. There seems to have been a quality about Riis—perhaps a misbegotten sense of noblesse oblige too openly assumed—that irritated many westerners with whom he came in contact. By his own accounts, he had trouble getting along with many of his Utah associates from the time of his earliest experiences at the Cunningham and Carpenter Ranch. Frictions continued to characterize his relations with people during his years on the La Sal Forest. Not unusual was a two-month period in 1909, when two new rangers and a forest clerk left suddenly, none of them serving more than three weeks. One of these men was from Wayne County, and two were from Sanpete. It may be assumed that they were all Mormons, which suggests one reason they left abruptly. Riis shared an idea with Inspector Robert R. V. Reynolds and other eastern foresters that Mormons could not be expected to perform well. While he made no reference to Mormons quitting almost before they began work, Riis did write the following on the matter:

> Some of the Mormons objected to my drawing most of my men from other states, and a delegation headed by Bishop Jones laid a protest before me. But I had tried several of the local boys with unhappy results. I was glad to use them as forest guards, but stuck to my guns in regard to the selection of my rangers, although the delegation carried its complaint to Secretary of Agriculture Wilson through Senator Smoot.[37]

---

35. *Cliffdwellers' Echo*, January 1912.
36. Because the matter of horse feed and its cost was a continuing problem, Henry Bergh addressed one of his "Cliffdwellers' Echo" items to the subject. Noting that policy permitted compensation when cost of forage and stabling horses exceeded $75.00 per annum, Bergh opined that all forage costs ought to be allowed. But since they were not indicated, his own policy had been to allow "an conservative allotment at the beginning of the fiscal year and allow him to spend that amount whenever he desires." Characteristically, Bergh required no receipts to be submitted. See *Cliffdwellers' Echo*, December 1912.
37. Riis, p. 57.

To Restore Lost Standing and Prestige

As unfortunate as it was, the Bergh affair was shock therapy for troubled La Sal. It finally brought the Ogden office more actively into personnel administration and pointed up that regardless of the La Sal's adverse status in relation to other forests in the district it could not, in effect, be used as a dumping ground for second-rate personnel. In accord with the latter realization, J. W. Humphrey was appointed supervisor. Moved in November of 1913 from the Cache Forest, where he had been assistant supervisor, Humphrey was a fortunate choice. He was born in Salina and was brought up in circumstances similar to those that prevailed around the La Sal Forest. Like J. A. and Jim Scorup, who also hailed from Salina, he had found little opportunity there and had held jobs around Utah as well as in the mines, railroads, and ranches of three neighboring states. His foundation in the Forest Service was sound, since he had been a ranger for several years on the Manti Forest. There he came under the influence of A. W. Jensen, whose administrative virtues included a close and demanding rein upon his rangers. Humphrey's assets also included a family relationship with the Scorup brothers—his sister was Jim's wife—that undoubtedly placed him in favorable standing with many La Sal forest stockmen.

As Humphrey assumed control in La Sal, he faced two immediate jobs: one was to placate Forest users, and to begin claiming a place of respect for the Forest; the other was to restore a degree of discipline and morale among Forest personnel. Although his stay on the Forest was short, he was eminently successful in the first job, and made some progress on the second.

His first step was to tighten up the operation generally. The staff was reduced to seven men from a high of thirteen in the booming days of Bergh's administration. Commensurate cuts were made in many other facets of the former supervisor's aggressive improvement program. Humphrey also undertook to enforce the game laws.[38] After acquiring some feel for the relationship of Forest grazing allotments to winter range on the public domain, Humphrey abandoned all effort to count cattle onto the La Sal. Contending that cattlemen actually could not control the number of stock that entered the Forest under existing conditions, he sought and won district approval for a three-phase program. First, he continued Bergh's effort to effect boundary adjustments. Second, he proposed that the entire Forest be fenced. Third, he called for the removal of all cattle permits and placed cattlemen on their honor to report numbers grazing on the Forest. The last two measures represented an about-face from the policy followed previously but had the merit of acknowledging reality with reference to the impossibility of control. Further, it resulted in greater revenues from grazing

38. Interview with J. W. Humphrey, Provo, Utah, 15 April 1971.

fees, as many users paid on the basis of the numbers they ran, rather than on the number permitted.[39] Another virtue of the Humphrey policy was its directness. Its assumption of honesty on the part of users led them to regard Humphrey and the Forest with favor. Where previous supervisors had faced contention, Humphrey found users quite willing to compromise and adjust.

However, Humphrey had little opportunity to see the fruits of his new approach, as he was transferred to the Sevier Forest in June, 1915. In terms of public acceptance, he had made real progress. Where internal administration was concerned, his superiors assumed that his performance could be improved upon by Samuel B. Locke. Locke's experience on the Sawtooth Forest, "where a very high degree of accountability was required of the men," seemed to promise well for finally bringing the field force of the La Sal under complete control.[40]

It would be a mistake to regard the years that followed 1915 as epilogue. As with the formative years, this time was important. An ebb and flow in the tide of Forest affairs continued. A variety of

Forest officers camped at the foot of Peter's Hill, about 1915.
U.S. Forest Service photo.

39. Statement of J. W. Humphrey, "Historical Information, La Sal National Forest," p. 24.
40. Homer E. Fenn, Inspection Report, 10 July 1915.

crises and external events affected its public image; and its supervisors and other personnel continued to vary in character. Samuel B. Locke, a well-educated and sensitive New Englander, performed well before going on in 1918 to the district office to head a new fish and game section. Intensely interested in birds, he amazed Humphrey on the occasion of a month-long inspection of the La Sal Forest in the fall of 1915 by lying in their tent in the early mornings and identifying birds by their calls. He later became president of the National Audubon Society.[41]

The appointment of Charles De Moisy, Jr. in May, 1918, marked a definite and long-term shift to Utah-bred supervisors. De Moisy, who came from Vernal, had been on the Uintah Forest prior to his La Sal assignment and returned there in 1921. Edmund B. Spencer, who was supervisor from May, 1921, to September, 1923, was a native of Cache Valley. He was a graduate of the Boston Conservatory of Music with a specialty in piano tuning and had been connected with the Thatcher Piano Company of Logan for a time. Attracting favorable attention by thorough work as a subordinate, he is said to have lacked practical judgment as a supervisor. Orange Olsen, a son of Emery County, was supervisor from May, 1923, to January, 1926, and was succeeded by Lewis T. Quigley for a period of one year. In 1927, Allan C. Folster of Salina took over, holding the supervisor's office until 1935, thus establishing claim to being the longest-lived supervisor in the history of the La Sal to that time. He was succeeded by Sidney S. Stewart, and he in turn, by Leland D. Heywood, bringing the Forest well into the 1940s. But the administration of J. W. Humphrey marked the coming-of-age of the La Sal National Forest. The role of subsequent administrations will be seen in the various functions of the Forest.

---

41.   Interview with J. W. Humphrey, Provo, Utah, 15 April 1971.

Chapter VIII

Boundary and Claim Adjustments

Fixing the Perimeter

A major concern of La Sal Forest administration during its first decades was the establishment and refinement of boundaries. The inspections upon which the Forest had been based were hasty and superficial, and presumed that subsequent surveys would complete the job. Complicating this situation was the fact that much, if not most, of the area embraced by the La Sal had not yet been surveyed by the General Land Office. Robert R. V. Reynolds, who had made the original examination on many western forests, including the La Sal, recognized the serious problems that resulted from laying out boundaries in country where survey lines were not fixed. As he pointed out in a 1910 memorandum, Forest examiners had tended to draw boundaries for unsurveyed sections by making a "traverse" from known point to known point, blindly ignoring the realities of topographic conformation and plant growth. In his opinion there was an urgent need to survey some 10,000 miles for Forest boundary— a job he calculated would cost no less than $125,000.[1] Although some areas contiguous to the La Sal Forest had been surveyed, the overwhelming majority had not. Relating this to Reynolds's estimate of surveying yet to be done, it seems that nearly the entire perimeter of the La Sal Forest—amounting to about 280 miles—required further definition. The process of working out its intricacies consumed fifteen years or more and involved numerous complexities. Related to this was the problem of adjusting homesteads and other claims falling upon Forest lands.

---

1. Robert R. V. Reynolds, Memorandum for District Forester, 6 October 1910, Proclamation and Boundary Folder, Manti-La Sal National Forest Historical Files.

From the beginning, the Washington Office placed much stress on boundary determination. W. W. Clark, field inspector, who assisted Orrin C. Snow in establishing the La Sal Forest in the spring of 1906, directed Snow to make boundary survey a major item of business. By July 2 of Snow's first summer, Albert F. Potter, chief of grazing, had written noting that the Forest would be difficult to manage because it was "so irregular in outline," and because unlike most forests it was not only surrounded by "leased and titled land," but was itself laid out so as to encircle a vast tract of private and state lands. Potter warned that Snow might find some tendency for private interests to encroach upon the Forest as they had moved into the public domain generally, by fencing, by monopolizing water, by controlling key ranges, or by other means. It was, he continued, essential that the public understand from the outset that the boundaries of the national forest could not be infringed upon by any of these devices.

Snow had not long to wait for an opportunity to assert the Forest's position. P. T. Stevens, a Montrose, Colorado, stockman with extensive interests on the La Sal Mountains, had recently built a fence running four miles along the state line between Colorado and Utah. This fence was on the Forest nearly a mile east of Stevens's east boundary line and allowed Stevens a grazing monopoly on the Forest between the state line and his property. Discovering this situation, Snow was directed to move aggressively to get the Stevens fence removed and locate Forest boundaries to ensure that similar invasions did not exist elsewhere.[2] As the next season progressed and problems growing from the ill-contrived boundary continued, Snow was promised that a "competent surveyor would be detailed" to work out the southern boundary of the La Sal, but no evidence exists to indicate that Snow got special outside help at this time.[3]

Boundaries also became an immediate and recurrent theme of the District IV office after it was created in 1908. Indeed, one of its initial efforts was a district-wide program "to determine positively and finally the proper boundaries of the national forests." Informing forest supervisors that by the end of the 1909 field season "we must be in a position to prove, by reports and maps . . . the character of the land and its ownership," the district forester set forth guidelines to aid in the survey. Having withdrawn some eight million acres of Utah lands from public entry during the decade just past, the Forest Service was under fire in 1909 for its seeming greed. Suggesting that District IV was not insensitive to this adverse public opinion, the district forester emphasized that the purpose of the field investigation was not only to determine proper forest bounds, but to seek out agricultural lands within the national forests and return them to public entry. The

2. A. F. Potter to O. C. Snow, 28 June 1906, G-Supervision Folder, Manti-La Sal National Forest Historical Files.
3. *Grand Valley Times,* 27 August 1907.

policy of the service was, as the directive pointed out, "to exclude from national forests all agricultural land except, as Congress clearly intended, areas so small that they can be handled more acceptably under the Act of June 11, 1906." Betraying a keen sense for public opinion, the directive continued: "Full consideration will also be given to the demands of the public for the retention of grazing lands provided they are set out in some written form. . . ."[4] Skilled aid in conducting the surveys was also promised, but appears not to have been made available to the La Sal Forest until 1910.[5]

With this kind of emphasis at the national and district levels, boundary surveys became an important element in the routine of La Sal Forest affairs. After a brief study following the creation of the Monticello Forest, Orrin C. Snow recommended that its east boundary be extended by 74,000 acres. Including timberland, watersheds for Monticello and Verdure, and grazing lands, Snow's recommendation was enlarged by approximately 26,000 acres and became part of the Forest on December 12, 1907.

It seems probable that even more acres would have been added had officers been in possession of sufficient information about the west line of the Forest. Following the "traverse" method of establishment, the original west boundary had been broken off bluntly midway in what was taken to be Range 18 East and, with no heed to elevation or topography, had been drawn in a straight line north and south. Writing about the question in 1908, John Riis noted that further additions had been impossible because "the Elk mountain vicinity is wholly unsurveyed and very rough and broken." He was, however, satisfied that "one or two small areas in this region should be added whenever we are able to locate them with sufficient acuracy [*sic*] to locate their proper boundaries."[6]

In 1909 Riis responded to the District IV survey directive by submitting a major boundary report. In it he called for adjustments around the entire Forest perimeter, including an arrangement to tie an alienated block of land east of La Sal to the body of the forest by the addition of two or three intervening sections. Riis also recommended that agricultural lands, particularly those in the neighborhood of Monticello, be eliminated from the National Forest and once again opened to entry.[7]

4. *See* Instructions for Examination and Report on Additions to and Eliminations from National Forests, 3 June 1909, Proclamation and Boundary Folder. The Act of 11 June 1906 was the commonly applied name of the Forest Homestead Act of 11 June 1906.

5. Robert R. V. Reynolds, Memorandum for District Forester, Proclamation and Boundary Folder.

6. Orrin C. Snow, Report on the Additions of the Monticello National Forest, and John Riis to the Forester, 13 February 1908, Proclamation and Boundary Folder.

7. "Historical Information, La Sal National Forest," p. 27. *See also* John Riis, Boundary Report, 12 October 1909, Proclamation and Boundary Folder.

The effort to resolve the boundary question continued in 1910 as Henry Bergh, incoming supervisor, made it a principal object of his administration, and the district dispatched a man to work on boundary surveys for about three months, evidently restricting his time to the Southern Division (Blue Mountains) portion of the Forest. In addition, Rangers R. E. Mellenthin, Edwin Taylor, and Fred W. Strong spent much of November surveying the Colorado boundary of the Northern Division (La Sal Mountains). Their report recommended that 9,000 acres be added to the Forest and that 1,000 acres of farm land in Sinbad Valley be dropped.[8]

It is impossible to indicate with complete confidence what came of the 1910 boundary recommendations. However, there is no evidence that any immediate changes were made, and it is certain that some of the proposals were not acted upon until 1914. Other elements appear to have been put into effect in 1913 when a small parcel of agricultural land—4,040 acres—was withdrawn from the Northern Division and opened for settlement.[9] Other modest exclusions of agricultural land continued to reflect the desire to define the Forest's bounds, but the major adjustment in the years after 1910 focused on the west boundary of the Woodenshoe and Dark Canyon allotments.[10]

The Woodenshoe-Dark Canyon Boundary, 1910-1914

In 1914, Executive Order 1264 eliminated 40,850 acres and added 33,640 acres to the Forest. Eliminated were the cedar slopes in the southwest corner of the Southern Division below the Bear's Ears and an area on Vega Creek northwest of Monticello. Added was the western part of the wild and spectacular Woodenshoe and Dark Canyon drainages. No other adjustment demonstrates as clearly the relationship of boundaries to the successful management of the National Forest as do the Woodenshoe and Dark Canyon additions. As indicated heretofore, the Forest boundary had been "traversed" without benefit of a survey. Worse, it had been done without benefit of a visit to the west end of Elk Ridge, which precluded any real understanding of the relationship of the Woodenshoe and Dark Canyon summer pastures to winter ranges in White Canyon, Beef Basin, and other desert canyons lying west and north toward the Colorado River. On paper, the original Forest line looked good. Unfortunately for the interests of the Forest, it made no sense whatever from the standpoint of practical grazing control. The line as drawn bisected a natural ranging unit that because of its topography could neither be fenced nor otherwise divided to control cattle movement.[11]

Until 1914 the Indian Creek Cattle Company and Lemuel H. Redd claimed that part of the Woodenshoe-Dark Canyon range lying

---

8. *Grand Valley Times*, 11 and 25 November 1910.
9. Ibid., 26 December 1913.
10. Manti-la Sal Historical Atlas.
11. Henry A. Bergh, *Cliffdwellers' Echo*, July 1912.

Scorup Brothers' line camp in Woodenshoe Canyon. U.S. Forest
Service photo.

outside the Forest, and under a grazing allotment used the portion
that lay within its bounds. In this situation, rugged terrain and divided control made it virtually impossible to control cattle moving into
the Forest. Even if the Indian Creek Cattle Company and Redd had
been ardent in their support of Forest policies—which they were not—
it seems unlikely that cattle drifting out of the rock mazes below
could have been limited to permit numbers. A further complicating
matter grew from the fact that the winter ranges dependent upon
Woodenshoe-Dark Canyon summer pastures had a much higher carrying capacity, adding the effect of drastic overgrazing to breech of
permit regulations.

Given these circumstances, it is not surprising that L. H. Redd
and the Indian Creek Cattle Company ran far more stock on their
Forest allotments than permits authorized during the years prior to
1914. Conservative estimates place the numbers they ran at double
their permits.[12]

The period of delay between the recommendation (1910) that the
Forest line be redrawn and its enactment was marked by continuing
friction. The largest Southern Division users were determined not

12. Simon Oliver to the Forester quoted in L. F. Kneipp to E. A. Sherman,
25 July 1912, and Sherman to the Forester, 31 July 1912, Records Relating to
Grazing Supervision, Region IV Papers, National Archives.

to lose another slice of grazing land to the Forest. In addition to Redd and the Indian Creek Cattle Company, the Scorup brothers appear to have been involved. Acting jointly, they used their connections with Senator Reed Smoot in an attempt to defeat the proposal. Quite naturally, La Sal Forest officers sometimes showed signs of frustration and impatience. Henry A. Bergh hammered continually on the theme of boundary adjustment, referring to it as the "burning question" in his administration. Three years earlier—before this particular question had become an issue—John Riis wrote the district forester a complaining letter in which he indicted the people of San Juan generally and, without naming them, turned special criticism on the large forest users:

> I think that one of the chief reasons that the people of the south division are so hard to deal with, is the fact that there are one or two large men in San Juan County and a very large percent of the settlers are in debt to those parties and therefore in a measure under obligation to them, this results in endless schemes by the large men, aiming to increase their permits, which are already above the maximum limit, by distributing the stock among the smaller men. This in connection with the natural clannishness of the settlers makes a pretty hard combination to buck.[13]

Even patient Will Humphrey thought that the big stockmen on the Southern Division made La Sal Forest administration more difficult than elsewhere.[14]

Reed Smoot, one of the most powerful conservation forces in the United States Senate, sought to control the La Sal Forest boundary matter at the service level, meeting with Albert F. Potter, Henry S. Graves, and possibly others. Officers and users both stood firm, and an impasse existed until 1913. However, late that year a break began to develop when Supervisor Bergh came to an understanding with Lemuel Redd. According to J. A. Scorup, Redd agreed to withdraw his opposition when Bergh promised: "I will let you have about what you want over here in the North Elk." Senator Smoot, who had invested a good deal of effort, was impatient at Redd's shift of position, but nevertheless took it to mean that the Scorups and the Indian Creek Cattle Company also were amenable to the change and dropped his campaign, permitting the boundary alterations to come into effect in 1914.[15]

If there is a lesson to be learned from this encounter, it is that when institutionalized and private interests came in conflict on the La Sal Forest, the advantage usually lay with the former. In this case, some of Utah's most powerful stockmen, arrayed with a senator whose interests and power were closely related to the public lands, held out for four years. Finally, one of them made a private deal, the line

13.   G-Supervision Folder, 5 April 1909.
14.   Interview with J. W. Humphrey, Provo, Utah, 26 March 1971.
15.   A. F. Potter to District Forester, 24 November 1911, Proclamation and Boundary Folder; and "Historical Information, La Sal National Forest," p. 56.

collapsed, and the Forest policy of restricted use made another advance. Where grazing is concerned, an examination of the Manti-La Sal records reveals a repetition of this process. The formula is simple and so obvious as to be undeniable: (1) policies adverse to the status quo of livestock operations are introduced in the form of boundary changes, permit reductions, shortened seasons, and escalating fees; (2) the stockmen protest; (3) concessions (often no more than token) are made; (4) the policy of restriction inches forward; and (5) the cycle begins again. Ignoring the vital question of where long-term gain lies, there is a quality of the inexorable about this expansion of power and control. Even the fact that there is fundamental progress in the process of moving from a free but unknowing use of a wilderness frontier to an increasingly rationalized and disciplined manipulation of natural resources—in which light this study has attempted to portray southeast Utah's development—does not obscure the growth of power nor the loss of personal liberty involved. This problem may well be among life's many imponderables; but, for all that, it is worth our time to recognize the process and to note that it constituted a problem in the developing La Sal Forest.

The Cottonwood-Allen Canyon Indian Allotment, 1923

In 1923 a final adjustment was made in the La Sal Forest boundary. This time approximately twelve sections—8,360 acres—spanning the Cottonwood-Allen Canyon drainages on the south slope of the Elks were eliminated and allotted to two small bands of Indians numbering about eighty persons. According to reports accompanying the request for elimination, Paiutes under the leadership of Mancos Jim and, more recently, Polk and Posey, had made the juncture of Cottonwood and Allen Canyons their principal place of residence for at least seventy years. It had been in this locality that Thales Haskell and other Mormons assigned as Indian missionaries in the 1880s had undertaken to instruct the Paiutes in the rudiments of agriculture and to establish permanent homes for them. The Paiutes were nomads in the full sense and had refused to be tied down by Mormon plans, but the Cottonwood-Allen Canyon area continued to be an important base for hunting forays when the Forest was created. Thereafter, eight sections of the same country had been allotted for Indian grazing purposes. Because of the continuous yearlong use by ponies and goats, the Indian allotment was "in a decidedly overgrazed condition." Small tracts along the streams had also been cultivated in a "desultory manner" and partial crops of "speckled Indian corn and melons" had contributed to the support of the Paiutes. The only access to this fantastically rugged canyonland had been via pack trails and stock driveways up the canyon bottoms.[16]

---

16. E. B. Spencer, Boundary Change Report, 25 June 1923, Indian Allotment Folder, Manti-La Sal National Forest Historical Files. La Sal Forest files

Several years of growing discord had culminated earlier in 1923 in the so-called Posey War when a notorious subchief and an unruly younger Paiute were killed by whites. The Cottonwood-Allen Canyon allotment withdrawal was in large measure the outgrowth of the Posey incident and represented an official effort to stabilize what had become a potentially explosive situation. Wearied by repeated acts of belligerence, most San Juan whites favored moving the Paiutes to a reservation. However, a strong minority argued for making the Cottonwood-Allen Canyon tract a permanent home for the handful of Indians still in the locality. Including many in whom the Indian mission commitment was still strong, whites of this persuasion could see no honorable alternative because Indian claims to the area had been guaranteed by General Hugh L. Scott when he settled an earlier dispute in 1915. Scott's agreement, together with matters of traditional rights and Mormon paternalism, constituted a conclusive argument.

After considering the question carefully, the Forest Service moved ahead to eliminate the Cottonwood-Allen Canyon tract from its jurisdiction. In endorsing the arrangement, Supervisor E. B. Spencer held that the area had been the customary home of the Paiutes, that it was well-adapted to their needs, that the area had little value otherwise, and that grazing and transportation facilities on the Forest would be improved. After some discussion of right-of-way through the allotment, the proposition was accepted by all parties, and on October 12, 1923, the area was withdrawn from the La Sal National Forest by presidential proclamation.

Prompted to passing zealousness by the general concern for the Paiutes, field officers of the Bureau of Indian Affairs made an abortive attempt late in 1923 to put a wagon road through to the confluence of the two canyons.[17] As the flurry of interest subsided, the lonely tracks of the Bureau of Indian Affairs road fell into disuse and pack trails continued to be the only access for several years.

Mountain Homesteaders

The elimination of the Cottonwood-Allen Canyon tract to accommodate the Paiutes was reenacted with variations and, on a smaller scale, in homestead and other agricultural claims upon the Forest. The twenty years after the La Sal's establishment constituted the great era of the homesteader in southeastern Utah. The American dream of free land, and through it economic independence and social position, was still a potent force. Science had begun to understand dry farming. Speculators and promoters were at hand to undertake

refer to the Indians involved in this case as Paiutes. The fact that two bands were involved and that one of them was headed by the subchief Polk strongly suggests that part of them were Utes.

17.   Ibid.

Remains of homesteader's dugout east of Monticello.

their development schemes. The end of World War I brought its flood of veterans. Seeking means to assist them, a grateful nation looked to the land, expecting it to receive the homecoming soldiers to its bosom as in past wars. Anticipating that the public domain would become a passing phenomenon before the onslaught of returning veterans, District IV made ambitious plans to establish a regional network of stock driveways, thus hoping to protect the interests of national forest users. Ranging from a half-mile to three or more miles in width, these prospective rights-of-way extended to all quarters of District IV, including the La Sal Forest.

More important in grasping the nature of the homestead movement of southeastern Utah is an understanding of the groups involved in the process. As we have seen, Indians, conclusively forced from their former patterns, sought solutions to their needs in the public lands. A few years earlier, the last generation of Mormon pioneers had squatted and homesteaded at Grayson, coming in such numbers as to claim all available land on White Mesa, and to make Blanding, as Grayson came to be known, one of the most promising spots in all southeastern Utah.[18] During this same period, other towns were laid out. Second generation Bluff residents were said to be planning a town on Spring Creek, a few miles northwest of Monticello. By

18.   Henry A. Bergh, *Cliffdwellers' Echo,* January 1912.

December of 1912, it was named LeVega, and the settlers started building a few dwellings. In the La Sal vicinity, brisk homesteading by Mormons expelled from the Mexican colonies caused speculation that "white Mexicans" would soon set up a community there. Reporting on this activity, Supervisor Bergh wrote:

> La Sal and Coyote are showing signs of thrift. A number of new settlers have gone in on Coyote flats and are there making themselves fine homes. It has been rumored that the Cunningham and Carpenter ranch may be purchased and a colony composed of refugees from Old Mexico may come in and divide up this large body of land into a dozen or more smaller farms. If this is done, it will mean that all must have some place to reside in. Such a change would bring about a demand for saw timber and all other Forest products. It would make business. We are favorably impressed with the proposition and trust that the change will come. White Mexicans are not hard to handle; we have now a large number of them and they seem to be thankful that they are alive. No fault is found with Cunningham and Carpenter Company but I would rather see ten families making a living than one man getting rich. The former is better for the country.[19]

By 1916 La Sal's growth had progressed so that 150 people met to consider the location of a school. J. W. Garman and Joseph Shafer relinquished 160 acres of land in the center of the farming community, and a committee was appointed to lay out the town site.[20]

Other groups, too, looked to the Four Corners area for prospective homes. Perhaps the most interesting of these was a colony of Hungarian immigrants. Following a fast-talking and free-spending promoter named Mortz, the Hungarians arranged to buy much of the land in Paradox and took over a sawmill as well as an ailing reservoir company on the La Sal Mountains before things began to go wrong. As with so many frontier ventures, the Hungarian colony proved to be a failure. La Sal Forest historical files include the following account of its fortunes:

> In 1918 they [a group of Colorado ranchers who had undertaken to develop the Buckeye Reservoir and Paradox Valley] sold to a Hungarian outfit managed by a Mr. Mortz, who brought in 150 to 200 Hungarians to colonize Paradox Valley. They bought the sawmill at Buckeye. They called Paradox, Titanic. The leader of the outfit was a grafter, he met P. W. Marsh [one of the Gunnison ranchers] on a train and bought Paradox interests from him and borrowed money from him to finance it. He borrowed money all over the country that was never repaid, Couraud's lost $500.00 in lumber to them and John Pace bought $2000.00 worth of hay which he never received. After three months Mortz disappeared by way of Moab where he cashed several checks on his way out. The Hungarian settlers were pretty much worked up about it but could never locate their former leader. The county finally financed the moving of the colony out of the country. The Buckeye and Paradox investments then went into receivership. . . .[21]

19.   Ibid., December 1912.
20.   *Grand Valley Times*, 16 June 1916.
21.   "Historical Information, La Sal National Forest," pp. 133-34.

Homesteaders were often credulous by nature and easily influenced by stories of the new farming El Dorado. And on the La Sal Forest, at least, many appear to have had little plan of operation beyond the most vague general guidelines. Indeed, some had little except their faith. This trusting quality quite naturally extended to their fellowmen—sometimes without justification. One wonders, for example, what led a group of Mexican homesteaders to Allen Canyon, an area isolated from society. A clearer case of segregation can hardly be imagined. Perhaps their exile was self-imposed. Perhaps elements of geographic determinism featured in it, as most of the homesteading Mexicans herded sheep for San Juan stockmen. A claim situated far into the Forest may well have placed them nearer their work and have been convenient from this standpoint. But it is difficult to escape the conclusion that the Mexican entrymen had been encouraged by dominating groups to take up their homesteads in virtual isolation.

No one was more enthusiastic about the influx of homesteaders than Forest Supervisor Henry Bergh. Using the "Cliff Dwellers' Echo" as his platform, he let his enthusiasm—which was always considerable—run at full speed. In the August, 1912, issue, he reported that the Dalton brothers had improved their claims, building fences and cabins; W. O. Knight had disposed of his Moab fruit farm to take up an entry; Brigham Spencer and his son, George, were busy

Cabin at Miner's Basin.

on their claims near Monticello with good crops to show for their first year's effort; George A. Stewart, mail contractor on the Monticello to Indian Creek post run, had taken up eighty acres on Spring Creek; and Mexicans at Allen Canyon, including Suzano Manzanares, Juan Trujillo, Gaspar Durand, and Abelardo Vijil, continued their homesteading. Requests for homesteads poured in, many asking for land on the "very tops of our mountains; no, not on Mt. Peale, but . . . at elevations of from 7,000 to 10,000 feet."[22] Bergh's buoyant mood pervaded even his official reports. In his Silvical Report for 1911, he expressed enthusiasm over the role the Forest would play as a basic natural resource when the country filled up. Southeastern Utah would soon, he predicted, "have thousands settle in it." Ignoring the realities of limited water supplies, he optimistically calculated land potential,

> Moab valley is estimated at 65,000 acres of arable land or 101 square miles; Castle Valley, 20,000 acres, 31 square miles; Paradox, 18,000 acres, 28 square miles; Coyote, 30,000 acres, 47 square miles including the dry farm land possibilities—the latter might be estimated at ⅓ of the total. Monticello 30,000 acres, 47 square miles of irrigable land and a quarter million acres or 1953 square miles of dry farm land. . . .[23]

One reason for Bergh's "homestead fever" was that as forest supervisor he surveyed sites, processed applications, and in other ways participated in the homesteading process. While southeastern Utah's homestead story was much broader than the La Sal Forest, the Forest was involved to a significant extent as scores and perhaps hundreds of entrymen took out mountain claims under the Forest Homestead Act, or the so-called Act of June 11, 1906. Under this law, forest officers assumed many of the duties ordinarily handled by the land offices. Entries were filed through the forest office, which also conducted surveys to determine legal location and made on-site examinations to determine the validity of the agricultural claims and sufficiency of improvements. In cases where hearings were required, forest representatives also supported reports and recommendations with testimony.

The earliest of the forest homesteaders were squatters whose date of entry extended back years and, in a few cases, decades prior to the Forest's establishment. Frederick I. Jones, an original Mormon settler whose Blue Mountain claim dated to 1888, is a good example. Running his place as a summer dairy, Jones had squatted on it until it came up for entry, at which time he filed under the provisions of the Act of June 11, 1906. One of the first official actions of John Riis as ranger on the new Monticello Forest was his examination of the Jones entry. With Riis's favorable recommendation, it was ac-

---

22. *Cliffdwellers' Echo*, August 1912.

23. Timber Management Folder, Manti-La Sal National Forest Historical Files.

cepted with no hearing and went on to be patented.[24] Another early squatter was Jones's eccentric neighbor, Louis Seyler. Acquiring interest in a rather substantial mining claim established in 1896 by George A. Jackson on the east slope of the Blue Mountains, Seyler had lived on the decaying premises year-round for twenty years when his patent was granted in 1917. While the entry was located at 9,000 feet elevation and obviously was more valuable for grazing purposes than for agriculture, examining officers accepted the obvious evidence that Seyler intended to make a home there as justification to recommend the place under a June 11 entry. One suspects that they also were influenced by admiration for the crusty old recluse. As one examiner pointed out, Seyler had been offered "good prices" for his claim but had emphatically turned them down. The examiner probably recognized the truth of the situation when he concluded his favorable report: "Claimant is rather eccentric and has become so attached to the place, that I doubt if he would be contented elsewhere."[25]

As suggested by the Jones and Seyler cases, the homesteaders who took out land within the La Sal National Forest were of widely varying backgrounds. Attention has been called previously to diverse national and ethnic groups involved in southeastern Utah's homestead movement. But mountain homesteading was predominantly a movement of individuals, and a potpourri of mankind participated. To be found were college men putting the theory of dry-farming to practical test, miners with a yen to settle down, wanderers who had reached the end of the trail, relatives of families already in the region, and others, including those seeking restoration of their health or escape from humanity in some forest fastness.

Most of them were alike in their poverty. This was manifest in numerous ways. First, their improvements were primitive—often in the most extreme sense of the term—with ditches, corrals, and fences frequently taking priority over houses. Yet, since a house was taken to be prime evidence of occupation, some sort of shack graced each forest homestead. Iowa Smith was a rare homesteader who lived in the comfort of his three-room log and frame house at the head of Pinhook Valley. Walter I. Smith also could boast of luxury, having a house twenty-two feet by thirty-six feet in dimension with three rooms and two porches. More characteristic was Juan R. Martinez, who for six months of the year lived with his wife and six children in a ten-foot by twelve-foot log cabin and a shed built of posts and willows, or Richard T. Swain, whose dwelling consisted of a fourteen-foot square tar paper shack and an adjacent dugout.

Few of the June 11 entrymen lived on their mountain homesteads year-round. As often the case in homesteading circles, residence was

24. F. I. Jones, Homestead Entry 15009, U-Adjustment Folder, Denver Records Center.

25. Louis Seyler, Homestead Entry 91359, U-Adjustment Folder.

for some a matter of sham—a pretense made only to prove up on their claims. Such individuals lived in town or elsewhere, and by camping now and then at their entry, sought to give the appearance of meeting the demands of the law. Others spent summer months on the mountain claim, retiring to lower elevations for sake of comfort and schooling in the winter. For many, living elsewhere was an economic necessity, and most entrymen worked outside in one capacity or another to support their homesteads. Albert Sidney Johnson, for example, had no family to require an annual exodus to school, but he worked winters regularly at Sunnyside in Carbon County to "make money to finance the development of his claim."[26] Along with mining and freighting, homesteaders turned to construction, ranch work, the Forest Service, school teaching, and various commercial ventures to maintain life. Almost none of them supported themselves entirely on their entry, although a few who had livestock came near being independent.

Among La Sal Forest homesteaders were a few pathetic figures. There were, for example, several widows, some of whom struggled to keep large families together. One or two claimants with nothing more to call their own than a few years of lingering life took refuge in this mountain clime in futile quest for restoration of their health.

While there was undoubtedly some prospect of ultimate reward— more in the hope of escalating land values than in the development of a home—the overall picture of homesteading on the La Sal is one of inconvenience and insecurity. By modern standards, mountain homesteading resulted in a squalid and unattractive life.

But for all the harshness of life on forest claims, the homesteader generally has enjoyed a special place in the heart of America. Somehow he has epitomized our great national dreams. The westward thrust of his quest for land has been at the forefront of the American mainstream. His concern for free land and opportunity has been among the most romantic and the least threatening expressions of a national obsession to get ahead. The homesteader also has been widely regarded, somewhat erroneously, as the arch-individualist, the prototype of America standing on its own feet. In recognizing that the homesteader's image is inextricably intertwined with many of our most potent values, we see him in yet another of his characteristics—as the underdog. He was, in short, the "little guy," totally without the threat of size and power, busily involved in a business intimately related to our national emotions. As such, his claim on America's sympathy has been secure and, as a phenomenon of history, remains so. Congress gladly legislated for him, developing first positive laws to guide his approach to the land and, as the era of our concern dawned, passed protective provisions hopefully designed to limit the shocking disparity between the fond myths and the

26. A. S. Johnson, Homestead Entry 031011, U-Adjustment Folder.

money-grubbing realities of our utilization of the nation's landed birthright.

It was, of course, in this latter connection that the National Forest system was created. Its affinity for the little man and its hope that it could place its trust in his wise use of natural resources, as well as its recognition that he constituted minimal threats to Forest Service regulations, were apparent in the sympathy of its policy and conduct toward homesteaders and various other small entrymen who filed on forest lands. As noted heretofore, service-wide and district directives emphasized the return of agricultural lands to an available status. While this may have been an attempt to curry local favor, it was also a genuine expression of sympathy for, and faith in the land-seeking little men of America. This attitude was manifested at the La Sal Forest level in numerous ways. There was, for example, a

Gatepost and cedar pole shed at Summit Spring.

dramatic difference in the spirit in which Forest officers approached the Lemuel Redds and the Harold Carlisles and the spirit in which they dealt with the underdogs. For the former, there was fear and presumption of wrongdoing; for the latter, there was sympathy and cooperation. While this proposition is oversimplified and ignores the fact that controls were placed upon both classes, it nevertheless describes a state of mind that influenced policy and conduct. Where June 11 entrymen were involved, locating surveyors often classified land as agricultural that had only the vaguest prospects of being farmed successfully. Forest examiners overlooked disqualifying features in homesteads if good faith were presumed. Grazing policy, related as it was to a base of land and crop production, favored the homesteader and other small users.[27]

While Forest sympathy for the little man knew few bounds, suspected bad faith was not tolerated even among individual homesteaders—especially if bad faith appeared to serve the interest of one of the large outfits. Files dealing with Mexican homesteaders reveal uniform sympathy for them except in those cases where the Mexican entryman was suspected of being the "dummy" for his boss. A situation in which such suspicion featured was that of Fernin R. Lopez. In 1919 he filed on a June 11 claim lying on the Forest boundary adjacent to the Old La Sal ranch of the La Sal Livestock Company, successor to Cunningham and Carpenter and managed by Charles Redd, son of Lemuel Redd. Lopez was a foreman and trusted employee of the company. The property in question had been filed on previously by two employees of the La Sal Livestock Company, lay under its general fence, and was farmed as part of its operation. Forest examiners sought and found further evidence indicating that Lopez had been "placed upon this claim in order to add this choice bit of agricultural land to the Old La Sal Ranch."[28] The Forest lost its case—possibly because of the restraint with which the case was prosecuted—but there was no sympathy for Mr. Lopez. The distinction in attitude toward large users and homesteaders is clearly apparent.

The irritation of Ranger John Riis at what he took to be a conspiracy between James Hicks and the Verdure Livestock Company to evade Forest regulations by manipulation of one June 11 entry is another case in point:

> . . . [I] urgently recommend that if it be not too late, the delivery of this patent be protested and an effort made to have it cancelled. This land is purely Forest land, not fit for cultivation and it is not the claimant's intention to establish a home upon it. He is at present in the employ of the Verdure Livestock Company, which concern has caused us considerable trouble by infractions of the grazing regulations, tho

---

27. I have elaborated on this theme in "Small Holding Land Patterns in Utah and the Problem of Forest Watershed Management," *Forest History* 17 (1973): 4-13.

28. Fernin R. Lopez, Homestead Entry 023661, U-Adjustment Folder.

up to the present date we have been unable to secure such positive proof as would enable us to prefer charges against them with any chance of success. This latter statement may not bear directly upon the claimant's case, but the granting of patent will have only one result i.e. the Verdure Live Stock Co. will rent the land from the claimant for grazing purposes and as it is not fenced, it will complicate matters and seriously interfere with our effort to secure an accurate count on their cattle, which we have not been able to do so far.[29]

Other Claims to Forest Lands

In contrast to the general sympathy for homesteaders, La Sal Forest officers were sometimes prone to regard the claims of big users to be unwarranted land grabs. This becomes apparent in a few private claims that were established on the Forest under provisions other than the homestead laws. Occasionally, small tracts were entered as lieu selections for land claims in other localities. One notable case of this kind involved Harold Carlisle and W. E. Gordon. As successors to F. A. Hyde and Company, they procured a tract of Forest land northwest of Monticello in a lieu selection for base lands in California. Suspecting that their claim to the California base lands was questionable, Supervisor Bergh investigated the Carlisle-Gordon claim from the standpoint of its local merits. He discovered that no improvements predated August 31, 1900, and that one Elijah Wilson had claimed it under squatters' rights at that time. Wilson had built a cabin and constructed a ditch, hoping to hold the claim with "a view of making a home" as soon as the land was surveyed. Before the survey was made, Carlisle and Gordon ran Wilson off; later his house was burned. The land was surveyed in 1902, whereupon J. H. Bankhead endeavored to establish a claim, but, like Wilson, soon succumbed to threats from Carlisle and Gordon. Having, as Bergh put it, become "all supreme in the matter," Carlisle and Gordon ran a herd of bucks on it in 1910 which were a nuisance to Forest management, and in 1911 the cattlemen fenced it and rented part of it for thirty dollars. While there was no reason why bona fide lieu selections could not stand, this one failed when it was determined that claims to the California lands upon which the selection was based were fraudulent.[30]

Another law that was put to occasional use was the Desert Entry Act of 1877. In the years after the establishment of the Forest, its usefulness appears to have been superseded by the Forest Homestead Act, but a substantial number of early claims were filed under its provisions. Perhaps the most important of these were filed by Edmund Carlisle and his employees during the late 1880s when the Carlisle Ranch was threatened by the Mormon village at Monticello.

A later instance of the Desert Act's use on Forest lands became a celebrated case in the annals of La Sal Forest claims adjustment.

---

29.   John Hicks, Homestead Entry 1500, U-Adjustment Folder.
30.   F. A. Hyde, Lieu Selection 3347, U-Adjustment Folder.

Involving thousands of hours of time and a major joint effort on the part of the Forest and district offices, this contest revolved around two desert claims filed at Mormon Pasture on the North Elks in 1903 and 1904 by David L. Goudelock, onetime county commissioner and largest investor in the Indian Creek Cattle Company, and his sister, Ella Kingsland. The site of Mormon Pasture had first come to vision in 1887, when F. A. Hammond, president of San Juan Stake, had chosen it as a prospective town, and two brothers, Joshua and

Homesteader planting grain near Monticello.

Alma Stevens, were sent out as the vanguard of a colonizing group that was to have consisted of at least four other Mormon families. For some reason, the larger effort fell through, but the Stevens brothers established a claim and, according to Alma's account, plowed about ten acres, developed water to irrigate the land, erected a cabin, and otherwise improved it. In October of the same year, a "stock company" was organized consisting of the two Stevens brothers, Brigham Young, Jr., and others. Bringing in about 600 head of cattle that fall, this company appears to have been among the first to run cattle on the North Elks, and to winter on ranges extending north and west to the Colorado River. In addition to the beef operation, the company developed a large summer dairy. For years thereafter, Mormon Pasture was marked by cheese presses and other dairying equipment that were scattered about the premises. In 1892 the Stevens brothers rented the ranch and cattle to Platte D. Lyman, who ran the operation until he was called on a mission for the Latter-day Saints Church in 1897. In the next year or so, one James Brewster established claim to the place. He in turn sold to Melvin Turner in 1901, who traded his claim to Goudelock in 1903. Moving to secure the claim thus acquired, the latter entered a desert claim on one piece in 1903 and had his sister take out a claim on a second site the following year. In both cases they took oath that they had made improvements that many evidences indicate should be attributed to earlier settlers. Prior to making final proof, it was necessary for Goudelock to file upon water rights, a process causing several years delay before patent could be conveyed.

The delay over water rights brought the Forest Service into the picture. Challenging the good faith of Goudelock's desert entry, as well as his contention that the land was desert in character, the Forest spent several years gathering evidence to support its position. Every Forest officer who had ever been at Mormon Pasture made depositions and otherwise contributed to the Forest's case. Correspondence and statements were collected from earlier claimants, and water and soil checks were made. But for all its effort, the Forest lost the case. Upheld in hearings at Salt Lake City, its protests were finally rejected when Goudelock appealed the case to the secretary of agriculture.[31]

Problems with the claims of big users, sympathy for homesteaders, and, indeed, the entire business of claims adjustment and definition of boundaries were part of the larger process of establishing the La Sal National Forest in the community of southeastern Utah. Along with its primary function of fixing the physical context of the Forest, this process helped delineate many of the human relationships in a society that was just emerging from its frontier status. Because of its

31. David L. Goudelock and Gertrude Goudelock, Deseret Land Entry, U-Adjustment Folder.

connection with a bureaucratic organization, the power enjoyed by the Forest was great. Although its officers functioned with restraint, and at times manifested most of the fallibilities of human nature, the impression of massive power persists. On the other hand, Forest officers were concerned with public opinion and were, in some degree, limited by it in their use of power. They also adhered to the rules and on occasion accepted defeat quietly.

It may be concluded that in fulfilling the district office's 1909 injunction "to prove by reports and maps . . . the character of the land and its ownership," the La Sal Forest had made more than a passing contribution to the growth of southeastern Utah.[32]

32. *See* Instructions for Examination and Report on Additions to and Eliminations from National Forests, 3 June 1909, Proclamation and Boundary Folder.

Chapter IX

Grazing and Range Management

On May 8, 1906, Orrin C. Snow was advised by the Washington office that all stockmen regularly ranging on the La Sal Mountains would be authorized to graze their stock on the new forest reserve without permits or fees during the 1906 season. In December, 6,100 cattle and horses and 21,000 sheep were authorized for 1907 at respective fees of twenty cents and eight cents per animal. Like their La Sal counterparts, stockmen on the Monticello Reserve were granted a grace period during the grazing season of 1907, at which time a blanket permit was issued covering all the stock running on the mountain.

By these acts, southeastern Utah's biggest business was gently initiated to the supervision of the Forest Service. Although protection of mountain watersheds lay at the root of the Forest Service's presence, it was in the control of livestock that this concern and most other activities of the La Sal Forest were most vividly reflected. More often than not, the problems of watersheds—or for that matter of transportation or even of mining and timber—were related to the predominance of livestock. The livestock industry was the main business of people in southeastern Utah and neighboring portions of Colorado, and livestock became the main business of the La Sal Forest.

Small Permits: Pattern for Utah

As the processes of range management became routine in the years after 1906, it became apparent that the La Sal Forest was unique in Utah, not so much in its preoccupation with livestock as in the size of the livestock enterprises which made up its permits. Unlike Utah generally, the La Sal had few permittees and these owned relatively large numbers of livestock.

From the earliest times, most other Utah forests were intensively used by extraordinarily large numbers of permittees with small average permits. On no forest was this phenomenon more apparent than on the Manti, where farm villages dotted both the west and east fronts of the Wasatch Plateau, and virtually every farmer ran a few cattle or sheep on the forest. The story is told that A. W. Jensen, first Manti supervisor, while on temporary assignment to the Washington office, continually objected to range management proposals as working injustice upon the great number of small grazers who used the Manti. After repeated objections, one of the Washington officers is said to have turned to Jensen and expostulated: "The Manti be damned, we'll do it anyway."[1]

As the years passed, there was a gradual trend toward fewer permittees and larger average forest permits, but Utah retained its reputation as the state of small users. In 1918, when livestock numbers were near their World War I peak, all Utah forests supported approximately 200,000 head of cattle and 802,000 head of sheep. Permits had been issued to 7,592 separate cattle grazers and to 1,406 sheepmen, making average operations of 24 head for cattle and 570 head for sheep. In 1939, by which time the Grazing Service (forerunner to the Bureau of Land Management) was issuing permits for rights on the public domain, a total of 202,777 cattle and horses and 2,618,918 sheep were permitted on Utah public lands, including the forests. By contrast to the forest count of 1918, stock numbers were up sharply and users had dropped modestly to 5,178, making for a considerably larger average unit. But Utah was still the obvious leader nationally in total number of users. The disparity with other western grazing states was dramatic. Arizona, for example, with public lands similar in extent and character, had no more than 603 or scarcely over 10 per cent as many licensees.[2] In Utah, some 2,368 forest permits, or 59.1 per cent of the total, were issued to owners of from one to twenty head of cattle in 1939. Only two permits were issued to owners of 601 to 1,000 cattle, and only one to an owner of 1,000 or more. The latter permit was to a La Sal Forest user and authorized upwards of 7,000 head.[3]

As A. W. Jensen had learned in Washington, D. C., Utah's dilemma complicated range management. Overgrazing persisted with all its related problems. Numbers alone made heavy demands upon forest administrators. C. E. Racheford, grazing inspector, pointed out

1.   Interview with J. W. Humphrey, Provo, Utah, 26 March 1971. For a more complete treatment of small permits and the problem they made for Utah, *see* Charles S. Peterson, "Small Holding Land Patterns in Utah."

2.   District Forester to Supervisors, 7 March 1918, G-Supervision Folder, Manti-La Sal National Forest Historical Files; and C. C. Anderson, "History of Grazing'" (original, Utah State University; copy, Utah State Historical Society), p. 9.

3.   Anderson, p. 17.

A La Sal Forest grazing allotment. U.S. Forest Service photo.

in a 1921 report that administrative difficulties could be appreciated when one realized "that the number of permittees on" at least one Utah forest "was pretty near equal to the total number of permittees on some of the other districts (forest regions)." With little grasp of the historical complexities out of which the situation sprang, Racheford laid the primary blame for Utah's dilemma upon Forest policy and conduct. Local officers were, he thought, too close to both the range and its users to apply necessary controls. Knowing, and too often sharing the problems faced by these struggling small users, and having memory of a time when ranges had been misused even more blatantly, local officers saw progress where little existed. But in Racheford's eyes, the gravest problem lay in the long-standing Forest Service policy of fostering the little man in agriculture:

> In our enthusiasm and earnest desire to help build communities and to foster agricultural development, we have encouraged every land owner in these valleys who has a few head of stock to put them on the National Forest. I think we have really gone so far as to say that the grazing of a few head of stock on the Forest is indispensable to the proper operation of the average farm in these communities. As a result of this propaganda and our desire to distribute our grazing privileges to the greatest number of people, we have probably gone to the extreme. We now have the distribution carried to a point where it is doubtful in my mind if the small number of stock grazed by the average permittee is of any real value to him.

Comparing the Utah forests with neighboring Idaho, where forest range conditions were much better, Racheford continued:

> I know the contention is held that the demand for range on the Utah Forests . . . is far more intensive than the demand on the Idaho Forests, and yet when you stop to consider that the Targhee, especially, is surrounded pretty much by intensive agriculture, that it has many intermittent valleys suitable only to the production of livestock, this contention seems to fall of its own weight. My belief is that the demand in Utah . . . has been encouraged and fostered, and that the demand in the Idaho Forests has been accepted as it is without any serious attempt to encourage or increase it.[4]

According to the Racheford analysis, livestock production in Utah was not a business but simply incidental to the main farming operations. Given these circumstances, the average user had little interest in the range and not only was unwilling to lay out much money in caring for his stock, but lost little if the range continued to deteriorate. Not surprisingly, transfers were frequent, with one forest allowing 232 permit transfers in two years. Inconsequential in terms of the number of livestock involved, these nevertheless demanded extensive accounting and administrative effort. Reductions in number or other range management measures were particularly susceptible to charges of oppressive action when invoked against small impoverished users.

Barn at Baker Ranger Station, with Blue Mountains' Horse Head visible in center background. U.S. Forest Service photo.

4. Memo to the Forester, 12 November 1921, G-Supervision, Region IV Papers, National Archives.

Utah senators and congressmen were quick in springing to their defense. Racheford thought the Mormon Church complicated the problem both directly and indirectly. Most Utah users were Mormon in background and, prompted by a long tradition of internal cohesiveness, "hung together," minimizing the success of what may be termed the Forest Service policy of regulation through a strategy of "divide and rule." Furthermore, the Church itself was not above asserting its influence in behalf of the grazing privileges of individual members. Thus, to at least one astute forest officer, the multiplicity of small permittees was Utah's greatest grazing problem.[5]

Large Permits: Pattern for the La Sal

As part of this state-wide picture, the large grazing permits and small number of users on the La Sal Forest stood out sharply. It is of special significance that for years the largest single preference issued in the United States is said to have been to the Scorup-Somerville outfit. During the period between 1910 and 1940, the La Sal never had more than 226 cattle permittees and 37 sheep grazers. During these same years, as few as 61 cattle and 15 sheep permits were issued at one time or another. With numbers permitted averaging at least as low as twenty four cattle and 500 sheep on all Utah forests, and dropping to fourteen cattle and 200 sheep on the Manti, La Sal Forest averages stand in contrast, never dropping below 110 for cattle and about 1,000 for sheep. Conversely, the average permit on the La Sal some years ran as high as 260 cattle and 2,650 sheep. In this connection, comparative figures from random years for the La Sal and the Manti Forests are instructive of the position occupied by the former, (shown in Figure 1).

Also useful in visualizing the relative position of the La Sal are figures from 1933 showing permit averages on Utah forests,[6] (shown in Figure 2).

But the story is only partially told by statistics comparing the La Sal Forest with other Utah forests. Within the five districts of the Forest itself there was much variation. Districts 1 and 2, which encompassed the La Sal Mountains, served proportionately more users who ran smaller numbers of livestock. The three Blue-Elk mountains districts served fewer users, including such large outfits as those of Lemuel H. Redd, the Indian Creek Cattle Company, and Scorup-Somerville.[7] Figures 3 and 4, giving permit data from 1912, will point up internal use patterns:[8]

---

5. Ibid.
6. Statistics were taken from C. C. Anderson's Miscellaneous Notes. They were originally compiled by K. L. Stewart of the Regional Forest Office in Ogden and used in writing Anderson's "History of Grazing."
7. While each of the above had La Sal Mountain interests, their major operations centered on the South Division.
8. *Cliffdwellers' Echo*, April 1912.

Figure 1

COMPARATIVE GRAZING DATA FOR THE LA SAL AND MANTI FORESTS

| YEAR | NUMBER PERMITTED | | | | NUMBER OF PERMITS | | | | PERMIT AVERAGES | | | |
| | CATTLE | | SHEEP | | CATTLE | | SHEEP | | CATTLE | | SHEEP | |
	*LS	M	LS	M	LS	M	LS	M	LS	M	LS	M
1909	15,770	19,764	61,509	191,984	157	1,031	25	583	100	19	2,460	329
1915	25,856	25,321	35,418	146,537	169	1,235	19	510	153	20	1,863	287
1920	23,560	21,987	37,987	128,209	150	1,600	37	644	157	14	1,026	199
1924	16,935	20,599	24,682	130,338	130	1,382	17	670	130	15	1,452	195
1929	13,430	15,945	40,970	139,412	64	933	36	826	209	17	1,138	170

*La Sal (LS) and Manti (M)

Figure 2

PERMIT AVERAGES

FOREST	YEAR	CATTLE	SHEEP
Ashley	1933	36	757
Cache	1933	22	732
Dixie	1933	23	440
Fishlake	1933	29	265
La Sal	1933	178	1,180
Manti	1933	17	184
Powell	1933	33	521
Uinta	1933	38	539
Wasatch	1933	20	780

Figure 3

CATTLE PERMIT DATA
La Sal Forest 1912

	Permittees	Cattle Permitted	Permit Averages
Dist. 1	48	3,191	64
Dist. 2	38	3,340	88
Dist. 3	21	3,022	151
Dist. 4	6	2,516	419
Dist. 5	53	6,164	117

Figure 4

SHEEP PERMIT DATA
La Sal Forest 1912

Permittees	Sheep Permitted	Permit Averages
9	5,995	666
5	5,325	1,065
2	10,773	5,385
5	7,038	1,408
9	12,122	1,335

Even the smallest of these far exceeds the average figures for Utah generally, and the two sheep permits in District 3 and the six cattle permits in District 4 emphasize the unique situation on the La Sal Forest.

The question may well be asked, why this dramatic break with the broad pattern of the state? The answer lies in large part in the unique natural and historical situations from which the La Sal Forest's grazing patterns emerged, and may be reduced to three inter-related factors. First, the country's terrain—its topography and the relationship of desert ranges for winter use and mountain pastures for summer grazing—lent itself to large operations. Second, the custom of sizable operations had been fixed on the country by the period of competition between ranch kings and the village-based livestock pools employed by the Mormons to enable them to contend with such giants of the range as the Carlisles or the L C Company. During the years of this competition, the strategy of range saturation adopted by the major participants tended to keep new small operators from coming in. It crowded out others, as evidenced in an earlier reference to the progressive (or more properly retrogressive) shifts of the Silvey family and other small cow outfits, to poorer and peripheral ranges as competition intensified.[9] Finally, southeastern Utah's population remained low, and the fragmentation of farmland, water, and range rights that attended population buildup elsewhere in Utah had not yet occurred when the La Sal Forest was established. Two primary factors explained this phenomenon. In the first place, the characteristic farm village approach of the Mormons had not succeeded. Consequently there was no great influx by voluntary immigration or mission calls. Furthermore, the late date at which the area was settled worked against its being overfilled by second and third generations wanting a stake in the family inheritance. Therefore, few people lived in the country to lay claim upon grazing preferences when the Forest was created, and those already there had well-established larger operations. Rather than the La Sal Forest contributing to fragmentation of permits, as suggested by C. E. Racheford, its management of grazing tended to limit permittee numbers at or below the pre-Forest use level. Indeed, if the La Sal Forest is used as the exceptional case by which the validity of Racheford's generalization is checked, it indicates that preexisting natural and social factors, rather than Forest Service policy, predominated in setting the small permit pattern on the one hand and the large user on the other.

Problems of Size

The Racheford report also expressed the strong opinion that increased size of operation would do much to facilitate range management and to alleviate problems of overgrazing on Utah forests. Experience on the La Sal Forest did not bear this out. Like Utah forests elsewhere, the La Sal was critically overgrazed and seriously eroded. Range users were slow to adopt managerial practices and vigorous in their resistance to boundary changes, reduction in numbers, and escalating fees. During the stormy first years, forest officers were agreed that the La Sal Forest was among the hardest in District IV to manage. A reason repeatedly advanced to explain this was the refusal of large outfits to comply with regulations. In the years before 1920, virtually every large user was charged with malpractice and deceit. As observed in an earlier chapter, the Indian Creek Cattle Company, Lemuel H. Redd, Carlisle and Gordon, and other large users opposed boundary changes and employed various tactics to hold or to claim ranges regarded by Forest administrators as more properly belonging to other parties.[10]

Some large users were also quick to employ various dodges to avoid the letter of the law with reference to permit numbers. Ran-

9. Silvey, *Northern San Juan County*, p. 36, and "When San Juan County Was Given to the Southern Ute Indians."
10. See pp. 153-55.

ger John Riis charged that the "large men" of his district engaged in "endless schemes" calculated to increase their permits by distributing stock among their families and to parties who were in their debt or employ.[11] Riis had almost no understanding of Mormon cooperativeness and may have taken some of its practices to be cases of large users manipulating their fellowmen for personal gain. Yet, there is no doubt that certain individuals who regarded themselves as scrupulously honest found no inconsistency in fictitious arrangements which had the effect of negating the essence of permit regulation. Lemuel H. Redd was included in this class. Running, according to some accounts, as many as 30,000 sheep and 2,000 cattle during the first decade of this century, Redd was hard hit by the first permits, which allowed no more than twice this number of sheep to all permittees. Redd's matter-of-fact manipulation of Forest regulations is attested in a recent biography by a son who wrote:

> In 1909 Mr. John Riis, Supervisor of the La Sal National Forest, sternly advised Father that he was considerably over the limit for which one man could hold permits, stating that 6,000 head were the maximum and he had run 10,788 head the previous year and it was reported that he had purchased the Decker sheep, totaling 1,581 head. They could not run on the forest if this was the case. This matter was resolved by running part of Father's sheep in the names of his sons.[12]

Others appear to have made even less pretense of abiding by permit regulations. The Southeastern Utah Stockgrowers' Association reported in 1909 that 2,000 unpermitted cattle ran on the North Division. But on the whole, North Division users were said to be more inclined to cooperation on the permit question than their South Division counterparts. As it worked out, the practice was evidently to accept the permits but refuse to make the adaptations in management required by them. Little users may well have been as guilty of this sort of fraud as were the large users, but it was the latter who attracted the attention of Forest officers. Suggestive of the problem's scope was John Riis's report that the assessor of San Juan County had informed him

> . . . that several parties on the south division are taxed as much as 50% more than they apply for on their grazing permits and it is not possible that they range the cattle in the summer on other range than the Forest. The Verdure Livestock Company, for instance, holds a permit for 410 head of cattle, is taxed for 800 head and recently considered an offer to sell their cattle on the range at 1800 head. This is of course an exceptionally large outfit, but the same condition prevails among all the grazers on the south division to a more or less degree.[13]

11. To the District Forester, 5 April 1909, G-Supervision Folder, Manti-La Sal National Forest Historical Files.

12. Redd, p. 141.

13. G-Supervision Folder, 5 April 1909.

For years, the Indian Creek Cattle Company appears to have been virtually beyond the control of permit regulations in the number of stock it ran on Dark Canyon, North Cottonwood, and Indian Creek drainages. It is in the context of Forest attempts to curtail the company's misuse of its preference that the boundary disputes of the Bergh era and the protracted Mormon Pasture case are to be understood.[14] Charges varied as to the extent of Indian Creek violations. Since these charges appear at various times, they may all have been more or less accurate. Homer Fenn of the district office thought that something like 2,000 unpermitted Indian Creek cattle ran regularly on the Forest. Other reports placed excess numbers at figures varying upwards from 1,500 head. A Simon Oliver made the most drastic charge, claiming that the Indian Creek Company owned no fewer than 10,000 cattle and that all of them ranged on the Forest under permits authorizing only 2,000 head. In response to Oliver's information, E. A. Sherman, district forester, admitted that the La Sal Forest was badly overgrazed and stated further that "overgrazing is not attributed to the number of permitted stock but to the drift of unpermitted stock of the same owners."[15] Whatever the reality of the numbers the Indian Creek Cattle Company ran on the Forest, there is evidence that it continued to ignore permit restrictions until 1918, when the Scorup brothers bought the entire operation. A few years later, Forest Supervisor Orange Olson traversed the former Indian Creek allotments. To his chagrin, he found it was still impossible to control the number of cattle entering the Forest in those quarters, but he did report conformity between permits and the actual number run. "It is believed," he wrote, "that at least 1,500 less cattle now occupy the range than a few years back. We are also quite certain that the number actually owned and the number (4,185) permitted are quite the same."[16] As it proved, it was a fleeting success.

Opposition to Controls

Throughout the correspondence of early Forest officers ran the expressed hope that users would recognize their own self-interest in permit regulations and reduce the numbers of their stock to bring the reality of grazing more into accord with the theory of the permit. In this desire they were long frustrated, and even the fact that they hoped for self-discipline indicates a lack of comprehension of the position and problems of the stockmen. The latter, big and little alike, were sure they understood the range business better than the Forest Service did. Most appear to have recognized that forage conditions had changed radically since the coming of the whites. Some, including J. A. Scorup, thought that the growth of brush and other browse

---

14. See pp. 153-55 and 166-67.
15. L. F. Kneipp to E. A. Sherman, 25 July 1912 and Sherman to Kneipp, 31 July 1912, G-Supervision Folder, Region IV Papers.
16. Memo on Grazing, 1924, Proclamation and Boundary Folder.

plants where grass had once been had resulted in added carrying capacity. As late as the 1930s others were determined that no change in capacity had taken place, or if it had, that it was of relatively recent origin. The majority, however, conceded that the capacity of the range

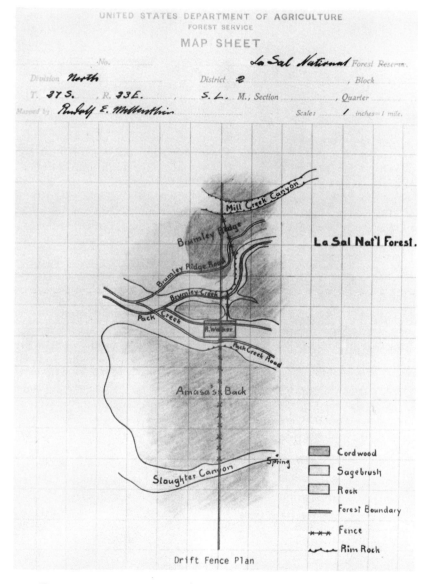

Range management map sheet of Mill Creek-Pack Creek area.

was down, and that weeds and other less nutritious plants had replaced grass. On the other hand, stockmen defensively insisted that deterioration was the result of adverse weather conditions rather than overstocking. There was little agreement among them as to when the deterioration occurred. J. A. Scorup laid depleted ranges to an extended period of drouth beginning in 1892 and ending in 1897. According to Scorup's memory, this period was followed by a cycle of good years ending during World War I after which another long drouth period set in.[17] Others thought the original drouth began in 1895 and extended to 1903. One Moab man was convinced that both drouth and range depletion were of recent origin, beginning only in the mid-twenties.

An additional problem stockmen faced as Forest permits were applied grew from the fact that in the early years, at least, there was genuine question as to how many cattle they actually owned. Open range conditions rarely provided opportunity for a controlled count, and most operators, especially the big outfits that ran in the rough country south and west of Elk Ridge, got along with approximations. What Forest officers sometimes took to be lack of cooperation was in reality little more than a reflection of casual managerial patterns. In 1910 Moab cattlemen admitted that some 2,000 head of unpermitted cattle had ranged on the North Division the previous season. But, as they explained, to charge them with lack of cooperation was "hardly correct."

> These unpermitted cattle have drifted onto the forest from the winter range. Their owners do not know exactly the number of cattle they have. No general count of the cattle has been made for years and the stockmen cannot without a count estimate within 20% of the actual number of range cattle that they have.[18]

The essential truth of their position was recognized by Works Progress Administration researchers in the 1940s as they collected data for a history of grazing in Utah that was never published. After hundreds of interviews with aging cowboys, the effort to fix cattle numbers at the turn of the century was dropped because "it is asking a lot to demand that a man tell you how many cattle he thinks his old boss or neighbor had when in the first place the owner didn't know himself, and in the second place the man being interviewed realizes that his statements might get into print and bring on controversies."[19]

Running in country that is among the world's roughest and with ranges extending over hundreds of square miles, southeastern Utah's big stockmen may have been hard pressed to get definite counts even far into this century. More important in this context is that vagueness was useful in dealing with Forest Service permits.

17. "Historical Information, La Sal National Forest," p. 53.
18. *Grand Valley Times*, 28 January 1910.
19. Anderson, "History of Grazing," p. 24.

Cattle Counts

While it may have constituted no excuse for ignoring grazing regulations, there was yet another impelling reason that stockmen tended to overfill permits. This grew out of the natural balance between summer and winter range and the necessary custom of holding public domain by utilization. Despite the barrenness of the region's vast deserts, they had a greater carrying capacity than did its limited mountain acreage. During the days of the livestock frontier, this had resulted in cattle numbers seeking a level consistent with winter range capacity, thus it placed the summer range under great pressure. Forest Supervisor Henry Bergh talked with old-timers who told of cattle coming off the summer range in the years before 1900 so poor that they could not be driven, but as soon as autumn rain and snow allowed the animals to get out onto the desert they would pick up and even get fat.[20] While this was precisely the problem Forest permits sought to redress, it was one that placed cattlemen in a dilemma. The Forest was the only summer range available. Maintaining herds at the maximum capacity on winter ranges meant overfilling Forest permits as it had meant overgrazing in the years prior to the Forest's creation. On the other hand, reduction of numbers to comply with permits relieved the pressure on the winter ranges, which, under the public domain conditions then prevailing, was one of the few valid claims a stockman could assert. Since surplus feed attracted new grazers to challenge established stockmen, there was an understandable reluctance to make the reductions demanded by the permit system. For many years, stockmen appear to have solved the problem by ignoring the real intent of the permit.

Beginning as early as 1909, Forest Service personnel made some attempt to count stock onto the Forest. This was apparently an easy matter with sheep, and violation of sheep permits never became a major problem. But cattle were another matter. After an abortive attempt to have stockgrowers' associations assume the task of counting stock entering the Forest, efforts were made to conduct a midsummer roundup at which rangers joined cattlemen in making a full tabulation. Because it was necessary to ride at that time of year to brand and collect steers, which in pre-World War I years were often shipped to summer markets, stockmen agreed to this practice; for several years it enabled the Forest to keep fairly close tab on accessible allotments. With violations still uninhibited among the large users in remote areas, all pretense of counting was discontinued in 1914 when Will Humphrey removed permit restrictions entirely.[21]

Concurrent with his discontinuation of cattle counts, Humphrey launched an all-out program to build boundary fences, and to reintroduce the permit system when they were completed. Apparently,

---

20. "Historical Information, La Sal National Forest," p. 35.
21. Interview with J. W. Humphrey, Provo, Utah, 12 April 1971.

boundary fences enabled the Forest to establish full control on some allotments within a few years, but sanguine expectations that counting problems would yield to boundary adjustments, fence construction, or other developments were still not realized in 1940 on other parts of the Forest. Even Orange Olson's expectation that Scorup-Somerville would manage their stock to comply with Forest regulations was premature. It would appear that his judgment that Scorup-Somerville had brought the number of their cattle running on the Forest into line with permits was based on a tally of steers and calves marketed and branded by the company itself. This technique was the basis of number estimates during most of the 1920s; but when Forest officers learned that it was often no more than 80 per cent accurate, and, as the budget increased, it was supplanted by counting during the 1930's. Actual counts regularly revealed that Scorup-Somerville ran from 300 to 500 head in excess of their permits. Considering that the company's permits approached 7,000 head during this period, this was a far cry from the freewheeling overfilling of the Indian Creek Cattle Company. However, the problem continued to exist.[22]

Trespass Proceedings

Trespass proceedings do not appear to have been a very effective tool in controlling stock numbers. While there was ample violation, no trespass cases were brought until 1912. Failure to act during the early years may have been partially due to the forebearance of Forest officers, but it was also the result of confusion about the legal validity of regulations based on the secretary of agriculture's authority. In 1907, one precedent was established when a South Dakota judge found a man guilty of trespass for running unauthorized stock on the Black Hills National Forest and fined him $100 and costs. The following year, the U. S. Circuit Court of Appeals in San Francisco upheld a decision which had found that stockmen could not allow their cattle to drift onto a national forest, and that regardless of state fencing laws, national forests need not be fenced to prevent such drifting. In March of 1910, the Supreme Court held that trespassing on national forests did not constitute a criminal offense but was subject to civil prosecution.[23] Even fortified with such decisions, the La Sal Forest did not bring trespass charges until 1912, when Rudolph Mellenthin, in what was widely considered to be a personal vendetta, reported seven trespasses on the south slope of the La Sal Mountains. Thereafter, occasional charges were made, sometimes for failure to obtain trailing permits, sometimes for grazing or bedding on restricted watersheds, and sometimes for drifting from one al-

---

22. "Historical Information, La Sal National Forest," pp. 44-46.

23. *Grand Valley Times*, 27 September 1907, 28 February 1908, and 18 March 1910.

lotment to another. Usually it was the big users that were involved in the infractions.

Interestingly, trespass action appears not to have been utilized as a means of controlling the major problem of running stock in excess of permitted numbers. Evidence of overgrazing and hearsay established violations beyond doubt, but rangers had difficulty in getting definite proof. Occasionally people accused others of trespass but were almost never willing to testify in court. Frustrated by these attitudes, Supervisor John Riis lashed out at the Southeastern Utah Stockgrowers' Association in 1910, charging:

> We are greatly handicapped by the attitude of the stockmen in the past and their cooperation with us has been of little benefit to either party up to the present time. This has not been the fault of the local office, but is due entirely to the small stockman who will sit tight and keep his mouth shut while his neighbor grazes stock in trespass.

Roused by this indictment, the stockmen defended themselves:

> We believe that the small owners who have "sat tight" and failed to notify the supervisor of trespass, have done so because their knowledge of such trespass was necessarily based on an estimate and not positive count, and further because they felt that the ranger in charge of their several districts was bound to know as much about trespass as they did, and that it was his duty as an officer of the forest, rather than theirs, to report it.[24]

During the late 1920s and the 1930s, more cases of trespass were observed and reported. In 1928, six trespass cases were initiated, and in 1929 charges were brought against five different operators for trespass of twenty cattle and 2,120 sheep. This flurry of activity notwithstanding, the most obvious trespass violations—overfilling of permits by Scorup-Somerville and other big users—resulted in no legal proceedings; only internal adjustments were effected, usually authorization for excess numbers under temporary permits.[25]

Permit System

The basis of the entire forest grazing program was the permit system. As noted earlier, it was initiated in 1907 on the La Sal Forest Reserve and the following year on the Monticello. Stockmen qualified for grazing privileges by prior use of mountain ranges and by possession of property adjacent to the Forest Reserve. Homesteaders and other "little men" were catered to. Grazing preferences (privileges) appear to have been denied to all stockmen who might be termed transients or whose major base of business was elsewhere. Subsequently, additional stockmen were admitted into the system by purchase of livestock under permit or as "new beginners" who entered homesteads or otherwise acquired land dependent upon

24. Ibid., 28 January 1910.
25. "Historical Information, La Sal National Forest, " pp. 44-46.

the mountains. In explaining this formula, Gifford Pinchot placed the "little man" first.

> In grazing, as in everything else, the little man and the home owner came first. Small nearby owners who lived in or close to the Reserve, whose stock had regularly grazed on the Reserve range, and who were dependent upon its use, were given preference over all others. Next came all other regular occupants of the Reserve range, and last of all the owners of stock who had not regularly occupied the range.[26]

Preferences for beginners were taken from two primary sources. Service-wide policy often allowed permit authorizations in excess of the numbers actually run, thus providing a margin from which local officers could draw—should conditions warrant it—to fill new applications or to increase established permits that fell below a minimum known as the protective limit. The other method used to fill the applications of beginners was to impose reductions upon large permit holders. To facilitate this process, protective limits were established in 1909 and were evidently part of the permit formula throughout much of the period of study. Set first at 150 head for cattle, protective limits later were reduced to 100 head and perhaps even lower. When applications exceeded authorized numbers, cuts determined on a sliding scale were sometimes imposed on users running stock in excess of the protective limits.[27] Preferences thus gained were distributed to beginners and to stockmen whose numbers were below the protective limit. A 1909 article in the *Grand Valley Times* explained that applications for permits below the protective limit were granted in full. Grazing applications for 150 to 250 cattle were reduced on a basis ranging from 5 to 10 percent; those asking for 250 to 500 head, by 15 percent; applications for 500 head and more were reduced 20 percent.[28] Similar reductions of large permits in an effort to stabilize small units were imposed well into the 1930s.

In spite of policies favoring beginning and small users, the number of permits remained low on the La Sal Forest. In 1909, the first year for which statistics exist, 157 cattlemen and twenty-five sheepmen were allowed permits. Reflecting the general good times, wet years, the homesteading boom, and favorable Forest policy, cattle permits reached a high of 226 in 1914 from which they fell to a low of sixty-one in 1930. Sheep permits remained remarkably stable, never falling below fifteen, and never rising above thirty-seven, between 1909 and 1939. Figure 5 portrays the stability of sheep permittees and fluctuation in cattle permittees.[29]

Turnover in permits was substantial—particularly among cattle owners. According to a 1935 study, a total of 576 La Sal Forest users

26. Pinchot, p. 269.
27. Orange Olson, Memo, 11 November 1924, G-Supervision Folder, Manti-La Sal National Forest Historical Files.
28. *Grand Valley Times*, 26 March 1909.
29. Data for Figures 5-8 is from Anderson, Miscellaneous Notes.

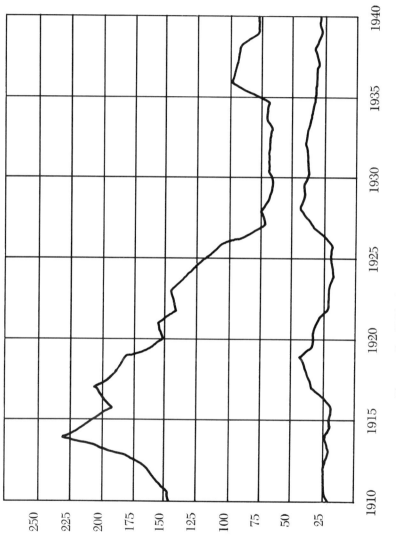

Figure 5: PERMITS ISSUED 1910-1940

had received permits up to that date. Of these, 516, or more than 89 percent, had lost or had sold their grazing privileges. Interestingly, large users had been the most stable element with the greatest incidence of dropout occurring among the smallest owners.[30]

Number Reductions

The most obvious pattern in the history of La Sal Forest permits was reduction in numbers. Substantial cuts were initiated the year after the Forest was created. Thereafter, with the exception of the World War I years, the trend was down. Permits for 16,518 cattle and 84,000 sheep in 1907 fell to 10,206 cattle and 30,985 sheep in 1939, or respective cuts of 38 percent and 63 percent.

But this sweeping generalization is far from the entire story. Cattle numbers were pegged at 16,000 head in 1910, but rather than sustaining immediate cuts, moved up moderately under Forest policy favoring exchanges from sheep to cattle and then soared during World War I. Reaching a peak of 28,468 in 1916, cattle grazed (actually there were more, but because of the counting troubles no one knows just how many more) began a long trend of cuts that was still in motion in 1939. (See Figure 6.)

Unlike their cattle-grazing contemporaries, early sheepmen suffered staggering reductions. They ran 84,000 sheep on the La Sal Forest in 1907, dropped to 66,000 the following year, and fell to 40,000 (less than 50 percent of their original number) by 1914.

With reference to the relative status of sheep and cattle in Utah, J. A. Scorup, who ran only cattle, once said that Utah laws always had discriminated against cattlemen and favored sheep and that as far as livestock matters went, the state legislature was the effective tool of sheepmen. If this be true, it was well for southeastern Utah's sheepmen, for they needed a friend in court somewhere—they certainly did not have one in the administration of the La Sal Forest. With little opportunity to have effectively evaluated the potential of the La Sal, early Forest officers declared the La Sal to be cattle country and made every effort to reduce sheep numbers and to encourage exchanges to cattle permits. Early sheepmen on the La Sal were under an onus that was multifaceted. Sheep there as elsewhere had never been regarded with favor, and had been blamed by someone or other for virtually every ill that had befallen the country. To some degree, Gifford Pinchot, himself, was responsible for a sharp lack of enthusiasm for sheep in Forest Service circles. In terms that definitely consigned sheep to an undesirable category, he later wrote:

> Perhaps I had better confess here that I hate a sheep, and the smell of a sheep, although many sheepmen were my good friends. I have seen

---

30. "Historical Information, La Sal National Forest," p. 49.

Figure 6

1910-1940

CATTLE PERMITTED

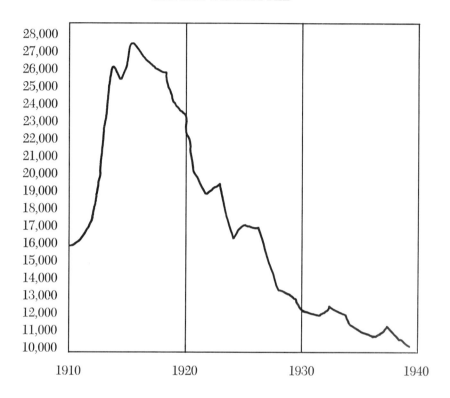

too much of the sheep's power to destroy. Yet I recognize (with regret) that sheep are necessary, and (with satisfaction) that good handling can make and keep them harmless.[31]

With such promptings at the top, it was easy for early Forest officers to see sheep as the real spoiler, largely responsible for overgrazing, erosion, water pollution, and for whatever else was wrong. As if the adverse image of the sheep was not enough, the sheepman sometimes bore the brunt of a tarnished reputation. The relatively large size of sheep operations often placed the sheepman in a position where he became the local manifestation of the "monopolist" so much the object of adverse attention during turn-of-the-century decades. Size also tended to place sheepmen outside the Forest Service concern for the little man.

31. Pinchot, p. 270.

Pushed by adverse exchange and reduction policies, sheep numbers continued to drop until 1915. The war years saw the downtrend arrested and even a weak resurgence before the downtrend was resumed in 1919. Sheep numbers reached a low of 23,594 actually grazed in 1925, after which sheep enjoyed a period of relative popularity and prosperity before falling again in the mid- and late-1930s. (See Figure 7.)

Stockgrowers' Associations

Permittees were, of course, a vital element in the management of ranges. Public opinion had been weighed, and the cooperation of potential users solicited even before the establishment of the original reserves, and public meetings and ad hoc committees had helped resolve the first problems of initiating Forest regulations.[32] But Forest officers deemed informal arrangements of this type to be inadequate or perhaps undependable or even dangerous, and from

Figure 7

1910-1940
SHEEP PERMITTED

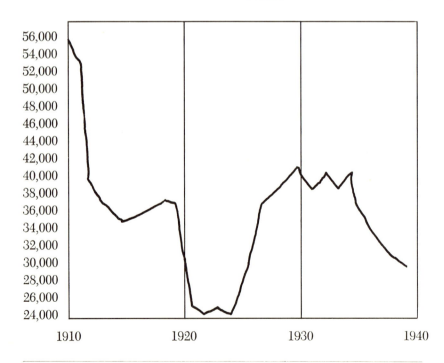

32. *Grand Valley Times*, 30 August 1907.

a very early time encouraged users to organize into permanent associations. Founded to "secure from the people collectively definite statements of their needs and wishes," associations often became no more than fronts by which Forest officers sought to manipulate grazers.[33] After initial experiences in which stockmen were enthusiastic enough, most of them regarded associations to be nuisances which, like permits and other regulations, were part of the burden of the new order.[34] So pervasive was antipathy by 1914, that J. W. Humphrey once reported he had "been unable to find one man who was favorable to the organization of an association."[35]

The first association to be organized formally was the Southeastern Utah Stockgrowers' Association, which was set up sometime prior to November, 1907, under the promptings of Orrin Snow. Snow obviously hoped to have the association become an effective instrument in policy formulation. Under his leadership it responded enthusiastically, meeting often, making boundary recommendations, setting permit levels, and, by counting stock on the Forest in 1908, actually enforcing policy.[36]

Based in Moab, the association was expansive in its aspirations, taking a name deceptive in its geographic spread and aspiring to become something of a Forest-wide advisory group. This self-image may well have originated at a time when the La Sal and Monticello divisions were separate reserves, but Forest officers soon recognized that the Southeastern Association did not provide representation for other localities. Thereafter, official policy encouraged smaller groups with purely local interests.[37]

After a year or so of effective work, the Southeastern Association began to fall apart. John Riis, who had found the Monticello Division users to be hard to deal with, initially thought that stockmen of the La Sal Division were cooperative and pointed to the association as a prototype of good management. But Riis was unable to countenance for long a group which expected to have its opinions make a difference. In 1909 he stripped the association of the right to count stock onto the Forest, noting with accuracy that its members were all interested parties. Thereafter, relations quickly deteriorated, coming to a hiatus early in 1910, when Riis hotly defended a raise in fees imposed by the district office as well as his own policy. A spirited exchange ensued, and in a suggestively short time, Riis was transferred to another forest. Under his successor, the Southeastern Association was split into sheep and cattle associations and was

33. J. W. Humphrey, Circular letter, 1 January 1914, Improvements Folder, Manti-La Sal National Forest Historical Files.

34. Fred W. Prewer to J. W. Humphrey, 28 January 1914 and Humphrey to Prewer, 4 February 1914, Improvements Folder.

35. Improvements Folder, 4 June 1914.

36. Improvements Folder, 8 November 1907.

37. Improvements Folder, 22 November 1907.

Pack string heading onto the Blues. U.S. Forest Service photo.

forced to elect members to a Forest-wide advisory group on boundary adjustments.[38]

These events not only resulted in the passing of the association as a real force but also set the pattern for other groups. Several organizations came into being over some specific issue. Once the issue was resolved, they limped along and passed completely from view unless roused from their lethargy by another issue. Later, as salting, water development, and other elements of range management were considered to be important, efforts were made to tailor associations to meet these needs.

As early as 1907 there was talk of a Forest-wide advisory group with authority to participate in policy formulation. But available evidence indicates that such a group did not come into being until 1937 by which time the Forest Service may have been prompted in its action by developments in the new resource management agencies spawned by the New Deal.[39]

Problems of Management

Range management became increasingly technical and complex as the years passed. Early management implied little more than

38.   Improvements Folder, 3 March 1911.
39.   "Historical Information, La Sal National Forest," p. 49.

permits, allotments, and a loose count, but later it came to include drift fences, water development, salting, reseeding projects, closer control of livestock to insure well-balanced use of ranges, and finally, during the 1930s, range analysis in terms of animal-unit months and other technical formulas.

The cooperative action by which these changes were implemented required untold hours of patient effort. An improvement program launched by Henry A. Bergh illustrates this. Twenty-six La Sal cattle permittees were involved, ranging in size from a struggling homesteader named Royal Larsen with seven head of stock to J. M. Cunningham, whose permits called for 895 cattle. The first step confronting Bergh was selling the program to this diverse set of users. This Bergh accomplished by working with an elective group he called the "advisory council," and by making promises as to total costs which proved hard to keep and which bred much ill will. Once users were committed, estimates were made and costs (less a portion to be paid by the Forest) prorated among the permittees. The program was then worked through the district forester and the solicitor's office. In due time the contractors finished the work, but, as might be expected, several stockmen failed to pay, throwing responsibility on the supervisor for collection and payment. Despite some ingenious dickering on the part of Bergh (or perhaps because of it), loose ends remained for J. W. Humphrey to write off as part of Bergh's maladministration.[40]

Another example of the difficulties implicit in changing managerial techniques grew out of the unfortunate coincidence of falling markets and prolonged drouth in the early 1920s. Stockmen kept their cattle, complicating an already adverse grazing picture. Accommodatingly, the Forest Service sought to soften the economic blow that a quick sell-off would entail, by enlarging permits through improved grazing management. For years district rangers had worked to distribute salt, to develop water and trails, and to build drift fences to spread cattle over entire allotments. These measures fell short because untended cattle moved by habit and convenience to the same overgrazed areas. To maximize grazing potential, officials distributed to permittees on the five South Elk allotments a special rule making them liable to a 10 percent reduction should they fail to make reasonable efforts to spread their stock into previously unused portions of their allotments. Users on three allotments failed to comply. Permittees on the other two allotments herded their stock with very favorable results. Acting on the basis of his directives, Supervisor Charles DeMoisy recommended cuts totalling 318 head, or 10 percent of the cattle, on the three allotments. After extensive correspondence, DeMoisy and C. N. Woods, assistant district forester,

---

40. Improvements Folder.

worked out a formula allowing violators to hold their stock until better market conditions prevailed.[41]

Certain patterns have emerged in the foregoing pages. Grazing continued to be the dominating activity of the La Sal Forest as it had dominated the frontier era. Unlike Utah generally, the La Sal was a place of a few large permittees. This made for problems of management which may not have been more serious than problems confronting other forests in District IV, but which were unique. Range management progressed slowly by means of a seesaw struggle between Forest officers and users. Successive reductions were hailed as the action finally necessary to redress nature's balance, but in 1939 evidence suggested that further cuts lay ahead. L. H. Redd, Cunningham and Carpenter, the La Sal Livestock Company, the Indian Creek Cattle Company, and Scorup-Somerville were among the great stockmen of District IV, and one or two of them may well have ranked among the largest in the nation. Taken all together, grazing during the first three decades of the Forest's history stands up well as the successor to the great livestock baronies of the late nineteenth century.

---

41. Wood to DeMoisy, 17 February 1921, G-Supervision Folder, Manti-La Sal National Forest Historical Files.

Chapter X

Wildlife

Game

Until well after 1940, the grazing situation on the La Sal Forest was not appreciably complicated by large numbers of big game. A few deer were to be found on each division; and until 1935, when they were killed, or were driven to lower country along the Colorado River, a handful of bighorn sheep maintained a precarious existence. Smaller game, too, was scarce. However, it would be a mistake to regard game as being unimportant to either Forest administrators or to the public. Indeed, scarcity may have been in some part the product of the importance of game to the livelihood of both Indians and settlers. When the whites first came, the country is said to have carried large numbers of wild animals, deer being especially numerous. A typical report was A. N. Ray's:

> There were a lot of deer when we first came to this country. One fall, just after the first snow, Buddy Taylor and I were riding the north end of the mountain [the La Sal Mountains]. We rode out onto a point overlooking Kirk's Basin and Buddy counted 300 deer just in the basin, and there were a lot more. I don't know what happened to them in later years, never did find many dead. The Indians killed a lot just for their hides but they had always been killing them.[1]

Within a decade of the first pioneers' arrival, deer numbers were evidently sharply reduced, and by 1900 they were almost wiped out. Overgrazing, and heavy hunting by Indians and whites kept the count low for many years thereafter.

It was into this situation that Forest Service personnel moved in 1906. During the first years it was a rare occasion when deer were sighted—a fact that occasionally led foresters to make special com-

---

1. "Historical Information, La Sal National Forest," p. 131.

ment. Indicative was one ranger's 1911 report that he had seen four deer on a recent trip. Encouraged by the event, he speculated that deer were on the increase. But even guarded optimism was premature. In 1916 the *Grand Valley Times* noted a special "scarcity of deer" and reported that "although several dozen hunting licenses were sold, and although many people went on hunting expeditions during the open season just closed, only a few men were successful in bringing back venison." In the face of this adverse return, Forest officials expressed "the belief that there are not as many deer in the country as in recent years. . . ."[2]

Statistics as to deer numbers do not exist for the years prior to 1917, when Supervisor Samuel B. Locke estimated there were 250 deer on the La Sal Division and 100 on the Monticello. Thereafter, more or less regular estimates show between 200 and 300 deer for the entire Forest until about 1925 when, following the statewide upward trend, deer began to increase. By the early 1930s sufficient attention had been attracted by this increase to occasion an effort to get more accurate information, and the counts of that year show a total of 1,225 deer. A grazing reconnaissance of the mid-thirties reported 700 head on the Northern Division and, in spite of general overgrazing, indicated that "twice that number" could be carried. In the opinion of Ranger Owen Despain, who was involved in the reconnaissance, deer were not increasing, which suggests that part of the upward trend in numbers may be attributed to better counts.[3]

Although the La Sal Forest's increase to 1,225 head of deer represents a substantial climb, its share of Utah's 1930 total was insignificant, as 54,749 deer were reported that year. The Fishlake Forest accounted for nearly 40 percent of that total, and together with the Dixie and Manti forests it had 80 percent of all deer reported. See Figure 8.[4]

By 1930 the Utah deer herd amounted to almost one-half of all deer in the intermountain area. Numbers continued to climb, reaching 80,000 head in 1934 and 99,000 in 1938. In the latter year there were also some 3,000 elk in the state, but there is no evidence that any of them were to be found on the La Sal National Forest. By contrast, Wyoming grazed more than 20,000 elk in 1930, 17,000 of which ran on the Teton National Forest.[5]

To some degree the low deer population on the La Sal Forest was the result of heavy hunting by Indians. As pointed out earlier the La Sal and Blue mountains had attracted Indians since time immemorial. In 1853 John Gunnison had found the Uncompahgre Utes

---

2. *Grand Valley Times*, 3 November 1916.
3. Owen Despain to the Supervisor, 22 October 1935, Range Management Folder, Manti-La Sal National Forest Historical Files.
4. Game census prepared by Carl H. Dopp, Region IV Office, for C. C. Anderson, "History of Grazing," Miscellaneous Notes.
5. Ibid.

Figure 8:

Forest	Deer Census		
	1921	1925	1930
Ashley	1,350	1,450	1,940
Cache	910	456	1,900
Dixie	1,750	2,500	13,000
Fishlake	3,735	6,375	20,700
La Sal	275	725	1,225
Manti	1,150	2,500	8,800
Minidoka	60	100	120
Powell	1,600	2,200	2,800
Uinta	1,750	1,515	2,075
Wasatch	650	600	2,189
Total	13,230	18,421	54,749

following migrating herds along the Gunnison River. Mormons of the Elk Mountain Mission had carried on a brisk trade for buckskin, and after settlers arrived frequent reference was made to Indian hunts. During the reservation negotiations of 1888, Utes were adamant in their demands that the La Sal Mountains be included in the proposed reservation because of their hunting potential. The commissioners refused to make this concession but did assure the tribesmen full hunting rights on the La Sals. Sensing that the La Sal Mountains would ultimately be off-limits to them, Southern Utes are said to have launched a hunt-to-extinction in 1884. By white accounts, 2,500 head of deer were killed in 1886, most of which were skinned and the meat left to rot. These big hunts were continued into the years after 1900, when Don Taylor of Moab saw one Indian with fifteen green deer hides thrown over his horse.[6]

Whites were always discomfited by the big hunts, protesting both the Indian's presence and the slaughter of deer. In June of 1896 the *Grand Valley Times* reported that a supreme court case involving Wyoming Bannocks had ruled that Indians living on reservations were amenable to the game laws of the state in which they lived. Although this ruling obviously did not apply directly to the La Sal Forest region, *Times* editor J. N. Corbin wrote: "It is now the duty of wardens to prohibit the Utes and Navajos from slaughtering the deer in this section."[7] Since there would be no game wardens—in the effective sense of the term—in southeastern Utah for upwards of twenty years, Corbin's injunction meant nothing. The hunting went on.

It is not clear just where the Indian hunters came from, but parties from three different groups probably hunted the region at varying

6. "Historical Information, La Sal National Forest," p. 131.
7. *Grand Valley Times*, 26 June 1896.

times. Traveling bands passing between the Uintah Reservation and the Southern Ute Reservation in southwestern Colorado undoubtedly levied something of a toll on the La Sal as did roaming tribesmen of the Weeminuches band. But probably the heaviest and most persistent tribute of game was taken by Paiutes, who by the first decades of this century made home base in the Cottonwood-Allen Canyon area and ranged throughout the Elks, Blues, and La Sals as the spirit moved. As the deer population decreased, Paiute efforts to glean a meager yield in wildlife intensified. John Riis has left a colorful account that makes clear the poverty in which Indians lived and the extent to which they had killed off all game:

> One day I rode into their camp on the south side of the mountains, before I was aware they were near. A few scrawny ponies, their backs raw from the saddle and covered with flies grazed under the trees. Perhaps a score of goats were foraging around under the watchful eyes of the squaws and on a hillside sat a lone Indian buck very busy doing nothing. Before the door of a wickiup a fire-blackened coffee-pot boiled over a little fire. Within the tent, the flaps of which were thrown back, half a dozen ragged Ute braves squatted on the bare ground and watched in stony silence, as I rode up and dismounted. Stooping over the fire I raised the lid of the coffeepot. A single egg boiled in the muddy brown mixture. Save for the Indians, the interior of the tent was bare of any furnishing or camp trapping. It was a shelter and no more. . . . Polk's gaunt bare shins showed below his ragged blue overalls. I had heard that the Utes were afraid of the water and some devil prompted me to find out, so I pointed my finger at his dirt encrusted shin. "Why you no wash um?" I demanded. Polk gave me a deadly black look but before he could answer there was a shrill yell from the lone Indian on the hillside. Bedlam broke loose in the camp. Squaws, bucks, papooses, all yelling and shrieking at once! The Indians in the tent leaped to their feet and charged out. I almost fell down before the rush but leaped to my feet, resolved to sell my life dearly. It looked like there was going to be a massacre with me as the victim. But it was something more important . . . The Indian on the hill had seen a rabbit; a pitiful little cottontail. After it they went with sticks and stones and wild yells that completely befuddled the poor bunny. In less than a minute it was skinned, drawn, and stewing in a pot; head, legs and all. They were not too choice in their culinary preparations. I was not invited to dinner.[8]

The Blue and Elk mountains were particularly hard hit by Indian hunters, a fact apparent in the consistently lower deer count returned for the Southern Division, which encompassed nearly twice the area of the Northern Division. But in the years after 1923 when the Cottonwood-Allen Canyon allotment was made, the Indians were less a factor in the continuing adverse game situation.

In relation to attitudes toward game, as well as conduct, southeastern Utah whites appear to have adopted much of the permissiveness of their Indian neighbors. Forest Supervisor J. W. Humphrey found little respect for game laws during his stay on the La Sal. One Pack Creek settler typified the predominating point of view when he

---

8. John Riis, pp. 53-54.

openly admitted to killing four deer per year. This was, he asserted, no more than the prerogative of the rancher on whose premises deer ran. Miners, too, often felt special right to La Sal Forest deer. One, a placer miner named Johnson from Gold Mesa, killed at least two deer out of season during the summer of 1914. Four men helped him carry the venison in, including Chester Wright, a deputy sheriff, and Ranger Fred Strong, each of whom received a quarter of venison in return for their services. Displaying no apprehension, Johnson tacked the green hides on his cabin, thus attracting Supervisor Humphrey's attention. Goaded by Humphrey, Henry Thompson, a Green River game warden, brought charges; however, in Humphrey's opinion, there was no sentiment anywhere other than in his own person to convict Johnson for the infraction.[9]

As suggested in the Johnson case, permissiveness often extended to officials. Humphrey recalls that Randall Turpin, a deputy game warden, charged one man with illegal trapping of eight beavers, bringing him before Justice of the Peace Charles Redd at La Sal. In spite of the fact that Turpin produced the pelts and the offender admitted to the violation, Redd acquitted him. In frustration, Turpin asked the justice if he wanted the pelts. Mr. Redd's answer was negative.[10]

Forest officers were not above reproach in this matter. John Riis writes of dropping a nice buck. He then emptied his carbine at "the three does who still stood gazing at the buck wonderingly" and rode on, leaving the buck briefly to take his pack into camp. Returning as darkness fell, he failed to find the deer. According to his account, other foresters "rode me pretty hard and swore that I imagined it all." However, his show of remorse extended only to having lost the animal, not to killing it in the first place.[11]

Furthermore, violation of game laws was not a passing phenomenon in the La Sal Forest area. The primitive days when wardens had to be brought in from neighboring Green River passed, and game numbers increased; however, poaching persisted. In an oral interview given in 1935, Berten Allred of Moab lamented a noticeable decrease in deer during years just past.

> There has been a very noticable decrease in game. Unlawful hunting has been the main factor. When one man kills 35 deer in one year the number is bound to be decreased. Some settlers have told of killing seven to thirty deer in one winter. The depression has had an influence on out of season kills due to the lack of other things to do and for subsistence. Livestock has not been a factor as the deer graze largely on areas inaccessible to stock.[12]

The present writer lived at La Sal from 1953 to 1956 during which time he heard of and observed a good deal of violation. One of the

---

9. Interview with J. W. Humphrey, Provo, Utah, 26 March 1971.
10. Ibid.
11. Riis, pp. 63-64.
12. Berten Allred interview, 10 October 1935, Range Management Folder.

Redd Ranches foremen frequently related that he had raised his family on "buckskin," and that particularly through the depression days venison had been a staple in the family's diet. A grey-eyed cowboy, whose aversion for "dude hunters" was proverbial, continued to live on venison at his summer camp on the La Sal Mountains. Carefully wrapping his meat in an alfalfa sack and hanging it on the north side of his cabin by day, he kept it good by taking it out of the bag at night, exposing it to maximum chill. Served with sourdough biscuits, fried potatoes and scorched-flour gravy, it made good eating indeed. Uranium miners and farmers took a heavy toll of deer, sage hens, and cottontail rabbits. Sage hens, which ranged in flocks numbering from a half-dozen to hundreds in the fields and adjacent brush, made easy prey, and farmhands sometimes killed dozens of them; however, pressure was not great upon the sage hens because they were neither good to eat nor much fun to hunt and kill. Deer grazed regularly at night on the ranches around the Forest. Many of the ranchers argued that a certain amount of poaching was necessary to the success of their farming operations. To them, the fact that they boarded large herds of deer was clear justification for killing an occasional animal. It also seemed to them logical and even necessary to chase the deer from the fields with rifle fire. So persuasive were the arguments of one rancher that a friend of his, who, after the fashion of Mormon elders, had just taught a ward teaching lesson on upholding the law, proceeded one early fall evening to make a spotlight kill on the fields at Rattlesnake Ranch, which lies about a half-dozen miles below the Forest boundary on the southwest slope of the La Sals. The fact that the venison was strong with sage, more than the hunter's pangs of conscience, kept him from returning for more.

It does not seem likely that permissiveness where game laws were concerned was entirely eradicated even among Forest Service personnel. It is the writer's opinion that the social climate in the La Sal Forest area generally has been more tolerant of this sort of infraction than in most other parts of Utah. Fish and game officials recognized at an early time that along with certain other outlying game districts, Utah's southeast tended to regard unlawful kills as minor violations not meriting punishment. Addressing himself to the problem of game law violation, the commissioner of fish and game came out strongly for a hardhanded policy in 1908. Diminishing numbers were forcing belated recognition that game might be hunted to extinction. With more than a touch of irony, the commissioner noted that it was often those who had earlier been the worst offenders who now cried loudest for control and criticized fish and game management most vehemently. Continuing in this vein, he leveled a strong indictment at people in the remote quarters of the state:

> . . . in some communities public sentiment tends toward excusing violations on the part of the citizens . . . Among this class of people in the more remote hunting districts of the state are people who feel that the

law as made by the legislature of this state did not apply to them. These certain few feel that they have a right existing from time immemorial to take what game they please for their own use . . . and they seem to think that any attempt to molest them in carrying out their desires is an infringement upon their sacred rights. . . . It is impossible to watch every settler in the more sparsely settled districts of our game country, and for that reason a great many take advantage of our inability to detect them in their violations and do very much as they please, but when detected and brought before a court and jury composed of his own countrymen it is too often the feeling of the jury that this individual should be excused, while if the offense was committed by a stranger in the land, or one coming from the town or city, the same jurors are only too glad to convict him for coming down and killing "their" game.[13]

Although the commissioner was not discussing southeastern Utah alone, it is certain that the region was beyond the pale of the fish and game commission. In 1905 four Utah counties had no game wardens; Grand and San Juan counties were among them. This condition continued for many years. In 1911 the record indicates that at least one ranger was serving as a deputy warden.[14] By 1915 all La Sal Forest officers appear to have been authorized to serve in this capacity.

That little control existed in at least one other remote locality is borne out by a recollection of Will Humphrey. While he was supervisor of the Sevier Forest, Humphrey accompanied the state sheep inspector to Kanab. The roads were bad, and Kanab, like Moab and Monticello, was considered to be the jumping-off place of the world. Anticipating no trouble with game officers, the Kanab hotel served venison as a specialty the first night Humphrey was in town. The next day Humphrey went to the forest supervisor in Kanab and asked if he knew the hotel featured venison. Humphrey always suspected that it was more than coincidence that he was served only stale salt pork thereafter at that hotel.[15]

Fish

For years the La Sal Forest also lay virtually beyond the fish stocking capabilities of the fish and game commission. In 1901, one plant of 30,000 fry was made in Mill Creek at the insistence of a Grand County state legislator. Although the stocking program was plied vigorously elsewhere in the state, there is no evidence of more fish being stocked on the La Sal Forest until 1911, when a total of 75,000 fry were planted in La Sal Mountain streams.[16] No fish appear to have been planted on the Blue Mountains prior to 1915, when 48,000 were placed in four separate streams.

13.   "Biennial Report of the State Fish and Game Commissioner," *Public Documents*, 1907-1908, pp. 6-7.
14.   *Cliffdwellers' Echo*, July 1911.
15.   Interview with J. W. Humphrey, 15 April 1971.
16.   *Public Documents*, 1901-1911.

The poor record of fish plants was in large measure the result of logistic problems. The La Sals were remote from any hatchery; Thompson was the closest railway station, and few roads existed on the mountains. Obviously there was much chance for slipup with the fragile young fish. Will Humphrey handled one small shipment during July, 1914. The man he sent to meet the fish and game delivery at Thompson (evidently a Forest guard rather than a ranger) was bent on celebrating his visit to the railroad station and dallied at the saloon. The outcome of the planting is unsure, but the fish and game man who waited for the guard to sober up was not favorably impressed with the whole affair.[17] Such incidents may have prompted fish and game officials to limit the number of fish assigned to La Sal Forest streams until roads and transportation improved. Later, when fish were regularly planted, transporting them the last miles into the Forest from Moab or Monticello was a matter of packing heavy, unwieldy cans. At Moab a rod and gun club helped officials haul fish onto the mountain and lobbied to get more fish assigned to the La Sal.[18]

Licenses

Another index of the fish and game commission's failure to penetrate southeastern Utah is to be observed in the poor sale of hunting licenses. In 1911 only eleven licenses were sold in San Juan County and fifty-four in Grand County. The next smallest county in terms of license sales was Kane, with 108. By way of contrast, Salt Lake County accounted for 9,901 sales. In 1913 San Juan licenses dropped to eight while Grand enjoyed something of an uptrend with forty-eight. Kane County accounted for 151 sales, and Emery, for 236. This pattern persisted until at least the end of World War I.[19]

Beaver

Beaver, which at one time existed in substantial numbers, were trapped to virtual extinction by the turn of the century. After many years during which no beavers were seen, the animals made a moderate comeback about the time of World War I and became sufficiently numerous by 1917 to be regarded as pests. In 1925 the Moab Fish and Game Association hired High H. Turner to trap beaver alive on Two Mile Creek and transplant them to Mill Creek on the assumption that it would "bring back the old days when the creek was a continuation of beaver dams, and thus improve the propagation of trout."[20] The spirit of conservation led

17. Interview with J. W. Humphrey, Provo, Utah, 26 March 1971.
18. *Grand Valley Times,* 30 April 1925.
19. "Biennial Report of the State Fish and Game Commissioner," for 1911 to 1919.
20. *Grand Valley Times,* 30 July 1925.

Moab to condemn a fish and game commission policy permitting trapping on the Colorado and Green rivers in 1927. Responding to this local interest, officials revoked all permits in the Moab vicinity for the time being.[21] But the withdrawal of permits was only a weak deterrent, and certain parties continued to trap. One Moab resident reported in 1935:

> "Beaver have been unlawfully taken throughout this region. As many as $3,000 worth of furs have been taken out at one time. One old trapper took $2,500 worth out of the Book Mountains at one time and three weeks later was back, broke, living on beaver tail soup and ready for further destruction of beaver colonies."[22]

Beaver appear to have done relatively well on the La Sal Mountains, and limited harvests were taken during the 1940s and 1950s by part-time trappers—often school boys—including Delbert Oliver of Moab and Albert Steele of La Sal.

Predators

Much more important than the beaver in terms of trapping were predatory animals. Originally not numerous in the country, coyotes, bears, and wildcats increased rapidly, until by 1892 they exacted a heavy tribute on livestock. Wolves—usually referred to as grey wolves—were also found from the first, but apparently not in great numbers until about 1910, when there was something of a population explosion of all classes of predators. The entire decade that followed was marked by unusual numbers of predatory animals, and the record is full of references to the problems they caused and to the effort to control them. Although they were brought under partial control after 1920, a continuing effort has been necessary to keep them within manageable limits.

Bears and mountain lions were the largest and, in some ways, most spectacular of the predators. Both animals existed in relatively large numbers and did enough damage to attract the full hostility of stockmen and foresters. In killing stock, lions and bears appear to have worked singly, but bears were at times found in groups numbering up to eight or ten. In 1922 Oscar Stewart and T. E. Lassiter reported meeting ten bears near the head of Pack Creek, four of which they killed before running out of ammunition.[23] A party of surveyors had been attacked by "a large number of bears" on the Manti Forest in 1901. Having routed the surveyors, the bears turned on a flock of sheep of which they reportedly killed fifty.[24] There may have been periods when bears and lions were unusually prevalent, but aside from the general in-

21. Ibid., 16 February 1927.
22. Berten Allred Interview, 10 October 1935, Range Management Folder.
23. *Grand Valley Times,* 26 October 1922.
24. *Emery County Progress,* 27 July 1901.

crease after 1910 it is impossible to determine when numbers were greatest.

Coyotes were probably the most destructive predators over the years, and existed in great numbers. Their depredations were in the main limited to sheep—particularly at lambing time. Some idea of their destructiveness may be gained from the fact that a bounty of five dollars was fixed for destroying them, but in general their killings attracted less attention than did those of the larger predators. Perhaps this is because coyotes were too much a part of everyday life to merit reporting.

The most spectacular predators of all were the wolves. Not a problem during the first decades, they became the worst killers by 1910. There is no way of measuring wolf population, but it is clear that numbers were up sharply during the second decade of the century. They ranged generally in the country around the La Sal Forest, doing as much damage in adjacent deserts as on the mountains, but it was thought that they were most prevalent on the Elk Mountains and its canyon drainages. According to local belief, wolves killed with a wanton joy that not only struck the rancher economically but frightened him as well. Because of this, and the farflung ranging habits of some wolves, reports likely tended to exaggerate wolf numbers; however, there can be no question but that there were enough of them to constitute a serious problem. The years of 1911 and 1912 probably saw wolves reach their greatest number—at least contemporary records refer to them most frequently during these years.

Unlike coyotes, wolves did not restrict their depredations to sheep and lambs but inflicted great damage on cattle as well. According to one account, eighteen adult cattle were killed in one vicinity in March of 1913. Evidently much of this killing was done for the fun of it, as only small parts of the slain animals had been eaten.[25]

In addition to their sheer destructiveness, wolves were reported to be brazen in their killings and, at times, ruthless and relentless in their pursuit. In December, 1912, a report appeared in the *Grand Valley Times* that illustrates this point. Victor Corn of Grand Junction left for his ranges in Utah with five horses. The second night on the road his animals were attacked by wolves. Three were killed outright and "almost entirely devoured." The fourth was hamstrung, which forced Corn to shoot it. Following Corn's trail during the next day, the wolves killed his last horse on the third night, and Corn beat a terrified retreat to Thompson the next day.[26]

Others had less devastating experiences. One such was John Jones, a Monticello cowboy, who came on a half-dozen wolves one winter day. The snow had a thin crust which slowed the wolves down. Putting the spur to his horse, he followed the slowest wolf, throwing his

25. *Grand Valley Times*, 21 March 1913.
26. Ibid., 17 December 1912.

loop over the agile animal six times before he could draw it closed. Once his rope was set, he turned his horse and dragged the wolf to death.[27]

Efforts to combat predators were various. Guns were carried by most stockmen and rangers. Undoubtedly a substantial part of the country's kill was accounted for, but never recorded by riders who broke the tedium of wilderness journeys shooting coyotes, wolves, lions, and occasionally bears. The latter two classes were sometimes hunted with hounds, but evidently this was not a common practice. Trapping and poisoning were probably the mainstays of the control program, with the former predominating; however, some ranchers, especially Cunningham and Carpenter of La Sal, favored poisoning. Interesting flourishes were sometimes added as in the case of a tame female wolf kept at Bluff for use as a decoy.[28]

Successful trapping required experience and certain natural gifts. In 1911 and 1912 Forest Supervisor Bergh hoped that rangers could become trappers in slack winter periods. After a few unsuccessful attempts, this effort was abandoned. Others were more effective, and many cowboys, miners, and farmers trapped as winter sidelines. A few full-time trappers may have supported themselves, but incomes were generally insufficient to attract more than a handful. Indicative of the common practice, Charlie Snell, a prospector, turned a few dollars by bringing in coyote scalps for bounty. On one occasion Howard Balsley staked Snell for a uranium prospecting trip into Lisbon Valley. Hearing nothing from Snell for some time, Balsley was surprised and more than a little perplexed when he received an unexplained check from San Juan County for twenty-seven dollars. Several weeks later the problem of the mysterious check was resolved when Snell inquired if Balsley had received payment from the county and told him he had found no uranium but had located a den of coyote pups. Since Balsley had financed the expedition, Snell took him to be a full partner in the bounty proceeds.[29] Soapy Perkins of Monticello tells an interesting story of similar nature. One trapper acquaintance of his made regular and unique use of Sugar Loaf Rock just north of Peter's Hill on the floor of Dry Valley. The large rock mound has steep sides and a rounded top with a deep hole scooped out in the center, which served dual purposes as a collector of water and a cage or pen. According to Perkins, the old trapper often brought pregnant coyotes to the mound and imprisoned them until they whelped and the pups grew large enough to qualify for bounties.[30]

Predators were regarded as a public problem from an early time. In the beginning, the responsibility appears to have fallen entirely upon the counties, and very modest bounty rates were established

---

27. Ibid., 21 March 1913.
28. *Cliffdwellers' Echo*, January 1912.
29. Interview with Howard Balsley, Moab, Utah, 23 August 1968.
30. Interview with Soapy Perkins, Monticello, Utah, 2 February 1970.

at least as early as 1891.[31] At the prompting of the Utah Wool Growers Association, a state bounty law was passed in 1903 which set $20,000 aside for payment of bounties for the next two years. This law had numerous defects. In the first place, the funds it provided proved to be grossly inadequate. Second, it was not efficiently administered, and bounty checks were notoriously slow in being paid. It is not clear when government trappers—other than forest rangers—entered the scene; however, it is clear that Works Progress Administration trappers were employed on the La Sal Forest during the 1930s. These were paid a salary of fifty dollars per month rather than bounties.[32]

Bounties provided by public provisions did not attract enough trappers or the right kind of trappers, and stockmen periodically resorted to hiring their own trappers or offering bounties and rewards. Sometimes these private bounties ran very high, amounting to thirty to forty dollars for lions and bears and from seventy-five dollars to $100 for wolves. An indication of just how serious stockmen took the wolf problem to be is the following:

> The timber wolves are becoming more and more a menace to the stockmen and with the small inducement the state offers in bounty, nobody seems to be willing to undertake trapping them. To illustrate what the up-to-date stockman thinks of the wolf, I will mention here that Pace Brothers and W. A. Doak of Rock Creek and Sinbad, offer a reward of $100 for each wolf captured on their ranges. These outfits are running their stock on an area of approximately two townships but little of which is on the Forest. The hide, and proof that the animal was caught on their range, is all these gentlemen desire, and the money is there.[33]

Much more than the going rate of $100 per wolf was paid when the situation seemed to demand it. In the years just before 1912, one particular wolf caused special havoc on the Elk Mountains. No reference is made to the amount of the reward attached to his scalp, but it was evidently substantially more than the going $100 rate because two trappers spent the entire summer and fall of 1911 running him down. An even more notorious case was that of "Old Big Foot," a huge wolf said to have left a trail of bloody destruction over a range of 700 miles during the years before 1920. That year Roy Musselman took the old predator and collected the $1,000 reward which had been raised jointly by stockmen in the area.[34]

Pests

Prairie dogs and other rodents also constituted a serious problem. State law made modest provisions to aid in poisoning rodents in 1903, and the state appears to have provided poisons and directives for

31. *See* Minutes of the San Juan County Court, 1880-1900, 2 June and 8 July 1891, pp. 97, 103.
32. Anderson, Miscellaneous Notes.
33. *Cliffdwellers' Echo*, December 1912.
34. Times-Independent (Moab), 15 April 1920.

their use during much of the period of this study. Rodent eradication had its local adaptations. On what later became the Cache National Forest, Albert Potter had observed the ravages of ground squirrels, and also he saw two men catching them with fishing poles and a string noose. Attracting them by spreading grain on a canvas, they caught "100 in about one hour."[35] Ranger John Riis found a more structured method—if not more ingenious—used to control prairie dogs at Monticello. What he terms "the dog war" was staged annually during the four weeks after water was turned onto Monticello's fields. The village was divided into two groups; the side turning in the greatest number of prairie dog heads at the end of the month was declared winner. His account of the hunt follows:

> Out of the muddy water stuck a little brown seal-like snout as the unfortunate dog sought to escape the deluge only to find himself the centre of an excited circle of men, women, children, and yapping dogs and to be dispatched forthwith with sticks or pitchforks. . . . There were several dogs in every hole and the casualties were heavy. The heads were cut off and thrown into a sack to be locked in the town jail where they lay until the end of the campaign. The dog war came to an end and the town turned out one night around a great bonfire to count the dog heads. The two captains were there with the sacks ready to hand. . . . More than a thousand 'dogs' had fallen in the campaign. There were accusations that the winning team had raided the sacks of the losing side locked up in the flimsy jail, but all was forgotten in the dance and supper that followed a few nights later. [36]

The La Sal National Forest was deeply concerned with both predators and game. For years, policing and managing game and fish fell directly upon Forest personnel. While forest rangers showed no capacity as trappers, much of the predator control program emanated from the Forest administration as the primary agents of regulation in the area. With the improvement of communications and the growing specialization of federal regulating agencies after 1930, the Forest Service function in the control of both game and predators became less general, though with deer (as herds expanded) it continued to play a crucial role.

---

35. Diary of Albert F. Potter's Wasatch Survey, p. 7.
36. Riis, p. 48.

Chapter XI
Timber

The Role of Timber

In his regional history, *The Great Plains*, Walter Prescott Webb holds that until the American frontier reached the Great Plains the three essentials of its experience had been adequate moisture, good soil, and woodlands. In the east, timber had been quite as indispensable to settlement as had soil and moisture. The pioneer built his cabin of wood—or at least laid his floor, built his window sashes, and sheltered his head with it. Too, wood was his primary fuel as it was the stuff from which he made his fences. According to Webb, colonization of the treeless plains lagged behind the rest of the country until improvisation, such as heating with buffalo chips, and the substitution of barbed wire for the split rail, made the plains a homeland instead of a barren waste.[1]

The mountains that comprised the La Sal Forest provided a supply of timber that enabled the pioneers of southeastern Utah to avoid the added hardship that developing wood substitutes placed on Great Plains settlers. But, like water, the supply and location of woodstuffs helped mold the character of the community that emerged from the pioneer period. Villages hugged the flanks of the mountains, because water was there but also because the mountains gave access to wood. Rarely has a community's dependence on local wood supplies been as total and as protracted as was the case on southeastern Utah's frontier. For contrast we may cite Salt Lake City, where pioneers pushed ahead of the general frontier by nearly twenty years into an area of scanty wood supply. As a result an adobe city grew up which drew the note of many a traveler. Under close regulation of the ecclesiastical authorities,

1. Walter Prescott Webb, *The Great Plains* (Boston: Ginn and Co., 1931).

canyon openings in the Wasatch Front provided sparse timber supplies, from which were taken roofing materials and other wood essentials. But even the use of adobe and the close control of timber failed to meet the city's needs for long. Church and civil authorities alike encouraged the discovery of coal and the development of roads to put it in reach of the population centers, but Salt Lake Valley's problem was not solved until 1870 when the Utah Central Railroad tied it to outside sources of fuel and building materials.

In years past, it was often said that Bluff was farther from a railroad than any other town in the United States. But even Moab, lying one hundred miles back along the road toward the Denver and Rio Grande Western Railroad, was sufficiently far removed to render shipment of lumber impractical. Roads were primitive, and the communities small and impoverished. The net result was that, to an unusual degree and until well into the period of automotive transportation, settlement was dependent on local wood supplies.

The reverse of the coin gives an equally valid picture. There were no external pressures on La Sal Forest timber. Distance and primitive transit conditions as well as the character of timber growth placed it beyond the realm of commercial lumber operations until a relatively late date. Furthermore, internal developments made few demands. No transcontinental railroad—nor even a spur—penetrated the country to require crossties and bridging timbers. Mining was a matter of much talk and little production. With the possible exceptions of Cashin on the southeast slope of the La Sals and the Big Indian Copper mine, the industry's draw upon La Sal Forest timber was limited to logs for a few cabins, the product of a few small sawmills, a few thousand mining props, and fuel for a thousand campfires that blinked briefly, marking the aspiration of a handful of dreamers. Village populations remained small so that even the demands of pioneering were limited. This led to uneven cutting, and the loss of mature timber to rot, and other problems of age.

Very little timber management and use data has survived. A few pages of general information, a few lonely statistics, and the record of an early timber reconnaissance tell the story. Even the story of modern developments is curtailed to what may be termed active files. The historical data that does exist tells two primary stories. The first is a scant history of small sawmills meeting local needs. The second is the narrative of a timber reconnaissance in 1911 by which the La Sal's timbered resources were measured.

Sawmills and Lumbermen

The first lumber produced in the region of the La Sal Forest was whipsawed. At Bluff, thirty miles removed from saw timber,

Yellow pines on Elk Ridge. U.S. Forest Service photo.

what one writer termed "a famine for lumber" existed which "induced certain men to slice up cottonwood logs with a whipsaw." Lumber so acquired was virtually without value. Cottonwood boards are said to have been "so determined to warp and twist like a thing in convolutions, they wouldn't lie still after being nailed down."[2] At Old La Sal, yellow pine yielded much better lumber under the whipsaw. The Silvey family and others sawed lumber to floor and roof their own cabins. By dint of much labor, two good men could produce up to 300 feet per day.

The first sawmill was brought from Colorado by T. W. Branson in 1881 and located at Mont Hill Spring northwest of Paradox Valley. Trees for this mill were cut before the time of the crosscut saw, or at least before one was available to the mill operators, as the stumps "show they were cut entirely with axes."[3] The first Blue Mountains mill was set up much later—in 1889 by C. R. Christensen and Willard Butt in Bulldog Canyon. During the 1890s there was considerable sawmilling, particularly in the La Sals. During this period and for the decades that followed, mills were usually located convenient to their markets. Some were in canyons adjacent to towns. More mill operators sought to exploit mining development;

2. "San Juan Stake History," p. 93.
3. "Historical Information, La Sal National Forest," p. 109.

their sets following the tide of mining fortunes. When a mine played out or was shifted to a new site, sawmill operators abandoned half-cut tracts of timber in order to follow, since it was easier to move the mill than to transport lumber.

At best, transportation was a serious problem. Distances were great, teams were slow, and in the early 1890s very few roads were to be found on either the La Sal or the Blue Mountains although crude tracks had been worked to the more accessible mines by about 1900. Indeed, lumbering operations with the related mining developments contributed much to road-building. For timber crews, road construction was lost time and usually was done in the quickest, most haphazard fashion. Levi Savage, a young mill hand in the Kamas area of Summit County, has left a diary of his experiences in the Uinta Mountains during the 1870s. While his period was much earlier, conditions on the La Sal were probably quite similar to those young Savage confronted:

> A miserable night spent and here we are to day pulling and tugging up through the timber with six yoke of oxen *doubled* on to each wagon. The whole of yesterday spent in moving six wagons probably not more than one mile and a half; and, in clearing away the timber and under brush for the road. Everything wet and miserable in the morning but through the middle and after parts of the day it was more dry and comfortable. A small shower last night; enough to give the grass and weeds another good wetting; and almost every time we stir this morning wet socks and pantaloons is the result.[4]

Sawmillers overcame the disadvantages of bad roads by various devices. As suggested previously, one common practice was to locate the mill in timber standing adjacent to the market. Occasionally timbermen on the north La Sals also availed themselves of the Grand River. T. W. Branson floated rafts from Castle Valley to Moab with good results. Hauling lumber from his mill at the head of Castle Valley, Branson put his rafts in the river just above where Castle Creek debouches into it. Carrying between 6,000 and 10,000 feet of lumber, the rafts were a quick and efficient means of transport to Moab. Branson's 1903 raft ran aground on a sand bar, forcing the raftmen to spend a miserable night in the sand, but river transit was sufficiently successful to cause the *Grand Valley Times* to extol it. According to its lines, the "great water-way of the Grand River" was "of inestimable value to this section of the country."[5]

Only small mills were used on the La Sal Forest with capacities capable of (but rarely achieving) up to 10,000 feet per day. At least

---

4. Diary of Levi Mathers Savage, Book A, 1873 (handwritten original owned by Joseph Savage of Chandler, Arizona; copy in present writer's possession), p. 24. A less detailed account of Savage's lumbering experience may be found in Charles S. Peterson, ed., "Book A—Levi Mathers Savage: The Look of Utah in 1873," *Utah Historical Quarterly* 41 (1973): 4-23.

5. *Grand Valley Times*, 13 November 1908.

one "up and down" mill was operated—at Bulldog Canyon. All mills appear to have been portable and powered by steam until the 1930s, when one or two gasoline engines are mentioned. No permanent waterpowered mills were used on the La Sals, but several of this type operated in adjacent Emery and Sanpete counties usually in conjunction with flour mills. One noted miller was Samuel Jewkes, who used the same water to power both a flour mill and a sawmill at Fountain Green. Immediately after moving to Emery County about 1880, Jewkes built another mill in the mouth of Cottonwood Canyon west of Orangeville. His son, Joseph H. Jewkes, left the following account of its construction:

> To build our mill, long leaf pine was brought from the head of Cottonwood Canyon. . . . It was hauled down by ox teams and was sawed by horse power. The mill was built by Brother Brigham T. Higgs . . . He was an architect as well as a skilled carpenter and supervised the entire construction. . . . When completed, it being the first mill in Castle Valley, a celebration was held.[6]

More commonly used for threshing purposes, sweep powers turned by horses do not appear to have been utilized for milling purposes on the La Sals.

Early La Sal Forest mills were manned by crews of no more than a half-dozen. For the most part these were occasional lumberjacks, unskilled and often willing to work only when other obligations permitted. Wages were said to be high, averaging from $2.50 to $3.00 per day in 1911. Lumbering was not an easy life. Serious injuries and deaths were not infrequent. Powered by steam and without inspections to force cleanliness, these small mills were very susceptible to fires. Levi Savage waxes almost lyrical as he tells of one conflagration:

> . . . after we had all quietly fallen to sleep last night, the noise of a fire in the thick timber near by awakened some of the camp. They gave the alarm and soon we were all out fighting it some with clothes on and some naked. The fire ran up through the oily leaves of the balsams and streamed out above, like a mighty plag of the *fairies* that was wafted in the night presenting most a magnificent spectacle. This was a beautiful scene. But not a very pleasant sensation to be suddenly startled out of a peaceful slumber and find a large fire raging so close to a thick grove of timber in which we were sleeping. The fire I suppose started from the bellows of the blacksmithshop a few yards from the mill lumber logs and etc. However, a few minutes of desperate exertion in felling trees and clearing away underbrush brought his majesty under our control.[7]

Most early mills appear to have been jerry-built contraptions put together from odds and ends of other mills and, in all too many

---

6. Joseph H. Jewkes, "Reminiscences" (mimeographed copy in writer's possession), p. 6.

7. Diary of Levi Mathers Savage, p. 38; and "The Look of Utah in 1873," p. 19.

cases, far past the point of serviceable operation. Illustrative of this situation was one La Sal Mountain mill that was abandoned for a time and was carried away a piece at a time until by 1940 the entire mill, including the boiler, had been removed. Given these conditions, breakdowns were almost continual. Savage's diary for September, 1873, makes the point. "On September 10 a wheel belonging to the Engine, which had been broken before and very poorly fixed up again came to pieces while she was under motion." With "chuncks of this hard stuff" flying around in a way that was "truly astonishing," the mill which had sawed no more than 10,000 feet since the last breakdown was idled while new parts were procured from Salt Lake City. Under way again by September 27, the mill limped along for a few days but was a sore trial to the patience of the crew. In Savage's words:

> The old mill does not come up to our expectations. She is nearly worn out, in some places and it is one continual 'toggle and tinker' to run her. Instead of six to eight thousand feet cut out in a day, about two is our largest.

But even two thousand feet per day was too good to last, and on September 30 the mill went down a third time. As Savage said: "It is very provoking to run an *old* saw mill always getting out of repair, and costing considerable to do anything at all with it."[8]

At least twenty-eight sawmills had operated on the La Sal Forest before 1940. Most were individual enterprises or partnerships, but Mormon cooperativism was expressed in the story of the Grayson Cooperative Mill. Henry Couraud, John Pace, James Stocks, William L. Young, Charles A. Burr, and the Innes brothers are among the names that recur in the lumbering record, but by all odds the most important were T. W. Branson and his sons, J. M. and John. They were among the earliest outfits involved, and the family continues in the lumber business in northern Arizona and southwest Colorado. At least one cattle company, Cunningham and Carpenter, ran its own sawmill, and one mine, the Interstate Mining Company at Gold Basin, sawed its own mining timbers for a few years. But for the most part early sawmillers were small jobbers supplying the demand of individual buyers on a retail basis or taking contracts to supply lumberyards in town, or providing lumber for projects such as the 1911 construction of the Moab bridge across the Colorado River.

All too often lumbermen did retail business on credit. Improvident settlers sometimes worked out debts by skidding logs or doing road work, but the general shortage of money was a continuing problem. Supervisor Henry Bergh thought it was the greatest handicap faced by La Sal Forest operators. Writing in 1912, he noted that timber sales had exceeded 300,000 feet. However, the mills

8. Diary of Levi Mathers Savage, pp. 37, 41; and "The Look of Utah in 1873," p. 19.

Logs for the Grayson Co-op Mill on the Blue Mountains. U.S. Forest
Service photo.

had been unable to run full time because ". . . they are unable to
collect cash for sales of lumber and they haven't sufficient monies
to put into the business or to carry so many patrons for any length
of time." One timber surveyor summarized the entire problem:
"Lumbering has always been . . . carried on wastefully and without
profit either to exploiters or to the forest."[9]

Until 1900, southeastern Utah lumbermen operated under few
regulations. In that year the Department of Interior promulgated
rules which it hoped would control the lumbering industry on
public lands.[10] However, controls had little impact until after the
creation of the forest.

In terms of management, La Sal Forest timberlands appear to
have caused few problems. Sales were small and of manageable
numbers. There is no record that the Forest actually processed a
timber sale until 1909, but it seems likely that earlier sales did take
place. The first recorded transaction was for no more than 25,000
feet and was made to the Grayson Cooperative Company. Most
sales were somewhat larger but still were below 100,000 feet. However, a few sales did involve larger amounts. In 1910 the Grayson
Cooperative Company purchased 434,000 feet (this may have kept

9. *Cliffdwellers' Echo,* December 1912; and Timber Management Report,
1911, Timber Management Folder, Manti-La Sal National Forest Historical Files.

10. *Grand Valley Times,* 2 March 1900.

the co-op busy for some time, as no other sale was awarded to it until 1912). In 1914 the J. E. Stevens mill purchased 515,000 feet, and in 1919 Charles A. Burr bought 404,000 feet.[11] These were all Blue Mountains sales. Transactions of similar scope were made on the La Sal division as is evidenced by a 1917 invitation for bids on a tract amounting to 600,000 feet.[12] Few statistics exist, but it seems probable that total timber production for the La Sal Forest ran about 1,000,000 feet during its first decade. Its productive capacity was said to far exceed this—optimists thought it could sustain an annual production of 3,000,000 feet—and logic suggests that footage escalated as the years passed.

Saw timber appears to have been limited to three main species: ponderosa or yellow pine, engleman spruce, and douglas fir. Of these, the ponderosa pine was the most important, while douglas fir provided relatively insignificant amounts. According to early reports all three species were scattered and with few exceptions not reproducing themselves. This was particularly true of the yellow pine. Although forest fires had not constituted a problem since the coming of the whites, timber experts were agreed that at an earlier time fast-moving brush fires had stripped the country of young growth and ground cover. Together with intensive grazing, this had almost eliminated the conditions necessary to natural reproduction. Thus, much timber, mature and even aging, stood in scattered growths over wide tracts. Major efforts were made to harvest spiketops and other partially defective trees and at the same time to provide ground cover by leaving lopped tops and branches where they fell and, in some cases, even scattering them.

Beginning at least as early at 1909, there was talk that reproduction could be stimulated artificially. Henry Bergh seems to have pursued this matter more energetically than any other forest supervisor. In his drive to establish a system of ranger stations, he planned to make the North Cottonwood Station a nursery to produce seedlings, and in 1913 he launched a program of reseeding and transplanting. In the fall of the previous year, rangers had spent several weeks cutting and drying cones, harvesting about 300 pounds of yellow pine seed—a disappointing yield in view of the time and energy committed to the undertaking. Since the only literature available on gathering seeds was designed for big operations, Bergh had found it necessary to feel his way into the seed gathering project. He quickly learned that trees from forty to fifty years old bore more cones than trees of other ages, and that their cones apparently bore more seed. Using pruning knives and hooks with handles about six feet long, the rangers pulled down limbs and picked or cut the cones. These were then dried on sheets stretched

---

11. "Historical Information, La Sal National Forest," p. 108.
12. Ibid., pp. 107-8; and *Grand Valley Times*, 23 February 1917.

Manti National Forest sawmill set. U.S. Forest Service photo.

over frames built about a foot from the ground, and the seed was shaken free.[13]

During 1913 the seeds were planted—again with disappointing results, as birds and rodents evidently picked out the sprouting plants. Somewhat more successful was Bergh's attempt to transplant seedlings. Some 45,000 plants acquired in two separate lots from a nursery near Kamas were set out by a crew of about a dozen men on the Blue Mountains in September and October. While no subsequent evaluation of the success of this project has come to light, Bergh himself was hopeful that it represented a good beginning.[14]

Free use of wood products was an important if not the most important aspect of timber utilization on the La Sal. In keeping with the Forest Service policy of extending help to individual settlers, regulations were worked out in the first years of Forest Service development enabling settlers to use such timber, wood, and poles as their own operation required. Indeed, the Act of June 4, 1897, establishing the forest reserve system, made the following provisions:

> The Secretary of the Interior may permit, under regulations to be prescribed by him, the use of timber and stone found upon such reservations, free of charge, by bona fide settlers, miners, residents, and prospectors for minerals, for firewood, fencing, buildings, mining,

13. *Cliffdwellers' Echo,* December 1912.
14. *Grand Valley Times,* 26 September and 17 October 1913.

prospecting, and other domestic purposes, as may be needed by such persons for such purposes. . . .[15]

Subsequent rulings refined the meaning of this law, placing emphasis upon individual use. Regulations required users to make application to forest supervisors and to remove the timber within the six-month time limit prescribed by the permit. Free use was clearly understood to be a privilege rather than a right, and permits were issued only on the supervisor's satisfaction that applicants qualified in the intent and locale of their use.

Free use drew heavily upon the La Sal Forest, but because of the small number of settlers it did not constitute an undue burden. This fact is attested by frequent reference to dead timber, poles, and other varieties usually used in meeting free use demands. Settlers hauled wood and cut poles as well as logs for houses. Rangers occasionally referred to spending much of their time administering free use permits.

The Timber Survey of 1911

Between April 21 and December 2 of 1911, a Forest-wide timber reconnaissance was conducted. A total of twelve men were employed with an average crew of about eight men in the field. Most survey personnel were assigned specifically to this job with the regular Forest force playing only occasional and minor roles. C. E. Dunston, who appears to have been a District IV deputy supervisor, launched the project and directed it during its first two months. On his departure Dunston placed S. S. Stewart in charge, and the remainder of the field work and the two surviving reports that grew from it were done under his supervision.

The party was in the field for more than seven months. During this period it was supplied by a string of burros purchased and trained for the purpose and later taken to Ogden for similar use elsewhere. While there was some turnover in personnel and members of the party came and went as required to transport mail and supplies, it was a hard-working group. S. S. Stewart and others appear to have stayed in the field during the entire field season, sometimes taking off on Sundays and holidays but often working seven days a week. The Fourth of July was spent in a wet camp. Stewart, who rarely recorded anything not strictly business, set the day apart with this entry: "July 4—Heap big celebration—like h--l."[16]

Stewart and his comrades spent the spring and summer months entirely on the Blue Mountains. Their function was two-fold, and the party worked as two crews—one estimating timber and the other running base lines and mapping. Completing work on the

---

15. *Compilation of Laws and Regulations, General Land Office* (Washington, D.C., 1903).

16. "Diury [Diary] La Sal Cruising Party 1911," Timber Management Folder.

Blue Mountains on September 11, they moved immediately to the La Sals and, with shortened days and cold weather confronting them, rushed to finish the job by December 1.

During their seven months afield, the Stewart party had subjected the La Sal Forest to its most careful and thorough survey. In addition to timber estimates amounting to 180,000,000 board feet, an area totalling 246,000 acres had been mapped. From data now available it is impossible to state with certainty if this mapping effort was merely an adjunct of the timber reconnaissance or if its careful triangulations, base lines, and measurements enabled Stewart and his colleagues to draw the first thorough map of the La Sal National Forest. It seems likely that their work made a major contribution to geographic understanding of the Forest.

The costs of the survey are interesting and important. Total expenditures for the field work, including all salaries, came to no more than $4,586. Stewart reported his expenses as follows:

Travel and subsistence	$ 490.70
Transportation of supplies	47.73
Equipment	221.47
Supplies	705.89
Salaries	3,120.81
Total	$4,586.60

In further analyzing costs he derived that the party's time had been applied to mapping as against estimating on a relative basis of 841 to 483. Translated to total costs, this ratio gave $2,913.40 for the mapping and $1,673.20 for the estimating. According to his statement, "average cost per acre of mapping in the field ($2,913.40 ÷ 246,900 acres) is $.0118 per acre. Average costs of estimating per M. ($1,673.20 ÷ 181,525 M) is $.0092."[17]

At least two major reports were written as result of the 1911 reconnaissance. One, "The Silvical Report of the La Sal National Forest," was technical and concerned with species, soil conditions, elevations, and their relationship to forage and timber types, fire damage, insect damage, lightning losses, and so forth. One extensive section dealt with various problems of management. The other report, "Timber Management Report 1911," covered much of the same ground but was more general in tone and included more data of a historical nature. Together, they provide a good look into the early timber conditions of the La Sal National Forest and were used heavily in formulating views advanced earlier in this chapter.[18]

In summary, the early La Sal National Forest may be said to have possessed what, in the light of the use burdens placed upon it,

17. Timber Management Report, 1911, Timber Management Folder. As used here, "M" indicates 1,000 board feet.
18. *See* Timber Management Folder.

Tool cache on Blue Mountains. U.S. Forest Service photo.

was a substantial amount of timber. Fire was not a major problem
although it did contribute to spotty reproduction. Heavy grazing,
drouth, and disease had also contributed to a scattered (but rather
extensive) timber stand. Local demands for free use and saw timber
were easily provided by the Forest, and until after 1920, little if any
lumber was shipped out. In terms of general importance, timber
management ranked high, not only because of local need for timber
products, but also because of its relationship to watershed management. However, compared with grazing it occupied relatively little
time and probably produced much less revenue.

Chapter XII

Transportation and Communication

Pioneer Roads

Among the overwhelming realities of southeastern Utah are its immensity and the need for transportation and communication—immensity's natural corollary. In effect, the pioneers of the area located themselves in the middle of nowhere. Magnificent canyons and deserts threw up barriers sharply limiting lines of travel and at the same time imposed an intervening distance requiring travel over untold miles for people who would come and go.

No more than a half-dozen paths have been found leading into the country. The Old Spanish Trail was, of course, the earliest of these. From the south came a trail passing from Tuba City and other points in Arizona to join the route of the Spanish Trail and proceed north via Green River. These trails and their branches are still followed by the region's highways. Less favored by history was the Hole-in-the-Rock road which extended east beyond Bluff to give the region contact with Durango and other Colorado communities.

Road construction and maintenance were undoubtedly the most important public obligations in the earliest pioneer times. They were also essentially local obligations, as pioneers were too few in numbers and too remote to attract territorial and state assistance. Thus, the counties shouldered the public burden of road development and, to the detriment of education and other functions now considered essential, devoted virtually all of their limited budgets to this purpose.

Public roads were designated by the county court and individuals were appointed to care for them. In some cases modest appropriations were made, and supervisors were directed to call upon private

Roadway up the Hole-in-the-Rock.

parties using the road to make contributions of labor. During the first years, emphasis was placed upon the lifelines running back to civilization; however, distance demanded self-sufficiency, and within a few years roads to timber and wood supplies were financed publicly. In time, special interests required that the major paths which crossed the region from north to south and west to east be supplemented. A road serving Castle Valley was necessary. Its approach was first from Cisco on the railroad line and later up the Colorado River. By 1900 Miner's Basin and other mining developments were served by roads—in reality little more than wagon tracks —which penetrated the north slope of the La Sals. About the same time a road was pushed up the easy southeast slope of the Blue Mountains to the Camp Jackson mines.

There was much private effort and participation. When roads were planned, subscriptions were called for. In some cases where larger interests desired roads, these interests undertook their own construction. In a few instances toll roads were developed. Among these was the Grand River road from Moab to Castleton. J. N. Corbin, editor of the *Grand Valley Times*, sponsored other toll roads. One projected a toll system from Thompson to Moab to serve as a special passage for "autos or other self contained motive power propelled vehicles."[1] In the last named case a franchise cover-

---

1. *Grand Valley Times*, 12 September 1904.

Early road grade along old Spanish Trail.

ing a period of fifty years was let by the county commissioners, but there is no evidence that the project was ever completed. Like Corbin's road for horseless carriages, other toll roads were neither successful nor important. Distances and cost of construction as well as limited use dictated that roads remain generally under public responsibility.

Ferries and Navigation

Tolls were used more successfully in connection with river crossings. A ferry appears to have functioned at least as early as 1881 at Green River, but travelers were forced to ford the Grand at Moab until about 1885. Later—probably after 1895—the Mail Ford Ferry was established at Dewey to serve Castle Valley. At Moab Lester Taylor owned land over which the road approached the Grand River crossing and for several years operated a ferry there under rates set by the county. Individual travelers occasionally reported fees as being somewhat higher, but the authorized list ran from a low of four cents for sheep in lots over twenty-five to a round trip maximum of $1.50 for a six-horse team and wagon.[2]

Ferry service was neither dependable nor safe. In 1897 the Dewey ferry slipped its moorings and ran downstream several miles before snagging, thus occasioning an interruption in service for several days. Escaping again, it got away permanently, requiring the construction of another boat. Drownings sometimes occurred. An unusual tragedy was related by Don Taylor, who as a boy ran his father's ferry at Moab:

> . . . I was only a boy when one day a group of Indians wanted me to take them across but would not pay toll. As I refused they started to ford the river. One old buck made his squaw trade horses with him as the one the squaw had was larger, and was more sure of getting across. As soon as he got into the water this horse reared over with him and he was drowned. They couldn't find his body that day but the next day I saw it caught above a small island a short distance below the ford.[3]

Bridges replaced ferries early in the second decade of this century. In 1910 a steel bridge was dedicated at Green River, and in the following year state appropriations made possible the construction of a bridge at Moab. Costing $45,000, of which the State of Utah put up $35,000 and the county $10,000, it was completed in December of 1912. Earlier the same year a bridge spanned the San Juan at Mexican Hat, built partly as a result of the San Juan oil boom of 1911.

River transportation attracted a surprising amount of attention in the years before good roads were developed. At least as early as 1896 there was talk of navigation on the Green and Grand rivers. At the turn of the century, a Captain F. H. Summeril carried tourists and freight on both rivers for a time before his boat, the *Undine,* overturned about eight miles above Moab.[4] Thereafter, river navigation lagged until 1905, when two groups, one with a gasoline launch and one with a steamboat, talked up the advantages of river transportation and made a few river trips. In Moab the prospects of water connections seemed brightest from Cisco, which lay on the railroad about four miles distance from the river some 40 miles upstream. According to the *Grand Valley Times,* Congress once appropriated $40,000 to develop that section of the Grand River, but President Cleveland vetoed the measure.[5] That the river continued

---

2. Ibid., 25 December 1896.
3. Historical Documents, Manti-La Sal National Forest Historical Files, p. 14.
4. *Grand Valley Times,* 13 December 1901 and 23 May 1902.
5. Ibid., 13 January, 7 April, and 21 July 1905.

to be recognized as an avenue into otherwise impassable country was evidenced by the activity of the Moab Garage Company during the 1920s. When geologists from the Mid-West Exploration Company decided to drill down river, the Garage Company had several boats with which it handled a contract to move 200 tons of drilling equipment to the site of the well.[6]

Railroad Dreams

Like most other Americans of the era, people of the La Sal Forest area dreamed of railroads and of prosperity borne on steel tracks. Predating the Forest by many years, the first of these dreams envisioned a Pacific railroad following the canyon of the Colorado River. Conceived by Frank M. Brown of Denver and nurtured by reports of gold, the Colorado River project actually got as far as an exploration of the river before Brown's accidental death forced the explorers back in 1889. Undaunted, the project's chief engineer, Robert B. Stanton, returned to complete the adventurous survey the following year, however, the railroad project proved to be dead.[7]

But visions of railroading refused to stay at rest. In 1900 the Rio Grande Western put parties in the field surveying a line from Cisco to the La Sal Mountain mines and led people of the area to believe that a branch would be built as quickly as mines could guarantee two carloads of ore per day. Thereafter, the railroad dream lay dormant until the fall of 1911, when a Mr. Wanemaker entered the country, promoting and surveying for a line which was to cross the west corner of the Forest on the South Elks and proceed to the Pacific coast via Hite's Crossing of the Colorado River. Among those excited by the prospect was Forest Supervisor Henry Bergh, who was approached by Wanemaker relative to the supply of timber available for use as ties. With characteristic disregard for fact, Bergh informed him that no less than 200,000,000 feet stood on the West Elks alone—actually the timber survey of that same summer had indicated some 180,000,000 feet on the entire Forest.[8]

Forest Trails and Roads

Logistics posed problems quite as severe for the Forest as for the population at large. With the exception of a few wagon tracks, the La Sal National Forest had been penetrated only by horseback when the reserves were established. Construction of trails and roads was

6. Virgil Fay Baldwin, "Freighting on the Colorado River," *Utah Historical Quarterly* 32 (1964): 122-29.
7. C. Gregory Crampton, *Standing Up Country, the Canyon Lands of Utah and Arizona* (Salt Lake City: University of Utah Press, 1964), pp. 131-34; and Dwight L. Smith, "The Engineer and the Canyon," *Utah Historical Quarterly* 28 (1960): 263-74.
8. *Cliffdwellers' Echo,* January 1912.

second only to personnel expenditures in the budgets of the early years; in the 1930s road construction may have become the largest single budget item. Given this emphasis, a complex system of stock driveways, trails, and roads was developed. The record is brief and usually makes only passing reference to this phase of Forest administration, but a few conclusions may be advanced.

Trail construction was initiated immediately after the Forest was established and continued throughout the period of this study as the Forest officers undertook to gain access to the various grazing districts and to provide trails to facilitate livestock management. Costs often were distributed among the stockmen benefiting from trail development. However, there appear to have been many trail projects undertaken entirely at Forest expense. In 1925 an especially vigorous trail program was carried on, with virtually every district on the Forest having a trails crew at work. Most trails constructed that

Over the Sandrock Trail, between Moab and Monticello. U.S. Forest Service photo.

year appear to have been devoted to improving accessibility of various rough parts of the Forest. A 1928 report laid out the entire system of trails and roads both as they existed at that time and as Forest projections set forth. Of a system totalling 364 miles, 342 had been completed at a total cost of $14,000, and twenty-two miles remained to be constructed at an anticipated cost of $1,000. That subsequent planners recognized other needed trails improvements is obvious in the fact that the decade of the 1930s saw at least fifteen separate projects undertaken.[9]

The 1928 report also indicated that the Forest system included 107 miles of completed roads, which had cost a total of $67,000, and that twenty miles were then on the planning boards at an anticipated expenditure of $11,900. The total figures involved are so small as to suggest the report did not include all roads, and yet contemporary accounts indicate that most La Sal Forest roads were constructed or substantially improved during the 1930s by the Civilian Conservation Corps and other federal programs.

As with the trails, Forest roads were sometimes undertaken as cooperative ventures with the Forest assuming part or all of the expense of roads passing within its bounds. Roads constructed from La Sal to Paradox and from Blanding to the Natural Bridges in the 1920s were typical. A 1916 *Grand Valley Times* article reported that the State Road Commission and the federal government had projected $10,000 on the former road on a matching basis for the 1919 fiscal year. Early in 1919 a series of articles disclosed Supervisor S. B. Locke's maneuvers to raise the Forest's share. The project was given wide publicity, and Locke openly urged residents to display their interest by petitioning Washington to make funds available. Evidently his efforts were successful because $5,000 was appropriated, and the project was promptly initiated.[10] Since its inception the Forest had promoted the Natural Bridges. Its assumption of the cost of construction from Cottonwood Canyon to the Kigalia Ranger Station and southwest to Maverick Point made it possible for the public to visit this natural wonder at a time far earlier than had it been left entirely to state and county funds.

Roads: Passenger Service and Recreation

Although regular mail deliveries date back to at least 1883, there is no evidence that public transportation was generally available in southeastern Utah until well after 1900. If travelers lacked conveyance, they appear to have waited to catch a freight wagon, or to have hired a buggy, and in more than a few cases to have walked. Writing in 1907, Burl Armstrong made the first note of travel by stage that

9. "Historical Information, La Sal National Forest," pp. 90-103.
10. *Grand Valley Times,* 1 December 1916 and 29 March, 4 April, and 18 April 1919.

has come to my attention. By contrast, dozens of earlier references provide evidence that for many years passenger service either did not exist or operated only infrequently. However, by the second decade of the century, a "horse and buggy stage line" provided regular mail and passenger service.[11] In 1910 the Allred Transportation Company obtained the post contract between the railroad at Thompson and Moab, and, combining it with daily passenger service, operated at sufficient profit to allow the company to extend its service to Monticello two years later. Using only horses until 1913 or 1914, the Allred Company offered minimum facilities, including Studebaker buggies, stations at several lonely sites on the long road between Monticello and the railroad, and "canned goods and crackers . . . as standard emergency rations . . ."[12] Fare from Moab to Thompson was three dollars and from Moab to Monticello, four dollars. Like modern air fare, a ticket entitled passengers to carry up to forty pounds of luggage. Travelers included salesmen, theatrical groups, members of Moab's 500 Club (a booster club), politicians, Forest Service officers, and, occasionally, far-ranging tourists. Beginning in 1913 automobiles were experimented with. At first they were a constant source of trouble, but by the end of World War I the automobile stage had fully supplanted horses.

As means of travel improved, the Forest Service became one of the earliest boosters of southeastern Utah and assumed considerable responsibility for drawing tourists into the region. We have seen Supervisor Bergh promoting railroads and using the "Cliff Dwellers' Echo" as a device to advance the country. In 1916 the Forest worked up the first of several tour guides. Recognizing that natural wonders were the country's main attraction, the guide extolled its beauty and played down the inconvenience of its frontier conditions. Two separate approaches were proposed to the traveler. One stayed with the main roads; the other suggested that special equipment and guides be hired to enable the real enthusiast to view the unique scenery and prehistoric sites that covered the hinterland.

Roads were important to this guide, and it was a time when sentiment and color were used freely in stirring public interest. Giving Moab as the focal point, the guide started travelers from Salt Lake City over the Midland Trail to Thompson. Taking the Sandrock Trail—a name used by John Riis as well—the tour guide directed the traveler to Moab, from which he was assured he could follow the Rainbow Route, a new road to be completed in 1917 to La Sal and thence to Paradox. If the spirit of adventure was with the traveler, he could then avail himself of the famed Rocky Mountain Highway to Durango, then loop back to Mesa Verde National Park, and then

---

11. B. W. Allred, *The Life of a Horse and Buggy Stage Line Operator,* Great Western Series, no. 11 (Washington: Potomac Corral, The Westerns, 1972).

12. Ibid., p. 3.

on to Bluff, Blanding, and Monticello and points north to the Glacier National Park for a total of 1,825 miles. Using more prosaic names, the guide then invited tourists to visit the various towns in the Forest's neighborhood and finally described the wonders of the mountains, uranium mines, the geological formations of Salt Creek and Beef Basin, the Natural Bridges, numerous cliff dwellings, the Colorado River, Monument Valley, and various other wonders.

By 1929 some of the names had changed, but the sentiment and color that characterized the earlier guide were still to be found. Travelers leaving Spanish Fork for southeastern Utah traveled over the Arrow Head Trail to Thompson where they took the Navajo Trail to Moab, "the northern Gateway to the scenic wonders of Southeastern Utah. . . ." Moving on over the Navajo Trail, they passed to Monticello through "a scenic panorama of rare charm and beauty . . . vari-colored cliffs, green-garbed hills, solitary monoliths and wide valleys conspire to make a journey of ever changing interest." Pressing on to Blanding, the hardy tourist took the last lap of his journey to the Bridges, crossing sixteen miles of the La Sal Forest, seeing the Goblet of Venus and Arch Canyon, "second in grandeur only to 'Bryce's Canyon.'" Now following the "Old Mormon Trail," the road proceeded through the Bear's Ears and on to the great natural bridges. Withal, the guide presented a use of color and sentiment quite as

Moab bridge, about 1912. U.S. Forest Service photo.

effective as in present-day advertising. In it, the primitive became a virtue and the rugged, a joy.[13]

Telephones

If 1916 travelers had paused to reflect that the country had been without benefit of telegraph or telephone until only twenty years before, the remoteness of the region would have needed little emphasis. J. N. Corbin was instrumental in organizing a telephone company in 1897 which brought service to Moab soon thereafter.[14] In 1903 the La Sal Mountain Telephone and Electric Company came into being with the stated purpose of extending the telephone lines to Castleton. The fact that the first Forest office was established at Castleton suggests that telephone service existed there by 1906, but no evidence has been located confirming this assumption. In 1906 the La Sal Mountain Company ran a line to a ranger station on Wilson Mesa and somewhat later to the La Sal Ranger Station and to Paradox. While the telephone was delayed in its extension to Monticello by numerous false starts, the Baker Ranger Station was equipped by 1909, and by 1914 much work had been done toward providing telephone services to other Blue and Elk mountains sites, including the one at Kigalia Spring. Even such isolated sites as the Mormon Pasture Station had a telephone by 1924.

Telephone communications were considered to be a necessity by the Forest Service from the very first. Speed was indispensable in case of fire, and good communications contributed to the general success of Forest administration. While some expenditures were incurred well into the 1930s for installation of telephone lines, the early arrangements seemed to provide adequate service and were subject to less elaboration and change than road and trail systems. Indeed, as late as the mid-1950s when I lived at La Sal, telephone calls were received on one ancient wall and earphone set, then relayed to remote ranches by the party taking the call. The relay was made over an equally ancient set that hung beside the first one on the wall of Redd Ranches' fine old ranch house.

Thus, the La Sal National Forest made an important contribution to southeastern Utah in the realm of transportation and communication. The Forest provided an additional public budget with which to develop roads over heavily used portions of the region. It also provided the impetus and organization necessary to motivate private interests. Furthermore, the multiple use policy of Forest administration led to road construction for recreational purposes in several important instances. The Forest's determination to have telephone service doubtless advanced its use in numerous mountain areas by years if not decades.

13. La Sal Recreation Folder, Manti-La Sal National Forest Historical Files.
14. *Grand Valley Times,* 17 December 1897.

Chapter XIII

Watershed, Federal Programs, and Merging Forests

In the foregoing chapters, the La Sal National Forest has been studied in its regional context. Attention has been given to the genesis of the society in which the Forest functioned, and the story told about the Forest itself has been one of interaction with and adjustment to the broader community. Many of the major themes of Forest administration have been examined. However, much has of necessity been ignored. In the main, choice of topic has been predicated upon two interrelated considerations. First—as in all history—it has been necessary to let the available data guide the flow of the study. Thus, important and perhaps even crucial themes have received scant attention because information has not been found. Second, other themes about which data does exist have been passed over because they seemed to fit only loosely. However, since the full picture can hardly be seen without some reference to them, several topics for which only limited documentation has been found will be incorporated in this concluding chapter.

Watershed Developments

The primary function of the Forest Service has been to regulate the use of natural resources in order to get the most from them for the greatest number of people and to perpetuate resources for future use. In the arid west, water has long been recognized as the key resource. Timber, grazing, soil, and recreation, each in its own way, take life from it. Under proper conditions it holds the potential of effective regulation of other resources. Out of balance, it leads to a wide variety of problems.

Rarely has water been more critical than for the area of the La Sal Forest. Petitions to protect Monticello's culinary water first called foresters' attention to southeastern Utah in 1902. A few years later the two inspectors upon whose recommendations the original forest reserves were created recognized the role of water. Since that time Forest officers have repeatedly stressed water management's central function. However, at times this appears to have been more a matter of lip service than of practice. This is not to deny it was an underlying principle. Yet Forest managers frequently were diverted from the major issue of water by various short-term considerations. Problems were dealt with as separate entities rather than as part of a water-related whole. Thus, grazing, boundaries, or Forest improvements became the real objectives while watershed management slipped into eclipse. Put differently, water was recognized as the essential problem, but because of the magnitude of its regulation and the immediate demands of other functions, it received much less direct attention than did a number of other activities.

This fact is apparent in the historical record of water on the La Sal Forest. There is considerable peripheral material—that is, frequent but passing references to various watershed problems appear in the record of grazing, timber, or other activities. These create a general impression of water's importance. On the other hand, there is very little information that focuses directly upon water. The data that does exist may be organized to point up several general divisions of activity. First is the regulation of watersheds for culinary purposes. Then follow irrigation, floods, erosion, and pond development.

Each homestead, ranch, and village was dependent upon its own watershed for culinary purposes. In the case of ranches and smaller communities, one spring often provided the entire water source. Towns drew from larger drainages. For most of them, irrigation ditches were for years the source of culinary water. But by the mid-1890s, some towns had begun to think of more sophisticated systems. Progressive for its time was Moab's 1896 plan to install a water system using pine logs for pipe lines.[1] Good intentions notwithstanding, most villages made slow progress in solving problems of pure drinking water. Epidemics were not infrequent. For example, typhoid swept Monticello in 1910, leaving seventeen dead and many more weak and crippled.[2] But some towns limped along decade after decade with no water system at all or with makeshift operations. Typical was La Sal where during the 1950s the state dairy inspector carried on a prolonged campaign to force Redd Ranches to put in proper settling facilities and a treatment plant in order to maintain its dairy at grade A standards. Water for La Sal's seventy-five people came from Coyote Spring through an open creek which transected a lambing ground. Water was often discolored, and lambs and other dead animals were sometimes found in the settling tanks. When I left

---

1. *Grand Valley Times*, 5 June 1896.
2. *See* p. 134. *See also* Brooks, *Uncle Will*, p. 128.

La Sal in 1956, after operating Redd's dairy for a period, the problem had still not been adequately solved.

The three major towns, Moab, Monticello, and Blanding, each had trouble developing culinary water. Moab depended upon Mill and Pack creeks; Monticello, upon North and other creeks on the east slope of the Blues; and Blanding, upon Indian Creek, Johnson Creek, and a number of springs and brooks that fed the latter stream. In each case some restriction of grazing had been practiced. Sheep had been barred from the seven-mile limits above Monticello at a very early time and together with cattle had been kept from certain limited areas at the head of Pack Creek and Johnson Creek during the 1920s. However, in no case had erosion, pollution, and other watershed problems been controlled. On each drainage grew considerable timber, but lumber activities had not been a real problem. Some efforts at artificial reforestation and erosion control were made at relatively early times—particularly on Monticello's watershed. But artificial development of ground cover had enjoyed no great success.

Perhaps most useful in terms of understanding the imperatives of water development was Blanding and its Johnson Creek watershed—a fact which was recognized when LeGrand Olson featured it in "Blue Mountains Water Is Liquid Gold," an article for the 1967 *Yearbook of Agriculture.* The town had been established in 1905, and from the first had trouble meeting its needs for culinary water, drinking progressively from a scum-ridden pond, Westwater Creek, the irrigation ditch, and cisterns. About 1920, growing concern led to a plan to bring additional waters from Indian Creek on the north side of the mountain by means of a tunnel. Begun in 1922, the tunnel took thirty-nine years to complete, cost $120,000 and was something of an epoch in sustained human effort.

Another sort of self-control was necessary where grazing on Johnson Creek was concerned. As a 1929 report made clear, "the community [Blanding] as a whole are entirely dependent on the livestock industry."[3] Quite naturally there was reluctance to reduce critically needed grazing allotments. In 1929 some 2,400 cattle and 1,000 sheep, belonging to fifteen permittees, most of whom lived in Blanding, ranged the Johnson-Recapture Creek drainages and produced a direct revenue of $1,050 to the Forest in fees. There was talk of withdrawing the Johnson-Recapture watersheds from the Forest and turning them over to the municipality to manage, but neither the Forest nor the community looked at this alternative with favor. After putting up with dirty water for nearly fifty years, Blanding at last in 1953 approached the Forest to exclude livestock. Some 900 acres were withdrawn immediately from grazing, including parts of both the north and south drainages of the Blue Mountains. By

---

3. Report on Municipal Watershed, 7 March 1929, Watershed Folder, Manti-La Sal National Forest Historical Files.

1956 the entire area had been terraced and fenced thus ensuring a source of pure water.[4]

Equally important to life was irrigation, as demonstrated by the untold hours put into water development in each of southeastern Utah's towns. The usual pattern was for a community's first settlers to bring out the water by means of an informal and cooperative effort. As changing times demanded, irrigation companies were created for legal purposes, to provide long-term organization, and to enhance economical potential. Blanding's experience again is instructive. The first settlers came in the late 1890s. Rather than building homes immediately, they worked at developing Johnson Creek as a source of irrigation water. For years their faltering efforts failed. Finally a degree of success was achieved after 1905, when canals were tacked to hillsides, and ditch courses were so precisely engineered as to cause passing cowboys to jeer that they ran uphill. The White Mesa Canal Company came into being, and tunnels and other developments gave relative insurance of water. Only then did the town itself take permanent form.[5]

Elsewhere, a patchwork of ditches and watercourses undertook to exploit La Sal Forest water. In some places ingenious and complicated systems were used to get water where people wanted it. Of this sort was the ditch John T. Loveridge made to take the water from Brumley Creek to the upper end of Spanish Valley. Running along the top of Brumley Ridge just below the edge of the aspens, it brought Brumley Creek water into Horse Creek, which in turn emptied into Mill Creek. The water ended its unnatural odyssey when it flowed through Mill Creek Pass, finally emerging far above and to the south of its natural course.[6]

By 1915 some 21,500 acres were irrigated with water running from fourteen different La Sal Forest watersheds. The largest single block of irrigated land was at Paradox, where 5,000 acres were cultivated. Blanding, with 3,500 acres, and Moab, with 2,577 followed. Ironically, the smallest plot of irrigated ground was at Bluff, where Cottonwood Creek watered only 300 acres. Several other drainages watered less than 500 acres. Values placed on this irrigated land varied dramatically, with Fisher Valley land going at thirty dollars per acre and Mill Creek farms averaging $200 per acre. According to one Forest report, all irrigated land was valued at $1,611,000 in 1915. Broken into costs per acre, the Vega Creek water system had been the most expensive to construct, costing fourteen dollars per acre, with the Blanding, Monticello, and Mill Creek systems all running more than eleven dollars per acre. In terms of total outlay,

---

4. U. S., Department of Agriculture, *Yearbook of Agriculture* (1967), pp. 98-100. More informative was Olson's manuscript; see Watershed Folder.

5. Lyman, *History of Blanding.*

6. "Historical Information, La Sal National Forest," p. 134.

Blanding led with a cost of $40,000, Monticello expended $25,000, and Mill Creek and Pack Creek required respective outlays of $15,000 and $10,000. There was little relationship shown between costs of development, or for that matter between productivity and the commercial value placed upon the water-per-acre unit. Blanding, with the greatest total outlay for water development set the value of the average crop produced at forty dollars, and the value of the water-per-acre unit at thirty-five dollars. Most other irrigation systems gave similar figures for production and values. Exceptions were the Mill Creek and Pack Creek systems, where productivity was up slightly but where the commercial value of water rose dramatically, being pegged at $100 per acre unit under the Mill Creek system, and seventy-five dollars under Pack Creek water.[7]

The report cited above indicates that most irrigation systems were maintained at a relatively low cost. Some listed no expenditures for maintenance. Others showed maintenance costs at fifty cents per acre, with the highest running no more than seventy-five or eighty cents. In the light of frequent reference to washouts, flood damage, and later—after beavers began to make a comeback—to beaver dams in ditches, these costs seem low and may represent costs for a run of good years.

Damage to ditches, coupled with the uncertainty of water supply based on diversion of natural runoff, led to a number of efforts to build dams and reservoirs. Perhaps the most ambitious of these was the Buckeye Reservoir, which eventually watered much of Paradox Valley. The first effort in this direction was a private project to dam and divert the waters of Geyser Creek in 1907. A thirty-five foot dam was built, and water was turned in the reservoir the next year. The dam collapsed shortly, sending a destructive flood down Geyser and Rock creeks. After this failure, work began immediately upon the Buckeye dam. After numerous reverses, it was completed under the primary direction of Henry Wilcox. In 1940 most of its stock was owned by a Paradox irrigation company.[8]

In addition to several smaller dams on the Forest, there were a number of promotional ventures to bring water to the deserts north of Moab. Two favorite proposals were to bring water out of the Grand River and to impound flood waters in the large desert watercourses. Projects of the former sort were avidly discussed before the turn of the century. In 1897, for example, a Colonel Balcom of New York pushed an enterprise—styled the Plateau Grand Canal project—to take water from the Grand River above Grand Junction to water 80,000 acres in Colorado, and no fewer than 200,000 acres in Utah. The Grand Canal boom evidently failed to pass the talking stage.

7. S. B. Locke, Report on Watersheds of the La Sal National Forest, 20 December 1915, Watershed Folder.

8. "Historical Information, La Sal National Forest," p. 133.

Among the obstacles contributing to failure was the reluctance of the state of Utah to underwrite two miles of tunnel.[9]

Only a little less grand in scope and equally abortive were attempts to impound flood waters in the washes between Green River and Moab. Of these, few were carried as far as the Valley City development. It was hoped that thousands of acres could be irrigated—some said as high as 250,000 acres.[10] Known under various names, including the Grand Valley Land and Mineral Company and the Valley City Reservoir Company, the project evidently was developed under private financing and in its last stages was backed by an Indianapolis bank. In the years prior to 1908 an earthen dam was built and people were encouraged to take up homesteads below the dam and to buy water rights in it. Among those who succumbed to the literature put out by the Valley City promoters was Howard Balsley, a young resident of Indianapolis, where the bank backing the project carried on a vigorous publicity campaign.[11] In 1908 the dam gave way and the hope of Valley City's future with it.

Floods have been a periodic problem for La Sal Forest administrators and for people depending upon its mountains for water. However, floods do not appear to have been frequent or as devastating as they were on some other Utah forests. No major projects were developed to control them, unless we consider the general effort to control erosion carried on by the Civilian Conservation Corps in the 1930s. Yet floods and erosion were regarded with deep concern and, if nothing else, were used by the Forest Service in its continuing campaign to reduce the number of livestock grazed on the Forest. It is certain that floods seriously damaged ground cover plants, and that unimpeded flood waters cut gullies in roads, along streams, and on mountain slopes generally. However, it is difficult to determine from the historical record just how severe damage really was. Two reports, one from 1915 and one from 1927, give some indication.

In the earlier report Supervisor S. B. Locke undertook to evaluate the overall problem of erosion, including damage caused by erosion in various critical areas. In his opinion, no damage had been done to timber and only "slight" injury to timber reproduction. He found that roads, trails, and irrigation systems had suffered to some degree and recognized some permanent loss in the form of irretrievable washing away of land. His statement on Pack Creek damages—where erosion was greatest—follows:

> The damage to timber or reproduction is very slight. Road repair made necessary on account of floods amounts to approximately $50.00 per year. The damage to the land at the head of the creek, which perhaps may be more cause than result, amounts to about 3 cents per acre on 1,000 acres or $30. The agricultural land on the lower creek has been

9. *Grand Valley Times*, 20 August 1897.
10. Ibid., 7 April 1905.
11. Interview with Howard W. Balsley, Moab, Utah, 23 August 1968.

Erosion near Pack Creek. U.S. Forest Service photo.

damaged to the extent of about 100 acres @ $50 per acre, or $5,000. There is a yearly damage to dams and headgates of at least $250. On account of the sand and gravel, it is impossible to get a firm foundation for a dam or headgate and these are destroyed by every flood.[12]

Locke concluded his report with the statement that permanent losses amounted to $9,250 and yearly damages to $890 and recommended that a more thorough investigation be made.

Like Locke's report, the 1927 report gives the general impression of limited erosion damage. Three distinct classes of erosion were found. These were described as sheet and shoestring erosion, typical gully erosion, and unusual gully erosion. The last-named type was found only in Dark Canyon and consisted of a subterranean oozing

12. S. B. Locke, Report on Eroded Areas, 1915, Watershed Folder.

with subsequent sloughing of topsoil. This phenomenon was of greater concern than erosion generally and occupied most of the report. Along with brief examples of critical erosion of the other types, the report suggested remedies. For the oozing Dark Canyon erosion, cribs and other retaining devices were proposed. Elsewhere, ditching and damming were recommended but, in most cases, were regarded as too expensive to justify any real effort. Grazing restriction seemed to offer the best long-term prospect.[13]

Watershed management also included a sustained effort to develop springs, waterholes, and troughs. No fewer than 218 sources of water were developed between the Forest's founding and 1940, with most of the work taking place in the 1930s. During the latter period, special emergency funding was used, but most projects were carried on under regular budgets.[14]

The Taylor Grazing Act

In 1929 Supervisor A. C. Folster submitted a report on several La Sal Forest watersheds. Made out according to a form set up by the district office, the report included one item on the "present attitude of local people" toward management of public lands. According to Folster, there was no sentiment favoring municipal management of their own watersheds. Furthermore, he reported that the people of Moab, Monticello, and Blanding expressed "a keen desire that all public lands be placed under federal control, preferably the Forest Service."[15] Similar expressions appeared frequently in La Sal Forest records during the years before the Taylor Grazing Act was passed in 1934. While not all Forest grazers favored extending federal control to their winter ranges on the public domain, many of them had come to feel that it would be necessary. People of this sentiment found much company among Utah stockmen generally, who did not take a strong position favoring cession of public lands to the states or outright management by private interests. That this was so was evidenced by Utah Congressman Don Colton's leadership in the federal control movement prior to his defeat in the election of 1932. Another general evidence of Utah's position was the Utah Wool Growers Association's endorsement of the Taylor bill at a time when its sister organizations in Arizona, New Mexico, and Colorado were strongly opposed to it.

Established stockmen in southeastern Utah had complained for years that their winter ranges were subject to invasion from various interlopers, including transient stockmen and foreign nationals. From time to time this led to suggestions that the authority of the Forest

---

13. J. P. Martin, Report upon Erosion on the La Sal National Forest, 4 April 1927, Watershed Folder.
14. "Historical Information, La Sal National Forest," pp. 92-96.
15. A. C. Folster, Report on Municipal Watershed, 7 March 1929, Watershed Folder.

Service be extended to the public domain. However, for many years these expressions fell far short of general agreement. Indeed, other solutions seemed to attract more real support, and by 1930 stockmen were organizing to meet the threat of range invasion at the local level.[16] But as the question of managing ranges on the public domain was argued nationally, latent sentiment favoring federal control took form in petitions calling for creation of grazing districts under national management.[17] Thus, many, if not most, stockmen in the region were in essential harmony with the Taylor Grazing Act, which was passed in June of 1934. By its terms 173,000,000 acres of unreserved lands were withdrawn from public entry and placed under the administration of the Grazing Service in the Department of the Interior in cooperation with local stockmen.[18]

During the months following the passage of the Taylor Act, La Sal Forest users cooperated when a southeastern Utah grazing district was established and helped create two grazing district associations. An advisory board worked energetically in issuing permits and laying out the procedures of the new organizations. Most stockmen gave the new program their support.

The Civilian Conservation Corps

Other evidences of southeastern Utah's increasing movement from a frontier isolationism to a national assimilation were apparent in the various relief programs of the 1930s. Times had been bad for stockmen throughout most of the 1920s but the depression resulted in the most adverse condition they had experienced. Responding to hard times, the La Sal Forest reduced fees, allowed permittees to postpone payment, and, in one or two cases, made blanket arrangements whereby only half of the fees owed would be required. With drought added to low prices and poor markets, a "federal cattle purchasing campaign" was launched in 1934 as the New Deal came into being. In September, 816 cattle were purchased in Grand and San Juan counties. It was announced that by the end of October a total of 5,000 head would be disposed of—mostly to eastern canneries.[19] Like many depression programs, this one appears to have fallen by the wayside, and little more is heard of relief livestock sales.

Of greater significance was the Civilian Conservation Corps. Attracting more public attention and favorable response in southeastern Utah than any other early New Deal program, the CCC was launched on the La Sal Forest almost before it had a name. The first camp was established at the Warner Ranger Station during the spring of 1933.

---

16. *Times-Independent,* 27 March 1930.
17. Ibid., 16 March 1933.
18. Joe A. Stout, "Cattlemen, Conservationists, and the Taylor Grazing Act," *New Mexico Review* 45 (1970): 311.
19. *Times-Independent,* 9 September 1934.

Eating time at a Southern Utah CCC project. U.S. Forest Service photo.

In those days of the nascent CCC, the Forest Service played an important role and was the immediate beneficiary of much of its effort. Supervisor A. C. Folster returned from an Ogden meeting in May of 1933 with the happy word that Forest District IV could immediately employ no fewer than 17,000 men in improvement programs. In terms of the La Sal Forest this meant at least one and probably two camps of about 200 men. With Camp Warner a quick reality, welcome levies were made on Grand and San Juan counties for "local experienced men" or "LEMs," as well as a fair share of young men. As it turned out, Utah's forests were authorized to establish only twenty camps, and the second unit contemplated for the La Sal Forest did not materialize. The Warner camp put in a long season working on trails, roads, and water development before moving to Moab in the late fall, where it took up a flood control campaign on Mill and Pack creeks. Detachments also were assigned to street projects in Moab and to the Arches National Monument. Later in the winter, contingents were put to work at Monticello on the Baker Ranger Station and in Castle Valley on the Castleton-Wilson Mesa Road.[20]

20.   Ibid., for the entire summer and fall of 1933; and Kenneth W. Baldridge, "Reclamation Work of the Civilian Conservation Corps 1933-1942," *Utah Historical Quarterly* 39 (1971): 265-85.

For the La Sal Forest, the CCC meant telescoping a ten-year range improvements plan into one year. For Utah forests as a whole, the CCC also made vital contributions, reducing fire hazard on 1.8 million acres, building hundreds of miles of roads, forest trails, telephone lines, and fences, and planting more than 100,000 trees during its first two years. In addition, over 1,000 acres had been improved as picnic and camp sites, and Utah men had allotted in excess of $1,120,000 to their dependents.[21]

After 1934, the CCC role in southeastern Utah was less closely connected with the La Sal National Forest. Camps were established on the public domain and worked under the auspices of the Grazing Service, the Bureau of Reclamation, and the Park Service. Nevertheless, camps were at one time or other located at Indian Creek, Monticello, La Sal, Blanding, and other places where part or all of the effort affected the National Forest.

The Emergency Relief Administration also did much to accelerate La Sal Forest improvement programs. An examination of improvement projects for the 1930s reveals that about 25 percent of the projects initiated were to some degree carried on under the ERA. In 1937 several ERA crews were busy on the Forest, and in 1938 upwards of 100 men were employed on ERA projects, including fire control and range and recreational improvements.[22]

As the depression ended, one more important land management agency made its appearance. On February 8, 1940, a meeting was held in Moab at which about fifty landowners discussed the question of creating a soil conservation district. An April referendum showed them to favor by a substantial majority the establishment of such a district.[23] Shortly thereafter, the Soil Conservation Service became an additional element in the move to federal management of public resources which had been initiated by the establishment of the La Sal Forest in 1906.

Consolidation

The 1930s, with their expansion of Forest programs and proliferation of resource managing agencies, were followed by a decade of adjustment and consolidation for the La Sal National Forest. Change came in large measure as the outgrowth of developments in transportation and communication, but it also came as a reflection of the relative decline of grazing and the growing tendency to emphasize big game and recreation in Forest budgeting.

The first indication that administrative changes were in the offing for the La Sal Forest—which because of consolidations elsewhere was the smallest forest in Utah—came in 1939. At that time Forest

21. Times-Independent, 25 October 1934.
22. Ibid., 14 April and 19 May 1938.
23. Ibid., 8 February and 18 April 1940.

officers considered shifting the supervisor's office to Monticello because of housing difficulties in Moab. While conclusive evidence is lacking, there was some hint that something more than the possible move to Monticello was involved in Moab's donation of a building site for new Forest offices, warehouses, and, tentatively, two residences. If vague questions were raised in 1939, a definite threat came into focus in 1943 when a full-fledged drive was launched to close the supervisor's office and consolidate it with either the Uinta National Forest, headquartered at Provo, or with some Region II forest in Colorado. Arguing that economy and manpower cuts due to military and war industry demands lay behind the move, Regional Forester C. N. Woods proposed that the Monticello Division be reduced from two districts to one, that the La Sal District be placed under a "principal forest ranger," and that all administrative and office functions be consolidated with the Uinta Forest. Lying 250 miles from the Monticello Division, Provo was not regarded as an appropriate headquarters by many San Juan permittees. Some thought it would be better to consolidate with the Montezuma or the Uncompahgre forests with the respective headquarters in Cortez or Durango. Moab, on the other hand, was opposed to the move in any form and particularly opposed to merger with the Montezuma Forest. J. A. Scorup, who still ran more than 4,000 head of cattle on the La Sal Forest, also was opposed to a transfer to a Colorado forest and, after initial concurrence, to the Uinta Forest as well.

Forced to proceed slowly, the Forest Service studied the administrative readjustment in all its ramifications. In May of 1944 W. B. Rice, who had recently replaced Woods as Region IV forester, and John Spencer, regional forester from Denver, met in Moab to check with various interests there. They considered all the possibilities discussed above plus the advisability of splitting the La Sal Forest and attaching the Southern Division to the Montezuma Forest and the Northern Division to the Grand Mesa Forest with headquarters at Grand Junction. In spite of many factors favoring merger with Region II forests, including the specifically stated fact that it would bring all of Charlie Redd's permits under one region and make for better control of his operations, Spencer evidently did not favor bringing the Utah forest into his unit.[24] Furthermore, opposition which the Washington Office was apparently unwilling to face developed in the Utah Congressional delegation.

In the meantime J. A. Scorup proposed that consolidation with the Manti Forest with new headquarters at Price might provide the best solution to the entire problem. In his letter recommending that the La Sal be attached to Region II, W. B. Rice developed some of the pros and cons of Scorup's proposal to unite the La Sal and Manti for-

24. W. B. Rice to the Chief Forester, 23 June 1944, O-Organization Folder, Manti-La Sal National Forest Historical Files.

Congressman Don Colton addressing stockmen. U.S. Forest Service photo.

ests and suggested it as an alternative. As it turned out, the chief forester favored the merger, but preliminary inquiry indicated that while Mayor J. Bracken Lee of Price and most other Carbon County interests were avid for the change, no facilities were available in Price to accommodate forest offices.[25] Consequently, the administrative functions of the La Sal were joined with those of the Uintah Forest and the office moved to "Provo as a temporary expedient pending further study of the desirability of consolidating with the Manti. . . ."[26]

When Scorup first brought up the question of combining the Manti and the La Sal there was little thought that the Manti Forest stood to gain by moving its offices from Ephraim. But as time passed, the merger began to look quite as desirable from the standpoint of running the Manti Forest as the La Sal. With three rangers, a supervisor, and several Great Basin Research Station employees all located within a twenty-five mile radius of Ephraim, Sanpete County was said to have more forest representation than required for political and administrative reasons. Related to this was the general decline of Sanpete's population and the passing of the days when John H. Seely, David W. Candland, and other greats dominated Utah's sheep industry.[27] Price, on the other hand, was on the ascendancy at the moment. With a population approaching 7,000 and a mayor already marked for bigger things, it was the most important Utah city without a functioning contact with the Forest Service. Given the shift to big game and recreation, Price's sportsmen also represented an element which the Forest Service was anxious to woo. Also important

25. W. B. Rice to the Chief Forester, 2 April 1946, O-Organization Folder.
26. Ibid.
27. Edwin M. G. Seely, "A History of the Rambouillet Breed of Sheep in Utah" (Master's thesis, Utah State University, 1956).

were Carbon County's mining interests, the heaviest users of timber in Utah during the postwar years. Furthermore, headquarters at Price had obvious political and practical advantages, as it was accessible to forest users on the east side of the Manti as well as the entire La Sal division. Finally, the relationship between the La Sal Forest and the Uinta Forest had not worked out satisfactorily.

With such considerations in mind, Forest Service officers soon convinced themselves that a change was necessary and moved to effectuate it. As it first became apparent that they stood to lose the supervisor's office, Ephraim interests objected strenuously, charging breach of covenant, but conceded to the change as the determination of the Forest Service became apparent. On November 28, 1949, the consolidation and transfer of the Forest office were effected by Public Land Order No. 618. The new forest was placed under the direction of Manti Supervisor Robert H. Parks, and, to the profound distress of Grand and San Juan counties, given the name Manti Forest. As Regional Forester Price quickly pointed out, precedent existed in plenty for keeping the name of only the major administrative unit. Supporters of the La Sal Forest, including Supervisor Parks, pleaded for the continuation of the La Sal name, and on September 2, 1950, Public Land Order No. 667 changed the name to Manti-La Sal, thus perpetuating the old southeastern Utah forest in name.[28]

A New Approach and the La Sal Forest's Role in a Passing Frontier

The telescoping of a ten-year plan into the accomplishments of a single year by the Civilian Conservation Corps had its broader parallel in the changes wrought upon southeastern Utah by the events of the quarter-century after 1930. Developments of the period, including the uranium boom, continued growth of governmental agencies, and technological advance in transportation and communication, molded the area in a less distinctive pattern but in one that nevertheless provided opportunity for an economic and cultural quality quite beyond the potential of the old system.

In a sense, this transition was the harvest of plantings made by the La Sal National Forest. As observed in earlier chapters, pioneers had progressed by 1906 from frontier self-sufficiency and ignorance as to the prospects of natural resources to a partial grasp of the country's economic potential and to a halting willingness to accept regulation in return for public services. From 1906 to 1930, the La Sal Forest and its region were in a developmental phase as the impulses of local progress and of external forces moved from the independence and unplanned condition of frontier isolationism toward full integration with American society.

The transition which came to fruition in the proliferation of federal

---

28. *See* Public Land Order No. 618, and Public Land Order No. 667, O-Organization Folder.

Dam on Mill Creek silted in from flood in 1930. U.S. Forest Service photo.

agencies and the move to forest consolidation marked the fulfillment of a larger meaning of the La Sal National Forest. In the limited and legal sense it had been created to manage the La Sal and Blue mountains, but in the broader context it brought a new approach that was not only antithetical to the frontier but so different in style as to be almost revolutionary. It was in effect an invasion of planning and organization on a national scale, and of regulated exploitation. It was the more complex moving into the less sophisticated and the simple. It was understanding of resources rather than urgent response to need. It was the substitution of multiple options for a system where options had been limited to cows and sheep and in which even these limited opportunities overburdened the resource which carried them. But most of all, the Forest Service represented the substitution of an economic approach characterized by planning and preparation for an approach that was part blind faith in the myth of free land and opportunity, part luck, and part unimaginative opportunism. Without recognizing that it was champion of a different life-style, the La Sal Forest had been extended, an outpost on the frontier.

In this connection it should be understood that it was not the only vehicle by which the new approach entered the region, but it was one of the most important. During its first twenty-five years, or to about 1930, the La Sal Forest was too limited in personnel and program and too much part of the prevailing way of life to effect the changes implicit in this broader meaning of its role. It failed to understand that the homesteader was the very personification of the unplanned, optionless method which the Forest was itself supplanting. For years it was unable to control grazing and hardly gave more than lip service to the management of its watershed and to erosion control. It failed to bring planning and cooperation to all Forest users, but it did keep the torch of the new approach aloft and in its long dealings prepared the people of the region to tolerate the concepts of planning, organization, and regulation.

However, with the depression and the multiplier effect it had upon the Forest's method, the new approach increasingly supplanted the old, and southeastern Utah entered what may be termed its modern period.

Bibliography

Bibliographical Note. This study has depended upon a wide variety of official and unofficial records and published works. Central to the entire project have been Forest Service records. These are located in depositories at four record-keeping levels. First, and undoubtedly most important, have been the Manti-La Sal historical files. Following in order of descending contribution are collections at the Denver Records Center, the National Archives, and the Region IV office in Ogden. The Denver Records Center has the greatest volume of Manti-La Sal and related papers. They are organized as they came out of the active files of the Forest and are accessible by means of shelf lists and much sifting. A thorough search of Manti-La Sal holdings at the center would yield much information in areas not covered by this study, but this would be a gargantuan undertaking, as records are not individually indexed or arranged. However, search into specific subjects may be handled without undue effort as evidenced by this study's extensive reference to boundary adjustment files housed at the Center. The Region IV office has scrupulously purged its shelves and has very little Manti-La Sal material that may be termed historical. One important exception is an extensive collection of labeled photographs dating back to about 1910 and covering the entire region, but which runs heavily to Manti Forest shots.

The Manti-La Sal National Forest historical files consists of approximately four linear feet of records. Perhaps three-quarters of these pertain to the old Manti Forest. Fortunately, the La Sal portion includes an excellent historical compilation, "Historical Information, La Sal National Forest," which was put together under the direction of Forest Supervisor Leland Heywood about 1940. Together with supporting data, it provides information from which a history may be formed. Some ranger districts have maintained historical files on the Manti-La Sal which have filled in scantily documented topics. Records from the Great Basin Research Station have added an interesting element, and Senate and House documents, and other official reports also have provided much useful information.

The Utah State Archives have been an invaluable source. *Public Documents*, published biennially until recent decades, contain many useful reports, notably the annual messages of the governors and reports from the Utah Conservation Commission, the State Land Board, the Fish and Game Commission and other agencies whose business brought them into contact with the La Sal Forest. Much more extensive, and, like material in the Denver Records Center, very hard to get at are the accumulated records of state, including papers of the governors and various agencies. The papers of Governors Heber M. Wells, J. C. Cutler, and William Spry yielded valuable insight into conservation's beginnings in Utah.

Next to official records, newspapers have been the most useful source of information. Absolutely essential to this study was the *Grand Valley Times*, later the *Times-Independent* of Moab. Also making major contributions were the *Durango Herald* and the *Emery County Progress*, published respectively in Durango, Colorado, and Castle Dale, Utah. The *Salt Lake Tribune*, the *Deseret News*, the *New York Times*, and the *Rocky Mountain News* all were helpful.

A large number of diaries and personal reminiscences and much oral testimony have been used. Large manuscript collections, including materials pertaining to southeastern Utah are at the Historical Department of The Church of Jesus Christ of Latter-day Saints, the Utah State Historical Society, Brigham Young University, the University of Utah, and Fort Lewis College at Durango.

The following list of titles has been selected because of its usefulness in studying this national forest in its regional context. Very few manuscript titles have been included. This does not imply that they have little value but simply reflects the fact that they can be more efficiently dealt with in connection with the body of the study where each is cited in full.

Alexander, Thomas. "John Wesley Powell, the Irrigation Survey, and the Inauguration of the Second Phase of Irrigation Development in Utah." *Utah Historical Quarterly* 37 (1969).
————. "Senator Reed Smoot and Public Land Policy, 1905-1920." *Arizona and the West* 13 (1971)
————. "The Powell Irrigation Survey and the People of the West." *Journal of the West* 7 (1968).
Allred, B. W. "Pioneering at La Sal." *Corral Dust* 5 (1960.
————. *The Life of a Horse and Buggy Stage Line Operator*. Great Western Series, No. 11. Washington: Potomac Corral, The Westerns, 1972.
Alter, J. Cecil. "Father Escalante's Map." *Utah Historical Quarterly* 9 (1941).
————. *Utah the Storied Domain: A Documentary History of Utah's Eventful Career*. 3 vols. Chicago and New York: American Historical Society, 1932.

Anderson, C. C. "History of Grazing." Original. Logan, Utah: Utah State University.

Anderson, Nels. *Desert Saints, the Mormon Frontier in Utah.* Chicago: University of Chicago Press, 1942.

Arrington, Leonard J. *Great Basin Kingdom, an Economic History of the Latter-day Saints, 1830-1900.* Cambridge, Mass.: Harvard University Press, 1958.

Athearn, Robert G. *Rebel of the Rockies: A History of the Denver and Rio Grande Western Railroad.* New Haven, Conn.: Yale University Press, 1962.

Auerbach, Herbert S. "Father Escalante's Itinerary." *Utah Historical Quarterly* 9 (1941).

———. "Father Escalante's Journal with Related Documents and Maps." *Utah Historical Quarterly* 11 (1943).

———. "Father Escalante's Route as Depicted on the Map of Bernardo de Miera y Pacheco." *Utah Historical Quarterly,* 9 (1941).

Bailey, Paul. *Jacob Hamblin, Buckskin Apostle.* Los Angeles: Westernlore Press, 1948.

———. *Walkara, Hawk of the Mountains.* Los Angeles: Westernlore Press, 1954.

Baldridge, Kenneth W. "Reclamation Work of the Civilian Conservation Corps 1933-1942." *Utah Historical Quarterly* 39 (1971).

Baldwin, Virgil Fay. "Freighting on the Colorado River." *Utah Historical Quarterly* 32 (1964).

Bancroft, Hubert Howe. . . . *History of Arizona and New Mexico, 1530-1888* San Francisco: The History Company, 1889.

———. . . . *History of Nevada, Colorado and Wyoming.* San Francisco: The History Company, 1890.

———. . . . *History of Utah, 1540-1886.* San Francisco: The History Company, 1889.

Barnes, Will C. "Mormons and Their Cattle." *American Cattle Producer* 18 (1936).

———. *Western Grazing Grounds and Forest Ranges.* Chicago: The Breeder's Gazette, 1913.

Bartlett, Richard A. *Great Surveys of the American West.* Norman: University of Oklahoma Press, 1942.

Beck, D. Elden. "Mormon Trails to Bluff." *Utah,* 4-5 (1940-41).

Beckwith, E. G. "Report of Exploration of a Route for the Pacific Railroad near the 38th and 39th Parallels of Latitude." *House Document 129* (1855).

Bender, A. B. "Government Exploration in the Territory of New Mexico, 1846-1859." *New Mexico Historical Review* 9 (1934).

Birney, Hoffman. *Zealots of Zion.* Philadelphia: Penn Publishing Company, 1931.

Bolton, Herbert E. "Escalante in Dixie and the Arizona Strip." *New Mexico Historical Review* 3 (1928).

———. *Pageant in the Wilderness, the Story of the Escalante Expedition to the Interior Basin, 1776, Including the Diary and Itinerary of Father Escalante Translated and Annotated.* Salt Lake City: State Historical Society, 1950.

Brooks, Juanita. "Indian Relations on the Mormon Frontier." *Utah Historical Quarterly* 12 (1944).

———. *John Doyle Lee, Zealot-Pioneer-Scapegoat.* Glendale, California: Arthur H. Clark Company, 1962.

———. "Lee's Ferry at Lonely Dell." *Utah Historical Quarterly* 25 (1957).

———. *The Mountain Meadows Massacre.* 2d ed. Norman: University of Oklahoma Press, 1963.

————. *Uncle Will Tells His Story*. Salt Lake City: Taggart and Company, 1970.

Buhler, E. O. "Forest and Watershed Fires in Utah." *Agricultural Experiment State Bulletin*. Logan: Utah State Agricultural College, 1941.

Carhart, Arthur H. *The National Forests*. New York: Alfred Knopf, 1959.

Carrol, William E. "Utah as a Livestock Center." Utah Industrial Commission *Annual Report* 18 (1916).

Carstensen, Vernon, ed. *The Public Lands, Studies in the History of the Public Domain*. Madison: University of Wisconsin Press, 1963.

Carvalho, Solomon Nunes. *Incidents of Travel and Adventure in the Far West*. Edited by Bertram W. Korn. Philadelphia: Jewish Publication Society of America, 1954.

Case, J. E., et. al. *Regional Geophysical Investigations in the La Sal Mountain Area, Utah and Colorado*. Washington: Government Printing Office, 1963.

Cleland, Robert Glass, and Brooks, Juanita, eds. *A Mormon Chronicle: The Diaries of John D. Lee, 1848-1876*. 2 vols. San Marino: Huntington Library, 1955.

Clepper, Henry, ed. *Origins of American Conservation*. New York: The Ronald Press Company, 1966.

Clyde, George D. "History of Irrigation in Utah." *Utah Historical Quarterly* 27 (1960).

Correll, J. Lee. "Navajo Frontiers in Utah and Troublous Times in Monument Valley." *Utah Historical Quarterly* 39 (1971).

Cortes, Phyliss, comp. *Grand Memories*. Salt Lake City: Utah Printing Co., 1972.

Coyner, David H. *The Lost Trappers: A Collection of Interesting Scenes and Events in the Rocky Mountains*. New York: Hurst and Company Publishers, n.d.

Crampton, C. Gregory. "Outline History of the Glen Canyon Region, 1776-1922." University of Utah *Anthropological Papers*, no. 42, Glen Canyon Series Number 9 (1959).

————. *Standing Up Country, the Canyon Lands of Utah and Arizona*. New York: Alfred A. Knopf, 1964.

————. "The Discovery of the Green River." *Utah Historical Quarterly* 20 (1952).

————, and Miller, David E., eds. "Journal of Two Campaigns by the Utah Territorial Militia against the Navajo Indians, 1869." *Utah Historical Quarterly* 29 (1961).

Creer, L. H., ed. *History of Utah 1847 to 1869 by Andrew Love Neff*. Salt Lake City: Deseret News Press, 1940.

————. "Mormon Towns in the Region of the Colorado." University of Utah *Anthropological Papers*, no. 32, Glen Canyon Series, no. 3 (1958).

————. "Spanish-American Slave Trade in the Great Basin, 1800-1853." *New Mexico Historical Review* 24 (1949).

————. *The Founding of an Empire: The Exploration and Colonization of Utah, 1776-1856*. Salt Lake City: Bookcraft, 1947.

Culmsee, Carlton. *Utah's Black Hawk War*. Logan: Utah State University, 1973.

Dana, S. T. *Forest and Range Policy—Its Development in the United States*. New York: McGraw-Hill Book Company, 1956.

Darrah, William Culp. *Powell of the Colorado*. Princeton: Princeton University Press, 1951.

Day, Franklin D. "Cattle Industry of San Juan County, 1875-1900." Master's thesis, Brigham Young University, 1958.

Dyar, W. W. "The Colossal Bridges of Utah." *Century* (1904).

Edgar, J. H. "San Juan County Experiment Farm Progress Report, 1925-30." Utah State Agricultural College, *Agricultural Experiment State Bulletin,* no. 230 (1931).

Ekker, Barbara Baldwin. "Freighting on the Colorado River: Reminiscences of Virgil Fay Baldwin." *Utah Historical Quarterly* 32 (1964).

Farnham, Thomas J. *Life, Adventures and Travels in California.* New York: Nafis and Cornish, 1849.

Forsling, C. L. "Erosion on Uncultivated Lands in the Intermountain Region." *Scientific Monthly* 24 (1932).

————. "The Water Conservation Problem in Forestry." *Journal of Forestry* 31 (1933).

Frome, Michael. *The National Forests of America.* New York: G. P. Putnam's Sons, 1968.

Frost, Melvin J. "Factors that Influenced Homesteading and Land Abandonment in San Juan County, Utah." Master's thesis, Brigham Young University, 1960.

Gillmor, Frances, and Wetherill, Louisa Wade. *Traders to the Navajos: The Story of the Wetherills of Kayenta.* 2d ed. Albuquerque: University of New Mexico Press, 1953.

Goetzmann, William H. *Army Exploration in the American West, 1803-1863.* New Haven, Conn.: Yale University Press, 1965.

Gottfredson, Peter. *History of Indian Depredations in Utah.* Salt Lake City: Skelton Publishing Company, 1919.

Greenwell, Scott L. "A History of the United States Army Corps of Topographical Engineers in Utah, 1843-1859." Master's thesis, Utah State University, 1972.

Greever, William S. *Arid Domain: The Santa Fe Railway and Its Western Land Grant.* Palo Alto: Stanford University Press, 1944.

Gregory, Herbert E. "Population of Southern Utah." *Economic Geography* 21 (1945).

Hafen, LeRoy R., and Hafen, Ann W. *Old Spanish Trail, Santa Fe to Los Angeles, with Extracts from Contemporary Records and Including Diaries of Antonio Armijo and Orville Pratt.* Glendale, California: Arthur H. Clark Company, 1954.

Hayden, F. V. . . . *Geological and Geographical Atlas of Colorado and Portions of Adjacent Territory.* Washington: Julius Bien, 1877.

————. *Ninth Annual Report of the United States Geological and Geographical Survey of the Territories Embracing Colorado and Parts of Adjacent Territories.* Washington: Government Printing Office, 1876.

————. *U. S. Geological and Geographical Survey of the Territories.* Vol. 10. Washington: Government Printing Office, 1878.

Hill, Joseph J. "Spanish and Mexican Exploration and Trade Northwest from New Mexico into the Great Basin." *Utah Historical Quarterly* 3 (1930).

————. "The Old Spanish Trail: A Study of Spanish and Mexican Trade and Exploration Northwest from New Mexico to the Great Basin and California." *Hispanic American Historical Review* 4 (1921).

Hill, J. M. "Notes on the Northern La Sal Mountains, Grand County, Utah." *U.S.G.S. Bulletin, no. 530.* Washington: Government Printing Office, 1912.

Hodge, Frederick Webb. "Ute." *Handbook of American Indians.* Washington: Smithsonian Institute, Bureau of American Ethnology, 1910.

Hunt, Alice. "Archeological Survey of the La Sal Mountains Area, Utah." University of Utah *Anthropological Papers,* no. 14 (1953).

Jackson, William Henry. *Time Exposure.* New York: G. P. Putnam's Sons, 1940.

James, George Wharton. *Reclaiming the Arid West, the Story of the United States Reclamation Service.* New York: Dodd, Mead and Company, 1917.

Jennings, Jesse D. "Early Man in Utah." *Utah Historical Quarterly* 28 (1960).

————. "The Aboriginal Peoples." *Utah Historical Quarterly* 28 (1960).

Jensen, Andrew. "The Elk Mountain Mission from the Official Journal of the Company by Oliver B. Huntington." *Utah Genealogy and Historical Magazine* 4 (1913).

Jensen, Bryant L. "An Historical Study of Bluff City, 1878 to 1906." Master's thesis, Brigham Young University, 1966.

Kane, Francis Fisher, and Riter, Frank M. *A Further Report to the Indian Rights Association on the Proposed Removal of the Southern Utes.* Philadelphia: Press of William F. Fell & Co., 1892.

Kelly, Charles. "Antoine Robidoux." *Utah Historical Quarterly* 6 (1933).

————. "Chief Hoskaninni." *Utah Historical Quarterly* 21 (1953).

————. "Lost Silver of Pis-la-ki." *Deseret Magazine* 4 (1940).

————. "The Mysterious 'D. Julien.'" *Utah Historical Quarterly* 6 (1933).

————. *The Outlaw Trail: A History of Butch Cassidy and His Wild Bunch.* New York: Bonanza Books, 1938.

Kneipp, L. F. "Utah's Forest Resources." Utah Industrial Commission *Annual Report* 14 (1916).

Korstion, C. F. "Making the Forests of Utah a Permanent Resource." *Transactions of the Utah Academy of Science* 12 (1918).

John H. Krenkel, ed. *The Life and Times of Joseph Fish, Mormon Pioneer.* Danville, Illinois: The Interstate Printers, 1970.

Kroeber, A. L. "Ute Tales." *Journal of American Folklore* 14 (1901).

Lambert, Neal. "Al Scorup: Cattleman of the Canyons." *Utah Historical Quarterly* 32 (1964).

Larson, Andrew Karl. *"I Was Called to Dixie," the Virgin River Basin: Unique Experiences in Mormon Pioneering.* Salt Lake City: Deseret News Press, 1961.

Lavender, David. *One Man's West.* New York: Doubleday & Company, 1956.

Lever, W. H. *History of Sanpete and Emery Counties, Utah.* Salt Lake City: Tribune Job Printing Company, 1898.

Lyman, Albert R. *History of Blanding, 1905-1955.* Published privately, n.o.

————. *Indians and Outlaws: Settling of the San Juan Frontier.* Salt Lake City: Bookcraft, 1962.

————. "The Fort on the Firing Line." *Improvement Era* 51-53 (1948-50).

————. *The Outlaw of Navajo Mountain.* Salt Lake City: Deseret Book, 1963.

McGue, D. B. "John Taylor, Slave-born Colorado Pioneer." *Colorado Magazine* 48 (1941).

McMechen, Edgar C., ed. "Jordan Bean's Story and the Castle Valley Indian Fight." *Colorado Magazine* 20 (1943).

McNitt, Frank. *Richard Wetherill: Anasazi.* Albuquerque: University of New Mexico Press, 1957.

Macomb, J. N. *Report of the Exploring Expedition from Santa Fe, New Mexico, to the Junction of the Grand and Green Rivers of the Great Colorado of the West, in 1859, under the Command of J. N. Macomb, with a Geological Report by Prof. J. S. Newberry.* Washington: Government Printing Office, 1876.

Mason, Fred. "Forests in the Desert." *Utah Magazine* 9 (1947).

Miller, David E. *Hole-in-the-Rock: An Epic in the Colonization of the Great American West.* Salt Lake City: University of Utah Press, 1959.

————. "Murder at the Rincon." *Salt Lake Tribune* (March 23, 1958).

Morgan, Dale L. *Jedediah Smith and the Opening of the West.* New York: Bobbs-Merrill Company, 1953.

Moseley, M. Edward. "The Discovery and Definition of Basketmaker: 1890 to 1914." *Masterkey* (Autumn 1966).

Nord, A. G. "National Forests, the People's Playground." *Utah Magazine* 5 (1941).

O'Neil, Floyd. "A History of the Ute Indians of Utah." Ph.D. dissertation, University of Utah, 1973.

Parkhill, Forbes. *The Blazed Trail of Antoine Leroux.* Los Angeles: Westernlore Press, 1965.

————. *The Last of the Indian Wars.* New York: Crowell-Collier Publishing Company, 1962.

Perkins, Cornelia A.; Nielson, Marian G.; and Jones, Lenora B. *Saga of San Juan.* Published privately, 1957.

Peterson, Charles S. "Albert F. Potter's Wasatch Survey, 1902: A Beginning for Public Management of Natural Resources in Utah." *Utah Historical Quarterly* 39 (1971).

————. "San Juan in Controversy: American Livestock Frontier vs. Mormon Cattle Pool." In Thomas G. Alexander, ed. *Essays on the American West, 1972-1973.* Charles Redd Monographs in Western History, no. 3. Provo, Utah: Brigham Young University, 1974.

————. "Small Holding Land Patterns in Utah and the Problem of Forest Watershed Management." *Forest History* 17 (1973).

————. *Take Up Your Mission: Mormon Colonizing along the Little Colorado River, 1870-1900.* Tucson: University of Arizona Press, 1973.

————, ed. " 'Book A—Levi Mathers Savage': The Look of Utah in 1873." *Utah Historical Quarterly* 41 (1973).

Peterson, Levi S. "The Development of Utah Livestock Law, 1848-1896." *Utah Historical Quarterly* 32 (1964).

Pinchot, Gifford. *Breaking New Ground.* (New York: Harcourt, Brace and Company, 1947.

————. *The Fight for Conservation.* Seattle: University of Washington Press, 1967.

Pinkett, H. T. *Gifford Pinchot, Private and Public Forester.* Urbana: University of Illinois Press, 1970.

Powell, John Wesley. *Report on the Land of the Arid Region of the United States, with a More Detailed Account of the Lands of Utah.* 2d ed. Washington: Government Printing Office, 1879.

Price, Virginia N., and Darby, John T. "Preston Nutter: Utah Cattleman, 1886-1936." *Utah Historical Quarterly* 32 (1964).

Redd, Jay Amasa, ed. *Lemuel Hardison Redd, Jr., 1856-1923, Pioneer-Leader-Builder.* Salt Lake City, 1967.

Richardson, Elmo R. *The Politics of Conservation: Crusades and Controversies, 1897-1913.* Berkeley: University of California Press, 1962.

Ricks, Joel E., and Cooley, Everett L., eds. *The History of a Valley: Cache Valley, Utah-Idaho.* Logan, Utah: Cache Valley Centennial Commission, 1956.

Riis, John. *Ranger Trails.* Richmond: The Dietz Press, 1937.

Robb, W. L. "Lumbering, a Home Industry on Utah's Forests." *Utah Magazine* 5 (1941).

Roberts, Paul H. *Hoof Prints on Forest Ranges: The Early Years of National Forest Range Administration.* San Antonio: The Naylor Company, 1963.

————. *Them Were the Days.* San Antonio: The Naylor Company, 1965.

Robertson, C. A. "Southeastern Utah, the Mecca of the Homeseeker." *Bureau of Immigration, Labor and Statistics.* Washington: Government Printing Office, 1914.

Rockwell, W. M. "Cowland Aristocrats of the North Fork." *Colorado Magazine* 14 (1937).

Rogers, A. M. "A True Narrative of an Indian Fight." *Cliffdwellers' Echo.* (April, 1912).

Roosevelt, Theodore. *The Winning of the West.* 4 vols. New York: The Review of Reviews Company, 1904.

Sanderson, M. H. *Western Land and Water Use*. Norman: University of Oklahoma Press, 1950.

Schiel, Jacob H. *Journey Through the Rocky Mountains and the Humboldt Mountains to the Pacific Ocean*. Translated and edited by Thomas N. Bonner. Norman: University of Oklahoma Press, 1959.

Scorup, Stena. *J. A. Scorup, a Utah Cattleman*. Published privately, 1944.

Scott, Hugh L. *Some Memories of a Soldier*. New York: The Century Company, 1928.

Seely, Edwin M. G. "A History of the Rambouillet Breed of Sheep in Utah." Master's thesis, Utah State University, 1956.

Silvey, Frank. *History and Settlement of Northern San Juan County*. Published privately, n. d.

Simpson, C. D., and Jackman, E. R. *Blazing Forest Trails*. Caldwell, Idaho: Caxton Printers, 1967.

Smith, Dwight L. "The Engineer and the Canyon." *Utah Historical Quarterly* 28 (1960).

Smith, Justin G. "Deer and Sheep Competition in Utah." *Journal of Wildlife Management* 17 (1953).

Smith, Joseph. *History of The Church of Jesus Christ of Latter-day Saints*. 7 vols. 2d ed. Salt Lake City: Deseret News Press, 1948.

Sniffen, M. K. *The Meaning of the Ute "War."* Philadelphia: Indian Rights Association, 1915.

Standing, Arnold R. "The Road to 'Fortune': The Salt Lake Cutoff." *Utah Historical Quarterly* 33 (1965).

————. "Through the Uintas: History of the Carter Road." *Utah Historical Quarterly* 35 (1967).

Steen, Charlie R., ed. "The Natural Bridges of White Canyon: A Diary of H. L. A. Culmer, 1865." *Utah Historical Quarterly* 40 (1972).

Stegner, Wallace. *Beyond the Hundredth Meridian: John Wesley Powell and the Second Opening of the West*. Cambridge, Mass.: Houghton Mifflin, 1954.

Stewart, George, and Widtsoe, John A. "Contribution of Forest Land Resources to the Settlement and Development of the Mormon Occupied West." *Journal of Forestry* 41 (1943).

Stout, Joe A. "Cattlemen, Conservationists, and the Taylor Grazing Act." *New Mexico Review* 45 (1970).

Tanner, Faun McConkie. *A History of Moab, Utah*. Moab: Times-Independent Press, 1937.

Thompson, Gregory Coyne. "Southern Ute Lands, 1848-1899: The Creation of a Reservation." In Robert Delaney, ed. *Occasional Papers of the Center of Southwest Studies*, no. 1. Durango: Fort Lewis College, 1972.

Towne, C. W. *Shepard's Empire*. Norman: University of Oklahoma, 1945.

Underhill, Ruth M. *The Navajos*. Norman: University of Oklahoma, 1956.

U.S., Congress, Senate. "Report of the Ute Commission of 1888." *Executive Document 67*, 50th Cong., 2d sess., 1889.

U.S., Department of Agriculture. *Yearbook of Agriculture*. (1967).

Walker, Don D. "The Carlisles: Cattle Barons of the Upper Basin." *Utah Historical Quarterly* 32 (1964).

Walters, Joel. "Utah's Humid Islands." *Utah Magazine* 9 (1947).

Webb, Walter Prescott. *The Great Plains*. Boston: Ginn and Company, 1931.

Wentworth, Edward Norris. *America's Sheep Trails*. Ames: Iowa State College Press, 1948.

Wyman, Walker D., and Hart, John D. "The Legend of Charlie Glass." *Colorado Magazine* 46 (1969).

Young, Karl. "Wild Cows of the San Juan." *Utah Historical Quarterly* 32 (1964).

Index

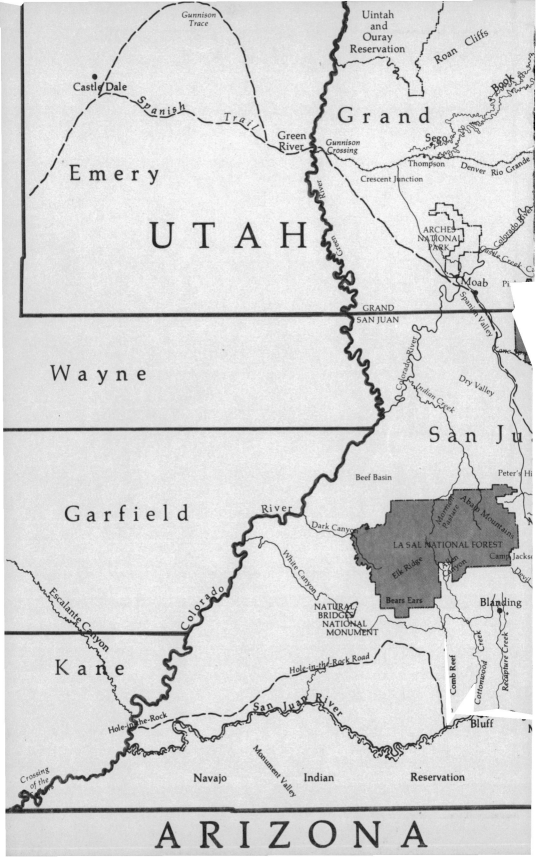